T0282925

IT TAKES TWO TO TORAH

IT TAKES TWO TO TORAH

An Orthodox Rabbi and Reform Journalist
Discuss and Debate Their Way Through
the Five Books of Moses

ABIGAIL POGREBIN | RABBI DOV LINZER

FOREWORD BY MAYIM BIALIK

BEDFORD, NEW YORK

For Devorah,
whose warmth, humanity, and deep wisdom
sustain and inspire me every day.

— Dov Linzer

For Dave,
without whom life would have less color,
clarity, fascination, safety, and joy.

— Abigail Pogrebin

Published in the United States by
Fig Tree Books LLC, Bedford, New York

www.FigTreeBooks.net
An imprint of Mandel Vilar Press, Simsbury, Connecticut

www.MVPublishers.org

Jacket design by Christine Van Bree
Design by Neuwirth & Associates, Inc.
Cover image: *On the Way to Sinai* by Yoram Raanan—www.YoramRaanan.com

Library of Congress Cataloging-in-Publication Data Available Upon Request

ISBN number 978-1-941493-34-2

Printed in the United States

Consortium Book Sales and Distribution

First edition

10 9 8 7 6 5 4 3 2 1

TABLE OF CONTENTS

Foreword *ix*

Introductions *xi*

GENESIS 1

EXODUS 75

LEVITICUS 137

NUMBERS 193

DEUTERONOMY 247

Acknowledgments *313*

About the Authors *315*

FOREWORD

by Mayim Bialik

An Orthodox rabbi and a Reform journalist walk into a podcast studio . . .

No, it's not the opening line of a joke. It's an opportunity to witness a living conversation about the most important book ever written.

The conversation is fifty-two weeks long, but it is also eternal; it is a conversation designed to get directly to the heart of the matter. The matter at hand for Abigail Pogrebin and Rabbi Dov Linzer is the Torah, aka the Chumash, aka the Five Books of Moses.

The Torah is the guidebook and jumping-off point for all the questions humans have and even those we don't yet know we have. You're not going to find anything in the Torah about how to get more followers on TikTok or how to use an AI algorithm to improve attendance in your synagogue. You also won't find anything about which $300 sneaker you should (or shouldn't) buy your teenager for their birthday, and you certainly won't find anything about which transcendental experience might help you overcome the pervasive anxiety that is with you for all of your waking hours and some of your sleeping hours as well.

What Abigail and Rabbi Dov both believe, albeit from different sides of the ideological and philosophical room, is that the Torah is a foundation and a scaffold for life. Everything is in it, and everything comes from it. It is from this shared conviction that they embarked on the conversation which you are now holding in your hands.

One of the most exceptionally unique things about the Torah as a foundational document of the Jewish religion is that it is prescriptively designed to not be studied in isolation. The Torah is said to be understood only by turning it over and over, inside and out, questioning and interpreting all of it and living it fully—but in order to do so, this should never be undertaken alone. Rather, the Torah must be studied with another person.

This kind of healthy confrontation of the text has historically occurred between two men. In addition, Orthodox Judaism tended to be the venue for this type of approach to interpretation of the Torah. However, the beauty of the Torah is that it allows for every conversation and every possibility in its understanding and analysis—especially those that shed new light on the wisdom contained within its letters and spaces.

What used to be a separation between men and women, between the Orthodox and the rest of us, has shifted and evolved as, similarly, so many of the black-and-white aspects of our culture have shifted and evolved. And what the Torah holds truest is that we are all united in our capacity to think and to learn and to question and find delight and joy in the Torah.

Abigail, a venerable and respected journalist and thinker, has decided to wade into the waters of Torah analysis with an Orthodox rabbi from another dimension of Torah teaching. This book is the product of two people literally meeting in the middle of all that there is and all there was and all there will be to bring us their most honest intellectual and relevant understanding of the Divine Torah.

Every chapter has a narrative as it walks us through each story and lesson, but consistent with any thorough analysis of Torah, each chapter also touches on hidden interpretation and insight into Divine meaning. Rabbi Dov and Abigail dutifully sift through their doubts, fears, and confusion together to find where they agree, where they disagree, and where they—and all of us—can be united. Where they find themselves united is in the most diverse of places: the place where we are all one.

For those of us who crave Torah knowledge, Abigail and Rabbi Dov deliver. For those looking for a deeper understanding of the mystery and beauty of the Torah, this conversation does not disappoint. And for all of us who picture a world where, despite our differences, we are drawn closer together to find greater understanding, a deeper sense of purpose, and an intoxicating blissfulness that only comes from the partnership of Torah analysis, Rabbi Dov and Abigail let us into their world. Which is also *our* world. In every chapter, they establish new branches on a thriving Tree of Life, and our wisdom, understanding, and joy grow with each branch we climb with them.

INTRODUCTION

by Abigail Pogrebin

I used to resist the metaphor I kept hearing from rabbis: that "we all stood at Sinai."

It wasn't just because I'm a literalist and know that we weren't there, 4,000 years ago. The symbolism felt remote, alien: How could I have inherited a document I do not live by? How can I possibly honor a contract I've never signed? I'm an involved Jew but not a *halachic* one. Sinai is more a parable than a pledge.

But instead of rejecting out of hand the idea that the Torah was given to me, too, I began a very simple act: talking about it. And lo and behold, doors started to unlock, windows started to swing open. I spotted or stumbled upon its verses and stories everywhere—in fiction, comedy routines, song lyrics, election stump speeches. In my quotidian activities and the hardest questions in my head. In my parenting and my politics, my friendships and my failures. This ancient, stubbornly enduring tome literally came to life—in conversation.

I admit it didn't hurt that the person on the other end of this dialectic was a rabbi who knows the document backward and forward and whose life's work is teaching it, but most importantly, he is someone who has a core belief in the God it describes.

Dov Linzer and I met back in 2009, when he was dean of the Orthodox seminary, Chovevei Torah (he's now its president), and I was a freelance journalist writing for publications about Jewish identity (or a lack of it). We were fortunate to be invited by *The Jewish Week* to a conference on Jewish ideas called—appropriately—The Conversation.

We've been talking ever since.

But our *chavruta* [study partnership] isn't an obvious one. We come from different ends of the spectrum when it comes to observance: Dov prays three times a day, I pray once a week if I make it to synagogue; he fasts six times a year, I fast once, on Yom Kippur; he is Sabbath-observant, I'm not; he keeps kosher, I don't; he sees the *mitzvot* [commandments] as binding, I do not.

We gently spar as much as we agree; part of what has kept us talking is that we push each other—often to a more honest realization of a personal roadblock we didn't admit or a spiritual challenge we share.

It's not a shock that an Orthodox rabbi would choose to parse Torah with a non-Orthodox Jewish journalist; of course, that's possible. What's less probable is that our partnership has endured on democratic footing. Neither of us claims to be teacher or student. Each of us listens as much as we talk (unless we're interrupting each other). And despite disparate perspectives of how this sacred text obligates us, each conversation feels sacred. Not just because it connects me to my heritage of learning and disputation but because it reminds me that this is what it means to sign up for meaning: It doesn't just land in our laps, but if we find a study-mate and prioritize the hours, this story can fire our brains and speak to our lives right at this moment.

Three years ago, Dov and I proposed a podcast that would allow us to take on one parsha at a time—with the discipline of just ten minutes each—zeroing in on one verse or passage that animated or flummoxed us both.

Tablet magazine graciously produced that podcast, called *Parsha in Progress*, and we're grateful to editors Alana Newhouse, Wayne Hoffman, Jacob Siegel, and producers Josh Kross and Shira Telushkin for all their wise support through that adventure.

But it felt like something was left unfinished. We kept hearing from friends, fellow congregants, and intrigued strangers, asking if our full Torah exploration existed somewhere in print in one place. They wanted the chance to walk through the entire Torah via these accessible ten-minute exchanges, perhaps using our discussions as springboards for their own.

Publisher Fredric Price of Fig Tree Books gave us the gift of making that book a reality, and he masterfully edited our real-time transcript for clarity and concision so that it has become a very different full journey on the page.

In the Torah-dive you're about to read, Dov and I disagree on everything from whether Reuben—Joseph's brother—is courageous or a coward, whether welcoming the stranger means welcoming the non-Jew or solely the convert, and whether Moses was unjustly barred from ever seeing the Promised Land.

We ask whether punishment can be holy, whether a loan preserves more dignity than charity, and whether faith can give us a kind of armor.

We try to square the *Sotah* ritual (I still can't), which forces a woman accused of infidelity to drink ink. We ask each other—when discussing the ornate Tabernacle—whether we personally need a fancy prayer space to feel prayerful. And we look at the key fact that human hands, not God's, were used to carve the second set of Torah tablets, just as Moses later instructed the Israelites to "inscribe every word."

What I took away from this ride was not just how relevant Torah remains, but how indelible the experience of traveling the entire story out loud, with someone else, is. Judaism has persisted not just through its study but through the interrogation it requires.

It also became clear to me that the Jewish tradition is an invitation. It beckons, in a sense, to get into the fight. Not to see the document as something fragile, untouchable, or fixed, but durable, reachable, and responsive to our struggles. "Kick its tires," Dov always encouraged me. "Wring every word."

These conversations proved again and again that the Five Books of Moses were meant to bring people together. We should not study in silence or alone. If you speak to these stories, they *will talk back.*

Torah lives on in repartee and in combat.

It takes two, indeed.

And of course, it took so many generations who came before us.

INTRODUCTION

by Rabbi Dov Linzer

"It's about being a lifelong learner."

That's what Abigail said to me when we reached the section in Deuteronomy that commands the king to keep a Sefer Torah with him at all times. It's right there in the verse: "And it shall be with him, and he shall read from it all the days of his life" (Deut. 17:19).

But here's the funny thing: Though I have been a lifelong learner—someone who has been immersed in the study of Torah since my teens, spending hours each day with my nose buried in one of the Five Books of Moses or Talmud, sometimes to the point of being so caught up inside my head with the ins-and-outs of a Talmudic discussion that I would bump into telephone poles—I never saw that verse in that way.

For me, the message had always been about what comes at the end: ". . . in order that he learn to fear God to observe all the words of this Torah." The point was that the king had to be constantly reminded that there is an authority and power greater than he, that even a monarch is under God and bound by God's Torah. And all of that is still true about what this text teaches. But how did I miss that key message of being a "lifelong student," which Abby rightly highlighted?

I missed it because I'd overlooked what it means to be a true learner. It's not just the hours one spends with their head buried in a book. It's about engaging with other people and ideas, which may be radically different from your own. It's about asking yourself: *What can I learn from this other perspective?* It's about cultivating genuine curiosity and stepping outside of your echo chamber.

In the world of the *yeshivot*, the learning of Torah is not an individual pursuit; it is always studied *bi'chavruta*, in pairs. Two people, often sitting on opposite sides of a table with the same text open in front of them, work together to plumb its depths and argue back and forth, even yelling at times, in the pursuit of arriving at the true meaning of a particular piece of Torah.

The daily partnership of study is a beautiful image and exhilarating to experience. And yet. The difference in viewpoints—which each member of the pair brings to the conversation—is often extremely slight. The *chavruta* arrives at a deeper understanding but within very bounded parameters of shared theological and religious commitments.

Abby taught me—through the many years that the two of us have been learning, laughing, sharing, and challenging one another—that to be a committed learner requires not only going deep but also going wide. Otherwise, your field of vision will be so narrow, you'll keep on walking into telephone poles.

That said, for me, learning Torah has always been more than an intellectual exploration. It is inexorably intertwined with my core religious beliefs and how I live my life. Like the king in the previously cited verse, I learn Torah "to fear God," because I believe that study is a *mitzvah* and orients me toward a constant and ongoing relationship with God.

Learning Torah elevates me out of the urgency of the moment, the busyness of the mundane. At the end of the day, the stories and laws in the Torah are all about what it means for us to be human and to be created in the Divine Image, with a mandate to choose good, to choose life. Making time to study a parsha [Torah passage], whether on my own, or—much better—with a *chavruta* and sparring partner, gives me the space and breathing room to be reflective about myself, my world, and the people around me.

The Torah pulls you in with its messy stories about imperfect human beings, doing what God wants them to do (or not), acting toward their spouse or a stranger in ways that are awe-inspiring or horrific or a little bit of both. And in the middle of all of that, I find it drawing me back to the same questions again and again: How would *I* act in these situations? How do these issues play out in my own family, friendships, and work? What are my values and priorities, and are they the right ones? What is it that I want from God, and what does God want from me?

Part of what it means to see the Torah as coming from God is that I approach the text with reverence, which does not mean silent submission. Learning Torah, for me, is an exhilarating experience of challenging and being challenged, of arguing and being persuaded, of struggling and embracing. But all are done with a deep recognition of this book as a God-given text, one that not just guides but also obligates me.

The Torah is a blueprint for how I should live my life: "He shall read from it all the days of his life . . . to observe all the words of this Torah." I am bound by its *mitzvot* and its laws. When a question arises about a commandment in the Torah, it will, in the end, directly impact my actions and practice. This makes it alive and pressing. Every minute detail of every law fully matters. It also makes it more than a little bit daunting, because there are some laws—for instance, stoning adulterers—which I am not so eager to incorporate into my daily life.

This is where "the Rabbis" come in. By "the Rabbis"—a phrase I use often in my discussions with Abby—I mean the rabbis who lived in the Talmudic period, from about 100–450 CE after the Second Temple was destroyed and after the locus of Judaism moved from the Temple to centers of Torah learning in the Land of Israel and the diaspora.

These rabbis of the Talmud were committed to the belief in a divine and binding Torah. And they understood that it was their task to interpret the Torah and its *mitzvot* in a way that was actionable and applicable while staying true to the text, true to life, to the tradition, and to its deepest values. Their commentary went a long way toward smoothing out the rough edges of the text.

I am trained to read the Torah through the lens of the Rabbis. This means a lot has already been "pre-solved" for me, whether morally vexing narratives or *mitzvot* that seem dated and alien. To some degree, the more the text matters, the more its difficult passages have been tamed.

Thank God, then, for Abby. She has shaken me out of my over-familiarity with one way of reading and learning the Torah. Abby is one of the most incisive, insightful, informed, and intelligent—not to mention kind, caring, and funny—people with whom I have had the privilege of learning Torah with. She is a woman who has devoted her life to thinking, talking, asking, challenging, and writing about what it means to be Jewish. And she doesn't let anyone—not the superstars whom she interviews regularly nor her Torah study partner—get away with complacency or wishy-washiness. Abby has kept me honest and helped make me, truly, a lifelong learner.

Our Rabbis teach us that when two people sit together to learn Torah, the *Shechina*, the Divine Presence, dwells among them. When two people challenge one another to understand Torah, they connect with something bigger than either one of them. They can even achieve a degree of transcendence. That has been my experience, and it can be yours as well.

I hope you will consider joining us as we talk and debate our way through the Torah. Pull up a chair—there's room for one more. Feel free to argue with us; we can take it. Better yet, find a study partner and read this book together—maybe a chapter a week, that's not a heavy lift—and see how the world opens. I guarantee you'll start to see Torah everywhere.

To cite the famous Rabbinic Chinese proverb: The journey of a thousand verses begins with a single word. So let's begin.

GENESIS

בְּרֵאשִׁית

Between each chapter, we've included a brief summary of key events that take place between where we leave off in one parsha and begin in the next—so that readers have a sense of the full narrative, even as we've chosen to zero in on certain central plot points or ideas.

This first parsha—the start of Genesis and of the entire Torah—opens with void and darkness until God declares: "Let there be light!" and there was light. This is the first act of the six days of the creation of the world, in which God creates: the heavens and the earth, the oceans and the dry land, vegetation and trees, the sun and the moon and the stars, the fish and the birds, the land animals, and finally, human beings. God rests from his work on the seventh day, the Sabbath.

BERESHIT

בְּרֵאשִׁית

AP: Let's start by asking why we are doing this. It may sound nerdy, but you and I have spent so much time together in past years talking about Torah.

DL: And God and the universe and everything.

AP: Just small topics. Over coffee. We have to go to kosher places, but we still have some very un-kosher conversations. And I guess we thought other people might be interested in these conversations because we come from very different ends of the spectrum in terms of observance.

DL: I agree with that.

AP: I don't think we subscribe to labels, but let's just say we're not exactly observing the same way—or as strictly—as each other. It's interesting to come at something as ancient and enduring as this text from different perspectives and ask why it matters.

DL: Because it does matter.

AP: Succinctly put, Dov. I'm looking forward to this ride together.

DL: Me too.

AP: So, let's start at the beginning. The first book of the Torah, Bereshit, literally means "In the beginning," and we've chosen to zero in on humanity—the creation of man and woman, Adam and Eve. Help us understand that there are two creation stories in Bereshit, or Genesis. This is not just a simple tale of "Eve emerging from the rib of Adam."

DL: When you look closely at the text, you realize the story is being told differently from the first chapter to the second. The second one is the most familiar: the Garden of Eden and the rib. But what is less well known is that, in the first chapter, man and woman are created *at the same time*; woman isn't created from man. It says they were created in God's image, they're completely equal, and there's no story about a garden. It was a shock when I first realized this, because the Rabbinic approach is to harmonize these two stories, so initially, I just saw the second story as an interpretation or a continuation of the first.

AP: You mean the two stories are married into a single narrative?

DL: Yes, exactly.

AP: Like it's one story told twice?

DL: It's more like they're telling the story in general terms in the first chapter and then adding specifics in the second. But when you pull back, you realize there are two very different stories being conveyed here.

AP: You and I are assuming people remember the second narrative, but let's just break that down a little more. God puts Adam to sleep and what happens?

DL: He takes a rib—or a side—from Adam and fashions it into a woman. Adam says, "This is now bone of my bones, and flesh of my flesh; she shall be called 'woman,' because she was taken from man" (Gen. 2:23). And then it goes straight to the snake and the Garden of Eden.

AP: It's kind of amazing that most people don't realize these two humans were created at the same time and instead digest this story as if the woman was an afterthought, or an addendum in some way.

DL: That second telling, which is the one that dominates in our mind because it's actually a story with characters, has allowed men throughout history to cite the biblical text to justify the subjugation of women.

AP: That's an important point, but before we get to it, let's focus on the rib for a minute, because it was another eureka moment to realize that there is no anatomical rib in the Bible.

DL: The Bible speaks only of a *tsela,* which can mean "rib," but just as often, it means "side." The classic Rabbinic tradition is that the first human being was created as an androgynous creature—half man, half woman—and that the creation of woman was a splitting of that being down the middle, making each half whole.

AP: That can also correlate to gender identity issues today, which we're seeing playing out across the globe.

DL: Absolutely. Does this first chapter signify that gender is strictly binary, or does it allow for an entire spectrum? In any event, in harmonizing the first and second chapters, the Rabbis acknowledge that man and woman were created equally and at the same time.

AP: I also heard that the apple is not found in the Bible. So, both the apple and the rib are fictions—a shock I'm trying to get over.

DL: That's true.

AP: I want to ask you about the line, "It is not good for man to be alone" in Genesis 2:18. That's God's determination, yes?

DL: That's a declaration, an existential statement.

AP: It strikes me as moving—and maybe I'm looking at it through too contemporary a lens—that aloneness is bad. God has created all these things before humans that are good, and this is the first thing that is bad, which is that man is alone.

DL: Right.

AP: When I think about Judaism, I find it kind of stirring and resonant that our tradition would say, "You should be with others and have companionship; we value partnership, you shouldn't live this life alone." Is that too contemporary a read?

DL: I don't think so. But first, I want to emphasize the power of what you just said—

AP: Are you dodging my question right now?

DL: I'm not dodging your question, but I need to underscore something you said. The entire first chapter is: "God creates the light and says it is good." God creates the animals, and "it is good; it is good; it is good." And then, all of a sudden, God sees that man is alone and says, "This is *not* good." That's really a big, existential, jarring statement—

AP: Crash the cymbals, pound the drums . . . .

DL: Exactly. Aloneness is not the way the world is meant to be. I've always read it with an implied context—that it's talking about man and woman coming together in a sexual union, through the sanctity of marriage.

AP: Where do you get the sex from this?

DL: When it says, "Man will cleave to his wife, and they will be one flesh" (Gen. 2:24), it's talking about them together in sexual union. Certainly, the Rabbis see it that way, so that's the way I am inclined to read it. But the point you've made is that it's a much bigger existential statement. It's not just about marriage; it's about how we fundamentally need partnership and connection. We aren't intended to live as solitary creatures. That's absolutely correct.

AP: Bruce Feiler wrote a book about Adam and Eve called *The First Love Story*. There's a line in it that I love: "Being alive is too overwhelming to be done by yourself." I think that's something a lot of us come to realize on our own, sometimes in the hardest possible way. But to your point, there's definitely Jewish pressure to not be by yourself.

DL: Yes, and in traditional, observant Jewish communities, which tend to be very family-centric, single mothers and single fathers are often seen as not full members, especially if they've never been married. That's something we really need to be attentive to and try to correct.

While we're talking about the importance of marriage, it's helpful to go back and read the first story, when man and woman are created independently and *at the same time*. The Bible never suggests that state of independence is fundamentally "not good." Sometimes, in relationships, people can lose themselves in the other person. I think the idea that you can also stand on your own two feet, separate and apart from your partner, is really important as well.

AP: Okay, Dov, it's your turn to ask *me* something.

DL: This is something that I struggle with: a lot of the Torah assumes a patriarchal society and is androcentric, meaning it sees things from the man's perspective. That bias is evident in the second creation story. Even if we say that Eve wasn't made from Adam's rib and she was, instead, half of him, it is still the man who is the main character, and it is a story about him finding his mate, his wife. How do you deal with text like that when it's not consistent with your values?

AP: I'm always resistant to looking for or interpreting text that supports one's politics, but I do think the first creation story is very encouraging. The equality symbolized by man and woman being created simultaneously is very significant and shouldn't be ignored. I may not be a rabbi, but I've learned that there's not an accidental word in the Torah.

DL: Hard to believe, but true.

AP: And because that's the case, there are also no unintended phrases or verses, which makes that first iteration of humanity very powerful.

DL: So you're saying it's significant that it's the *first* story that has man and woman being created equally.

AP: Yes, I think that matters. I'd add that Judaism itself, our tradition, has already proven how important both the man and woman are in this story. I believe that, whether it's ritual, relationship, or tradition, Judaism, Jewish life, and our personal lives benefit from one another. That's not to say that there is only value in a relationship between a man and a woman. I'm conscious that it could also be a woman and a woman or a man and a man.

DL: That's the heteronormative part of the verse.

AP: Right, but before we get into that, in terms of the sexism of the second story, in a way, I acknowledge that it's simplistic. It's not how we've evolved to think. It's not what gives magic and meaning to relationships and our tradition.

DL: Personally, I'd hesitate to say, "The sexism of the verse . . ." My relationship with the Torah would compel me to say, "What appears to me to be sexist . . .," and then I'd task myself with figuring out how to come to grips with it.

AP: Are you objecting because "sexist" is a facile, modern term?

DL: No, it's that I don't like to take a stance as if I'm in judgment of the text.

AP: I didn't mean to judge it. You had phrased it as something that has been used to justify the idea of a man's superiority to, or the subjugation of, women.

DL: I did, but even if it has been used by men to serve sexist ends, that doesn't make it objectively sexist. But to turn back to the point you were making . . . are you saying that you would, in effect, bracket those parts and say the evolution of our tradition has really been more about the equality of men and women. You really think that's correct? If you look at 3,000 years of tradition, where are you seeing the equality?

AP: We're in a very different place today, and it's no accident we arrived here. Look at everything you've done personally to further a more egalitarian brand of rabbinic education, which we'll hopefully talk about at some point. You obviously still live your life in a very *halachic* [based on Jewish law] way, but you also stand for a more equal model. That's a very different place than where my grandfather's rabbi stood.

DL: I agree with you, but I'd add that the *second* creation story reflects the reality of human society. The first story is sort of the divine perspective, which fundamentally says each person is created equally in the image of God. There's no image of God in the second story. But the way we've structured society for millennia has been patriarchal. By placing the two in tension, the Torah is calling on us to realize the *ideal* of the first story even while we grapple with the *realities* of the second.

AP: I think we can put the frame of this Creation story into the intention of our dialogue here: just as it's not good to be alone, it's also not good to explore Torah alone. How do you like that for an ending button?

DL: That's just great.

AP: Which is why I'm glad we're doing this.

DL: Well, it's our *chavruta*.

AP: It's a beginning.

DL: Yes, it is.

Bereshit to Noach

ADAM AND EVE's time in the Garden of Eden comes to an end when they succumb to temptation and eat from the forbidden Tree of Knowledge of Good and Evil. After God banishes them from the Garden, Eve gives birth to two sons, Cain and Abel. Resentful that Abel is favored by God, Cain kills Abel and is sentenced by God to a life of wandering. Adam and Eve bear another son, Seth, and from his and Cain's descendants, the earth fills with people. But as it does, people begin spreading evil throughout the earth, and God realizes that something must be done.

NOACH

נֹחַ

AP: We are in Noach, in the Book of Genesis.

DL: Or "Noah," without the guttural "ch" for English speakers.

AP: Why don't you anchor us in the story?

DL: Well, in the previous parsha, Bereshit, God created the world and looked at everything and said, "It is good; it is good; it is good." But that parsha ends with something *not* good.

AP: Yes, the first humans have already misstepped.

DL: Bereshit ends by saying that once human beings got to doing actions and deeds, they were doing evil, they were doing wrong—bad as opposed to good.

AP: So God creates humanity, and they immediately start screwing up.

DL: Exactly.

AP: Just to clarify the verse, "The earth became corrupt before God"—that means corrupt in God's eyes?

DL: Yes.

AP: "I have decided to put an end to all flesh, for the earth is filled with lawlessness because of them: I am about to destroy them with the earth" (Gen. 6:13). It's unbelievable to think that God is about to wipe out everything that He or She made. Sometimes I think we don't pause long enough to ask what that says about God.

DL: You mean about Him or Her giving up on humanity?

AP: Well, yes, but humanity is also God's creation, so is there not some culpability that God shares for its flaws and its lawlessness? You made this mess, God!

DL: I think that gets to the question of human beings and free choice, of their becoming divine-like after that first sin.

AP: Wait, why do you say humans became divine-like?

DL: If you go back to Bereshit, the snake says, "You'll be like God if you eat from the tree," and then, after they do, God says, "Behold, man has become like one of us."

AP: Does being Godlike mean being able to choose between good and evil?

DL: I think that's a compelling way to interpret the story—that God creates, acts, and makes moral judgments. God looks at everything and says, "This is good." God then tells us what to do—"Don't eat from the tree"—and when we disobey, we choose our autonomy and independence; we choose to decide what is good and bad and to act accordingly. This gave us free choice, which is an amazing thing to have—we became Godlike!—but when we use this choice, we often choose the wrong path.

AP: But God gave us the agency to do so.

DL: Exactly.

AP: Can you summarize the idea that we have evil and good born in us, that we're predestined to have both sides?

DL: Last week's parsha ended with God saying, "The inclination of man's heart is evil from his youth."

AP: So, as humans, we have both good and evil in us, but everyone up to this point was choosing evil . . . except Noah. But even though he wasn't actively engaged in evil deeds, he wasn't so righteous himself. After being told by God that a catastrophic flood is coming, Noah doesn't even resist God's plan that he and his family will be the only ones spared; Noah doesn't argue on behalf of his people.

DL: The Rabbis do hold Noah accountable for that. He was happy to obediently follow God's command and save his family, and he felt no responsibility to argue with God on behalf of the rest of creation. A good contrast is with Abraham later on, who argues with God to save the people of Sodom; Noah didn't try to persuade God that there were people worth saving, nor did he try to persuade his fellow citizens to better their ways.

On Yom Kippur, we read about the prophet Jonah: God sends him to Nineveh—the sinful city. Jonah tries to avoid that responsibility, but ultimately, he does preach to Nineveh's citizens, and they repent. By contrast, it is enough for Noah to know that he and his family will be safe. There's a Yiddish expression—a *tzaddik in peltz*—which means, "a righteous person wrapped in a fur coat." The point is, if you're cold, you can build a fire and make everybody warm, or you can get yourself a fur coat, and you alone will be warm.

AP: Noah just got himself a fur coat.

DL: Yes. Noah is a righteous person to a degree, but he's a righteous person in *peltz*—in a fur coat.

AP: Why is he considered righteous then? It doesn't make sense that Noah is picked for being superior in some way or for having an absence of corruption. It seems kind of corrupt to be so selfish.

DL: We also don't see any evidence that would demonstrate he *is* a righteous person. On one level, it could be God deciding, "We have to start again; we have to take the one person worth saving." Perhaps Noah happened to be the one who most closely fit that description. The verse does say, "He was righteous *in his generation*."

AP: So by comparison, it was a low bar?

DL: Exactly.

AP: Does the idea that humans started with this predisposition to be bad resonate for you, Dov? What about when you think of your children—do you accept the idea that evil is in us from the start, almost as a given, that we must counter? I resist that. Not that I'm perfect, or even good for that matter, but I don't think I started out evil.

DL: I think Judaism is different from Christianity in the sense that Christianity speaks about how after the Fall—Adam and Eve's transgression—humans are forevermore born in a sinful state.

AP: Don't duck my question. What do you think?

DL: No, I don't think we start out as evil, but we do start with an *inclination* toward evil. That's what the verse is saying. When babies are born, they're very selfish. That's natural; they have to worry about only themselves; they need to be fed, warm, loved. Our concern for others, our empathy, and our desire for a common good in society have to be taught and learned. So, are human beings inherently good or inherently evil? I tend to believe the traditional Rabbinic teaching, which is that we have strong impulses in both directions.

AP: But I think evil is also taught, not just goodness.

DL: I don't think selfishness has to be taught, but I do think evil has to be taught, yes.

AP: Further on into the parsha—after the flood and the destruction of the world—God says essentially, "I'm never going to do that again." I want to ask, "Where's your moral compass, God? How can you obliterate humanity so easily?"

DL: Or, for that matter, "What's making anything better now that You have destroyed everything? What are You going to do differently this time around?" I'm thinking about how, when you're trying to make something—cook a dish, say—and you botch it. It's like, "Oh my God, this is ruined! I'm not going to fix this. I'm just going to toss it all and start over again." That may be one way of looking at why God wiped out the world, but then what? God isn't now going to start making humans any differently. The one big change I see is that after the flood, God starts legislating for humanity. He says, "Anybody who spills the blood of another person, his blood shall be spilled." It's very legalistic, it's almost—

AP: Like God is saying, "There are going to be rules now. I'm not leaving it up to you anymore, because when left to your own devices, you cannot manage yourselves."

DL: Exactly.

AP: These new rules are not like the Ten Commandments, which we hear about in Exodus . . . .

DL: No. In this verse, there are only two: don't murder and don't consume blood, which represents life. The Rabbis, in their interpretations, add more. They say there are seven Noahide laws that were given to Noah and his descendants: don't murder, don't steal, don't commit idolatry, don't commit adultery . . . .

AP: So they're like a preview of the Ten Commandments.

DL: They are very similar. Some people—such as eighteenth-century German philosopher Moses Mendelssohn—viewed these as natural laws and not divine command. But I always found them very powerful as divine laws, because it's rare, if not unique, that a religion says, "There is a path to living a righteous life, even if you're not part of our religion." And Judaism says, "You can be a Jew and do 613 *mitzvot*, or you can be a non-Jew"—

AP: You're saying these laws apply to everyone.

DL: Everyone, yes. The Rabbis understood these divine laws to be given to all of humanity.

AP: Essentially, God is saying, "I am giving you agency, but I am not leaving you on your own. You need guardrails. You need rules. You need laws."

DL: That's the best of both worlds: giving us total freedom of choice but saying, "If you want to choose rightly, I'm going to make it clear to you what I, God, think are the right choices." So, to me, that's the precursor to God choosing Abraham and us receiving all the *mitzvot*, which are part of the Torah. The Torah ends with, "I'm giving you life and death and the good path and the bad path. You should choose life, choose the good path. I'm going to spell it out for you, but in the end, it's your choice to make."

I'd like to return to an earlier point in the story, if I may.

AP: You may.

DL: Before the Noah story, the Torah says that men saw beautiful women and took them—wives of other men—and raped them, and it was after this that God declared mankind evil. Did you see the movie *Noah* that came out a couple years ago?

AP: The one where they really created the flood cinematically in this dramatic way, with the roiling water—

DL: For me, the most arresting image of that movie was the hand reaching for the apple in the Garden of Eden. It symbolized the premise that our desire is to just take, take, take—even things that are not ours, that we're not allowed to have. And that mirrors what is happening today—humanity's despoiling of the earth—which will bring about its ultimate destruction.

AP: Isn't that the same lesson of the defilement of the Garden of Eden? We took too much?

DL: Yes. And I think we're doing the same thing right now in our own lives. It's so easy to criticize Noah and say, "Oh, I can't believe he was so self-concerned that he didn't bother telling anybody about the coming flood; he didn't do anything about it." But I sometimes think that's precisely what we're doing today. How are we changing our own actions to make even a little bit of a difference? How seriously are we taking our responsibility to the earth and to mankind?

AP: That makes me imagine the miraculous moment after the flood when the passengers of the ark are waiting for some sign that there is dry land so they can disembark. It makes me think about images we've seen recently of desperate people after a hurricane or flood waiting to find dry, solid land.

DL: Or what about the polar bear on that tiny ice floe? It's easy to blame Noah's shortsightedness, but have we done what *we* need to do in terms of our own responsibility?

AP: Well, here's to the good half of us.

Noach to Lech Lecha

Noah builds a seaworthy ark per God's instructions, brings his family inside, and fills the ark with a male and female of each species of animal. Having secured a future for human and animal life, God floods the earth with water, wiping out every person and animal outside the ark, and all that existed on the planet. After more than a year, the flood subsides, and Noah, his family, and all the animals exit the ark onto dry land. God vows to never again destroy humanity and places a rainbow in the sky as a symbol of that promise. Sometime later, the earth's inhabitants, all speaking the same language, join forces and attempt to build a tower—the Tower of Babel—so they can all dwell in the same place. But God, wanting the entire world to be inhabited, causes them to speak different tongues, sowing division and confusion, and they become different nations scattered across the earth. Ten generations after Noah, a child named Abram (later called Abraham) is born in the land of Haran.

Lech Lecha

לֶךְ-לְךָ

AP: We are talking about going forth today: Lech Lecha.

DL: Lech Lecha was my *bar mitzvah* parsha.

AP: Well, that has great meaning for us all! Lech Lecha means what?

DL: *Lech* means "go" and *lecha* means "for you." God is saying to Abraham, "Go forth, for you, from your native land and from your father's house to the land that I will show you" (Gen. 12:1). And that's an interesting second word—what did God mean when he said, "Go *for you*"? Rashi says—

AP: Rashi was a medieval commentator.

DL: Yes, he was a classic French commentator on the Bible in the twelfth century.

AP: And his commentary appears on every page of the Talmud.

DL: Correct. Rashi says it means, "Go for your sake. What I'm asking of you is going to be hard." God is telling Abraham to leave his father's house, leave his family, leave his homeland, and go to this new land he knows nothing about, but that it will, ultimately, be better for him.

AP: Let's talk about who's going where. We have God instructing Abram—he's not called Abraham yet—

DL: Good point. Good correction, Abby.

AP: Contextualize for us; where are we in the narrative?

DL: This is ten generations after Noah came out of the ark. Since the flood, humankind has sinned again, this time by building the Tower of Babel and trying to dwell in one place when God wanted them to spread out and inhabit the earth. Though things aren't as bad as they were in the period leading up to the flood, people just keep on sinning. And then, at the end of last week's parsha, we hear that there's this person, Terach, who takes his son, Abram—whose name becomes Abraham twenty-four years later when he's circumcised at ninety-nine years old—to go together with their family toward the land of Canaan—

AP: Later called the Land of Israel.

DL: The Torah doesn't tell us why Abram and his father are going. That story just ends. They were taking that journey, on their own, before God spoke to Abram, and it says that they stopped halfway there. And then, this week's parsha opens with God saying to Abram, "Go—*lech lecha*—to the land that I will show you." This begins a new chapter in Abram's life. Now he is going because God has spoken to him.

AP: Let's read the verse. We're at Genesis 12:1:

> God said to Abram, "Go forth from your native land and from your father's house to the land that I will show you.
> I will make of you a great nation,
> And I will bless you;
> I will make your name great,
> And you shall be a blessing.
> I will bless those who bless you
> And curse the one who curses you;
> And all the families of the earth
> Shall bless themselves by you."
> Abram went forth as God had commanded him.

I feel like singing Debbie Friedman's "Lech Lecha."

DL: The refrain of her song is: "You shall be a blessing."

AP: She sings, "L'chi lach, to a land that I will show you/Leich l'cha, to a place you do not know/L'chi lach, on your journey I will bless you/and you shall be a blessing . . . ."

DL: Do you see this refrain of, "You shall be a blessing" playing out in Abraham's life?

AP: I certainly think there will be riches at the end of the rainbow, but there's a long way for him to go. There's a blessing, I think, in what he has been tasked to carry. He's going to suffer along the way, but he's making a people, and there's blessing in that. And later, he argues with

God on behalf of his people when God is going to destroy Sodom and Gomorrah in Genesis 18. There's a definite leadership moment there.

DL: That's true, he's not just a blind follower, whereas Noah only knew how to follow rules. Abraham—

AP: Well, he's a blind follower, too, when he agrees to sacrifice his son later in Genesis 22. That's the same guy.

DL: Yes, but in general, Abraham is self-driven. He and his father and family start going to the land of Canaan before God even commands him to, so I think that helps us get a sense of who he is. One of the most profound teachings I've read on this opening verse comes from the *Sefat Emet*, the commentary of the third Hasidic Rabbi of Ger, Poland. He asked this question: "Why, of all people in humanity, did God choose Abraham?"

AP: And . . .?

DL: He says, God did not choose Abraham. God did not say, "*Lech lecha*" to Abraham alone. God said it to *all* of humanity.

AP: But . . . ?

DL: But Abraham was the only one who was listening. He, alone, of all humankind, heard God's *lech lecha*.

AP: I love that.

DL: *Sefat Emet* continues and says this call did not only happen this one time. Rather, a call goes out from heaven every day, saying "*lech lecha*." Follow your calling; follow your destiny. The question is—are we listening?

AP: And it means any one of us could be an Abraham and can listen for that mandate in some way. What are we called for? Maybe it has nothing at all to do with what we have accomplished or earned that makes us able to hear it.

DL: I think that's maybe the meaning of "*lecha*": You have to hear this voice, this calling, and know what it means *for you*. Where you should go and what you should do is different for each person, but we have to listen for it.

AP: But there also is a sense that we need a leader to go ahead of us. You couldn't have the rest of the story without Abraham, and in some way, it feels like we can't do it on our own. Even though God's voice is in all of us, we kind of need a rabbi.

DL: There are trailblazers, but you're right, most people are not prepared to be an Abraham.

AP: One of the things that has been used against Jews is the idea that we feel entitled to the Holy Land because of these verses. Particularly, the idea that we were predestined for a place based on divine mandate, and we are trying to fulfill or claim our inheritance. But that is a Torah that many people don't live by.

DL: As soon as Abraham enters the Land, God says, "All the land that you see I will give to you and your descendants," and that is consistently repeated through Bereshit, the first book of the Torah.

AP: And it's repeated today.

DL: Yes. It is used by people to dictate their politics and to defend actions that others think are unjustified, immoral, and violent—all because God promised us this land.

AP: And some people say those believers in God-given property are *meshugenah*, like, "They believe this made-up story?" The Torah is not a verifiable text.

DL: I think the more pointed response is, "Even if it *is* a divine promise, that doesn't give you license to perpetrate violence unto other people."

AP: What do you mean by that? Even if you believe that God—

DL: Even if you believe that God promised the land, that does not give you license to act in ways that violate morality and *halacha*. I think that's a core message of traditional Judaism: we're not biblical Jews. We're Rabbinic Jews, or *halachic* Jews, and that means we do not live in a world of divine promises. We live in a world in which we are responsible for our actions.

AP: But when some say it's a given—and I know you don't want to get political—that we can annex the West Bank because God commanded it of us . . . .

DL: That's not *halacha*. Going back a few decades, when there was a major debate about giving back the Sinai as part of brokering a peace with Egypt, some rabbis said, "You can't give back one inch of the land; this is the most important value; this is the divinely-promised land." But this great rabbi, Rabbi Ovadia Yosef, who was the Sephardi chief rabbi—

AP: You're dropping a lot of "rabbis" there, Dov.

DL: What can I tell you, these are my pals.

AP: What did Yosef say?

DL: He said, "You're totally wrong! We have a *halachic* mandate to protect life and ensure our own security, and that is our obligation much more so than fulfilling divine promises. Securing peace is of utmost importance.

AP: But wait, couldn't that *square* with the divine promises?

DL: I want to cite another rabbi—Rabbi Yosef Soloveitchik. Rabbi Soloveitchik was the Torah leader of Modern Orthodoxy in the last generation, a towering Talmudist and Jewish philosopher. When this issue came up, he once said that when you need to decide whether it is good or bad for your security to give back land, you do not ask a rabbi. You ask the generals, and politicians, and the people who know if that is in the country's best interest. That is what Rabbi Ovadia Yosef was saying: put the divine promises aside—*halacha* obligates us to first determine whether this is in our best interest for security.

AP: In other words, it might be in our best interest to *give over* some land.

DL: Exactly. If God wants this divine promise to be fulfilled, that's God's responsibility. Our obligation is to live a life of morality and *halacha*. Rabbi Yosef's position was that, from a *halachic* perspective, our prime responsibility is to the people and not to the land.

AP: So, if the people are safe because some land was relinquished, that is a higher mandate.

DL: A divine promise is not a mandate, and it's not a *mitzvah*. It is something God says that God will do. When God makes a promise, it's for God to see whether it gets fulfilled or not. We take our marching orders from the *mitzvot*, from what God *tells us* to do, not from what God *promises us*.

AP: What do you think about that, personally?

DL: It totally speaks to me. It's the reason I love *halacha*, because it's not saying, "We're going to take these broad religious ideas and just live them in a vacuum and not care about those whom we're impacting and affecting." No. We're going to have to own the messiness of our lives and contradictory demands and navigate them with a full sense of responsibility for the choices we make.

AP: But many people would say they think of *halacha* as being immovable: "It is what it is. This parsha tells us the land is ours, and that's where we stand."

DL: Yes, but again, that's not *halacha*. It's a divine promise, and we're not biblical Jews; we're Rabbinic Jews—*halachic* Jews. That's the Judaism I believe in.

Lech Lecha to Vayera

After having been commanded by God to leave his home for "the land that I will show you," Abram, with his wife Sarai and nephew Lot, arrive in Canaan. Abram builds altars and proclaims his faith to God, goes to Egypt in a time of famine to later return with much wealth, and fights a war to rescue his nephew, Lot, who had been taken captive. God promises to give the land to Abram's innumerable descendants but warns they will first undergo exile and slavery. When Sarai is infertile, Abram takes Sarai's maidservant, Hagar, as a second wife. Hagar becomes pregnant, and after being treated harshly by Sarai, runs away from Abram's home only to be told by an angel to return. She does so and gives birth to a son, Ishmael, when Abram is eighty-six years old.

God later makes a covenant with Abram, commanding him, as a sign of the covenant, to circumcise himself and all his male offspring, which Abram does. God changes Abram's name to Abraham and Sarai's to Sarah and tells Abraham that Sarah will bear to him a son, Isaac, who will be his heir.

Three angels visit Abraham and Sarah's tent to inform them Sarah is about to become pregnant, despite her old age. Abraham is also told of God's plan to wipe out the sinful cities of Sodom and Gomorrah. Abraham protests the death of the innocent people that will result, and argues with God to save Sodom if even ten innocent people can be found. Despite Abraham's best attempts, angels travel forth to destroy Sodom and to save Abraham's nephew, Lot, and his travel forth. Sarah gives birth to Isaac. Soon after, Abraham expels Hagar and Ishmael at Sarah's direction, and Isaac becomes Abraham's uncontested sole heir.

VAYERA

וַיֵּרָא

AP: Today we're going to be talking about one of the hardest chapters in the Torah, which is the "Binding of Isaac," often referred to as the *Akedah* or "Binding."

DL: It is a hard chapter. Genesis 18 is where this story starts.

AP: Translate the word *vayera* for us, Dov.

DL: It means "and He appeared." God appeared to Abraham. This is when the angels come to tell him that his wife Sarah will give birth to a son, Isaac, after decades of infertility.

AP: Even though she's ninety. God then appears to Abraham at the end of the parsha to stop him from murdering Isaac—which God had told him to do in the first place—and which any of us who are parents cannot fathom.

First, let's remind ourselves what is happening here: Abraham has taken his blessed, precious son up Mount Moriah.

DL: Yes. Abraham does this after God tells him, "Take your son, your only son, Isaac . . . and offer him up as a sacrifice" (Gen. 22:2).

AP: But he doesn't explain why.

DL: Correct.

AP: How do we know Abraham is actually preparing to do this? He goes with a knife and a donkey and—

DL: Fire. The meaning of sacrifice in this context is a "burnt offering," so there's a fire there as well. Abraham binds Isaac, and then he raises his hand and is ready to slaughter him.

AP: Then what happens?

DL: An angel comes from heaven and says, "Abraham, Abraham!" and he answers, "Here I am." The angel says, essentially, "Don't cast your hand against the child. Now I know that you are truly God-fearing."

Abraham looks around and sees a ram caught in the thicket, and he offers it up as a sacrifice in place of his son.

AP: This is obviously a very challenging story for any of us to imagine. Why would Judaism require a moment like this, a symbol of faith like this? It's too much to ask. What positive message could possibly come out of such a disturbing story?

DL: Different people struggle with it in distinctive ways. I think the thing that smacks us in the face nowadays is murder in the name of God—believing God has commanded you to do something that justifies not only martyring yourself but also taking somebody else's life.

AP: That sounds like a suicide bomber's justification.

DL: Exactly. So, is that the lesson the Torah is trying to teach us? That if God speaks to you and says, "Commit murder in my name," you should do it? I would say, absolutely not.

From a traditional perspective, the central message of the story can be found in the verse where God says, "Take your son, your only son, the one you love . . . ." It is meant to teach us that we should be prepared to give up what is most dear to us to serve God. In the end, God doesn't want to take Abraham's child or any child. That is the key teaching at the end of the story, when the angel stays Abraham's hand: God does *not* want us to take a human life in God's name.

I think this story is telling us two things. One, is in the message of the angel stopping the sacrifice: do not take a human life in God's name. And two, the message at the beginning of the story: be prepared to give fully of yourself and make sacrifices to serve God.

AP: Is it possible that this was God's way of testing Abraham and saying, "I *want* you to defy me. I *want* you to refuse me. This is to show you that your agency—your moral compass—matters, and you should not just blindly follow me."

DL: Certainly that's a contemporary read of the story. But if so, Abraham fails the test because he was ready to go through with the sacrifice.

AP: Wait, when you say, "a contemporary read," is that derogatory?

DL: No, not at all! But do I agree with that perspective? No, I don't. I think it violates the plain meaning of the text. Because the angel appears and says, "Now I know that you're truly God-fearing because you did not hold back your son, your only son, from me" (Gen. 22:12). So, I can't see how one can interpret it in a way that suggests Abraham failed because he was supposed to refuse the task.

The viewpoint I'm suggesting is a very traditional one. In our liturgy, we have a prayer that references the Binding of Isaac, and it goes something like this: "The same way that Abraham did not hold back that which was most dear to him, God, you should not hold back your compassion, your kindness from us." This almost ignores, or at least isolates, the fact that there was a human life at stake. It's more a symbol of being willing to give anything to serve God.

AP: But that also feels like a simplistic way to get out of a very hard thing. The text is the text. It's not symbolic; it's an assignment to kill.

DL: Yes, I think the text is morally challenging with any reading, contemporary or traditional. I think it needs to remain so. And we need to continue to grapple with it.

AP: So for a person who has no faith or struggles with faith, is this story irrelevant to them? Is there something in it for someone who struggles with the concept of God?

DL: I have to think about that one. You are right that my focus has been on someone who believes in God and can learn from this story that sometimes, serving God can require serious demands of us, and we have to strive to live up to them. But what might this story say to a non-believer? I guess I would still focus on the importance of sacrifice, even in the absence of God. I'm reminded of the quote—I don't remember who said it—that "If you don't have anything you're prepared to die for, then you don't have anything you're prepared to live for." If there's not something you are willing to sacrifice for, then what is your life about? I think that's a challenging question for a lot of us nowadays.

AP: I guess what it would mean to me—and I am a person of faith, obviously, but I know a lot of people who aren't—is a sense of the stakes being *that* high. That you would do something that hurts or inconveniences you for the sake of something bigger. Obviously, killing your child is more than an inconvenience—but if we're going to accept the metaphor, it's that you would do something that isn't easy for you or in your best interest because there's a greater kind of devotion, a higher obligation.

DL: If you ask most people, "What would you give your life for?" I think the first thing most people would say is, "My family or my kids," you know—

AP: But that's the irony—

DL: Yes, I was going to say that too. It's so ironic. But yes, I think that is a really good point. There's power in having something that you're willing to give everything for.

AP: Is it ever asked in the Orthodox community, or assumed, that ultimately, your love of God is greater than your love of your children?

DL: Well . . . wow, that's . . . .

AP: Let me ask that differently. It's a little unfair. Is it ever discussed, explicitly and literally, that your devotion to God must come before your devotion to anything else, including the love for your children? Is that a conversation that happens because of this parsha?

DL: Well, not because of this parsha. But here's something that connects to your question. In Talmudic times, many Torah scholars would be absent from their home and shirk their responsibilities to their spouse and their children for the sake of learning Torah. Some sages were okay with that, and some deeply condemned it. The twentieth-century historian of religion, Daniel Boyarin, has a chapter about this in his book *Carnal Israel*, called, "Torah as the Other Woman." Consider Moshe—

AP: Moshe, just to remind folks, is Moses—

DL: After Moses goes up to Mount Sinai, God says to him, essentially, "Go tell the people to return to their tents. But you stay here with Me" (Deut. 5:30–31). The Rabbis interpret this to mean that Moses was told to separate from his wife and devote himself to God. Nobody else, though, was given that license. The rest of us are supposed to live our lives in this world.

AP: What about Rabbi Akiva? Didn't he disappear to go study for many years?

DL: Yes, for twenty-four years. So you're right, it wasn't just Moses. That's always the question, though: who is entitled to act like that? Who is permitted to devote themselves to God at the expense of their family?

AP: That's not good for a relationship.

DL: No kidding! Are those people glorified as ideals that other people—usually men in this case—should strive to be like? Or are they the exceptions and not indicative of how the Torah really wants us to live our lives?

AP: All right, we should challenge each other with a surprise question. Why don't you surprise me first?

DL: My question to you is: When you confront a challenging text like this, do you try to view it in a historical context so you can see how this could have worked for people in the past, to keep it at arm's length, or do you ask yourself, "What meaning can I get out of this in the present?"

AP: I would say it's the latter. I want to see if there's meaning that resonates for me. But I'm also aware that this parsha is the very beginning of a long, unfolding story. Everybody's working it out for the first time—and not just Abraham but God, too. We've already seen how God created humanity and then wiped it out with the flood. So, I understand that God is learning along the way, just as the patriarchs and matriarchs are learning. In that sense, I'm fascinated by the *Akedah* being a very early incarnation of what it means to prove your faith. Because I'm not sure God made the right decision here. I'm not sure Abraham did either, by not protesting. I don't think God should have asked Abraham for this sacrifice in the first place, and I don't think Abraham should have said yes. But both did. In that sense, I am riveted by the extremes of this story.

DL: You're sort of seeing this in the arc where God realizes he needs to start over again and destroys the world. And then, "Wait a minute, human beings actually have an evil inclination, so I've got to figure out a new way of dealing with them." And here in this parsha, we also see God demanding unthinkable sacrifices and realizing, "Maybe I don't have to make these demands going forward." Is that how you're reading it?

AP: Yes, partly because I have evidence. I mean, in the Noah story, God says, "Well, that flood thing . . . I'm not doing *that* again. I'm not wiping out humanity again." That seems to indicate a pretty big regret after losing an untold number of people whom you just created.

DL: Right.

AP: There is a kind of proof in the text for God wanting a do-over or saying, "I'm not going to repeat that." It makes me think that, in this parsha, God is in the nascent stages of managing the first Jew—Abram or Abraham—and maybe God still hasn't gotten it quite right. You said something that I think is very strong, which is that Abraham was listening when God was talking.

DL: Yes.

AP: But suddenly, there was silence after the *Akedah*. Even after this dramatic near-murder of his child, and after affirming his faith *exactly* the way he was told to . . . . Abraham did everything right, and then God just stopped talking to him.

DL: That is a great point. And thank you for mentioning it, because I think God's silence is something a lot of people struggle with. I think some people live their whole lives believing God isn't talking to them. How do you deal with that emptiness if you want God to be talking to you? Your religion might talk to you, but you never feel that's the same as God.

Something closer to the Abraham experience would be someone who leads a deeply religious life and has heard God talking to them and then some tragedy happens. Say they lose a child, God forbid, and then they feel they're not hearing God anymore. God's silence is definitely one of the challenges we face nowadays.

AP: But I also see so many people going through impossibly hard things who seem to find a kind of strength or calm in the idea that God, or some larger force, is walking with them. So some do continue to hear God.

DL: I truly hope so.

Vayera to Chayei Sarah

SARAH DIES IN the city of Hebron at the age of 127. After weeping over and eulogizing his wife, Abraham negotiates the purchase of the Cave of Machpelah in Hebron as a burial plot for Sarah, himself, and their descendants. Just before Sarah's death, Abraham received news that his sister-in-law Milkah had given birth to eight sons, the last of whom had a daughter named Rebekah.

Chayei Sarah

חַיֵּי שָׂרָה

AP: We are in Chayei Sarah, which translates to . . . .

DL: "The life of Sarah." Abraham's wife. But it really opens with her death.

AP: Right . . . that's so Judaism.

DL: It basically says, "She lived 127 years and she died." And then it opens with the story of Abraham looking for a place to bury her.

AP: I'm going to be reading not about her burial, but later when Abraham says to his son, Isaac, "It's time for you to get a wife. I'm sending my servant to look for one for you."

DL: Abraham doesn't even discuss this with Isaac; Isaac is just talked *about*. He's offstage, and Abraham calls his servant over—

AP: That's putting a lot of faith in the servant.

DL: He says, "I need you to go find Isaac a wife." The verse says it's his trusted servant, because you're right, sending someone to find the right woman for his son *is* putting a lot of faith in him.

AP: You've teed us up perfectly, Dov. Genesis 24:13 reads, "Here I stand by the spring . . . ." Who is "I" here?

DL: The servant.

AP: The servant continues:

> As the daughters of the townsmen come out to draw water, let the maiden to whom I say, "Please lower your jar that I may drink," and who replies, "Drink, and I will also water your camels"—let her be the one whom You have decreed for Your servant, Isaac.

Meaning, the person who offers water—not just to him but also his camels—is the woman for Isaac.

DL: Yes, and the servant continues:

AP: "'Therefore shall I know that You have dealt graciously with my master.' He had scarcely finished speaking when Rebekah, who was born to Bethuel, the son of Milcah, the wife of Abraham's brother Nahor—" That's a lot of names, but we don't need to keep track. Rebekah came out with her jar on her shoulder. "When she had let him drink his fill, she said, 'I will also draw for your camels until they finish drinking.'" Ding, ding, ding! She passed the test!

DL: Superbly!

AP: And she went on, "There is plenty of straw and feed at home and also room to spend the night." So she even invites him to stay with her family. Her hospitality goes above and beyond.

DL: And although the servant prayed to God for help, he already knows what type of person he is looking for: someone of enormous caring and kindness.

So, Abby, can you think of any instances when you did something Rebekah-like?

AP: I think it would take hubris to say so, but in my own private compass, I am trying to do that at least once a week.

DL: Really?

AP: Yes, just in terms of volunteering to mentor underserved high school seniors and knowing that when I have to show up, it's not always convenient for me. There are times when I don't feel like going or times the kids I'm mentoring aren't really responsive. It's not always perfect, but that's not the point. It's not about my convenience or my comfort or the ease of it. We're supposed to go beyond just providing water to drink.

DL: That's a great analogy. You also make a good point about structuring your time. For me, the hardest is when you're busy and somebody interrupts, and you have to redirect yourself. I remember one time when I was downtown, an elderly woman asked me for directions. I could have just given them to her, but I wasn't sure she'd be able to find her way, so I walked with her for about twenty minutes to make sure she knew where she was going.

AP: That's a Rebekah moment.

DL: Sure, but all along I was thinking, *Oh my God, I can't believe I got myself into this*. But I was also thinking, *No, I'm supposed to be doing this. It is the right thing.*

AP: You didn't invite her home for lunch, though.

DL: Ha! Very true. But I think you're right—we need to structure time in our day when we do things that are not about our convenience or our needs, but about giving to others.

AP: We always think, *I can't possibly add anything else to my plate*, but then you realize—of course you can.

DL: There's always time for kindness.

AP: What about the fact, though, that Rebekah, for all this kindness, or *chesed*, is the one who goes on to deceive her husband, Isaac, and entreat her son Jacob to steal the birthright from his brother by engaging in a very deceptive plan? Squaring her as both a role model and a manipulator is hard for me.

DL: Well, let's also remember that she is the one who gets the divine message that Jacob will be the chosen son. So, the dynamics playing out there—

AP: You mean, she's fulfilling some divine direction?

DL: Yes, that's next week's parsha. It starts by telling us that the twins she was pregnant with were causing her agony, and she seeks out the Lord, and the Lord speaks directly to her and says, "The older one will serve the younger one."

AP: But that doesn't mean she had to engineer some kind of deception to make it come about. Rebekah is the person who draws water for this stranger and all his camels. She presumably knows the difference between doing something good and something you wouldn't want your kids to emulate. I guess it goes back to what we were saying about Abraham: He's not perfect. He's chosen, but that doesn't mean he is without blemish. He argues on behalf of humanity in Sodom and Gomorrah, but he doesn't argue when God tells him to sacrifice his own son. I guess Rebekah is human, too, in that sense.

DL: Yes, they're complex characters. I'm sure you know people who can be very generous one minute and callous, maybe even manipulative, the next. I certainly do.

I want to ask you a question. Rebekah's kindness wasn't just an exemplary quality—it was *the* quality that Abraham's servant was looking for in a mate for Isaac. Do you think kindness is the core quality that we should look for in a mate? If you had to pick just one test, what would it be?

AP: That's a surprising question. Now that I have kids in their twenties, I do think about what I would want them to look for in a life partner. I feel lucky to have found a husband who is consistently kind. But when I think about how I evaluated David when I first met him, it wasn't necessarily about his kindness. I mean, I thought he was a nice guy, but there are so many other things that society tells us to look for in a mate: someone who's a self-starter or does interesting things, is a good communicator, has a sense of humor . . . . Eventually, you see someone's kindness over time, and it's something you value and fall in love with, but I'm not sure it was the first test.

DL: So, if you had to tell your kids the most important thing to look for in a mate, what would it be?

AP: I would say, "Choose someone you want to talk to everyday," which, in a way, encompasses kindness. But a person can be very kind and also very dull, honestly, so they may not be the best match for you.

DL: That's an interesting take.

AP: What about you?

DL: I think I would tell my children to find somebody who's totally devoted to them, to their success, and their self-actualization. I think that can be a real issue in marriage. I would say to look for generosity of spirit—if not exactly *kindness*—to others. Marriages present challenges, and maybe that's somewhat related to the importance of a sense of humor, but I think generosity of spirit is key.

AP: I certainly feel that my husband is kinder than I am. And I'm so glad my kids have grown up with someone who has a bedrock sense of what's fair and what's good. And it's not something that even has to be said—it's just what they see in him every day.

DL: Amen to kind spouses!

Chayei Sarah to Toldot

Rebekah accompanies Abraham's servant back to the land of Canaan, where she marries Isaac. She becomes pregnant with twin boys, and God tells her that the older child will serve the younger. Esau is born first and becomes a hunter and a "man of the field." Jacob, who follows him, is "a simple man, one who dwells in tents."

One day, Esau returns from a hunt exhausted and ravenous. When he sees Jacob cooking a lentil stew, he begs his brother to feed him. Jacob agrees but only on the condition that Esau sells him his birthright. Esau agrees.

As Isaac nears death, he asks his son Esau to hunt game and bring it to him so he may bestow upon him his final blessing. After overhearing this, Rebekah tells Jacob to disguise himself and approach his father as if he were Esau. Isaac, nearly blind, is tricked into bestowing his blessing on his younger son.

Toldot

תּוֹלְדֹת

AP: This week's parsha is Toldot, which means . . . .

DL: "Generations."

AP: And we're talking about how we might be able to square the moral actions of Jacob and the patriarchs.

DL: Yes, that's right.

AP: Let's summarize the basic story. Jacob, at the behest of his mother, Rebekah, who is scheming and telling her son to pull the wool over his father's blind eyes—

DL: It is Jacob's father, Isaac, who is blind—

AP: Rebekah essentially says to Jacob, "Go to your dad and pretend you are your twin brother, Esau, who's the firstborn and therefore entitled to the birthright. Your father will bless you instead, and you'll go on to great things."

DL: Like any good Jewish son, Jacob listens to his mother.

AP: And he cheats Esau out of something that was rightfully his.

DL: Esau finds out, and he's murderously angry. He exclaims—and here I'm paraphrasing from Genesis 27:36—"Ah, this is why he's called 'Jacob,' because he's tricked me twice." Jacob's very name is associated with deceit. The Hebrew word for Jacob—*Yaakov*—comes from the word meaning a heel, something bent, rather than something straight and honest.

The question this parsha raises for me—and for a lot of people, I think—is: What should we infer from the fact that the Bible includes this story of our patriarch, Jacob? Is it that the Torah holds this type of behavior up as a model, as an exemplar, or, at the very least, condones it?

AP: It's especially curious because it's not the only instance of deception in the Bible. It's almost like duplicity gets passed down through the generations. In Toldot, Rebekah gave this idea to Jacob, and Jacob is later tricked himself. His uncle Laban engineers a switch of his daughters under nightfall, so that Jacob sleeps with Leah instead of Rachel, and later Jacob's sons trick him into thinking his favorite son, Joseph, is dead. Then, even later, Joseph tricks the rest of his brothers when they come to him for help. It's almost like deception is in this family's DNA now.

DL: By extension, this becomes the stereotype of the Jew as the trickster, the schemer, willing to do anything to make a profit. We are criticized, and we've suffered because of this stereotype, and this story seems to confirm this ugly trope. Christians in the Middle Ages *used* this story to say, "You Jews are tricksters. You are schemers. Just like your forefather, Jacob."

AP: "The Torah says it, so it must be true . . . ."

DL: Yes, they use the Torah's words to justify this belief as if it applies to all Jewish people. By the way, a fascinating aside—in the Rabbinic mindset, Rome descended from Esau, and therefore Christianity, which was adopted by the Roman Empire, also becomes identified with him. So the enmity between Esau and Jacob from the biblical period later returns in the forms of Christianity and Judaism.

AP: Interesting parallel. But I still have a problem with Jacob being held up as a role model, whom, as a patriarch, we're presumably supposed to emulate. I'm uncomfortable with how Christians have used the story to fuel their antisemitic bile, but that doesn't exempt us from having to wrestle with Jacob's behavior.

DL: I totally agree. And, as you know, the traditional way of dealing with this problem is to excuse it, to paper over it to some degree, to—

AP: When you say "traditional," what do you mean?

DL: The medieval commentators—

AP: The rabbis—

DL: Yes. To defend Jacob's honor, and probably in response to Christian attacks, these rabbis said, "What he did wasn't so bad. It was actually totally moral." But when Jacob comes in and presents himself as Esau to his father, Jacob flat-out lies. Isaac, who can't see, says to his son, "Who are you?" And Jacob says, "I am Esau, your firstborn." But then these commentators say, "He didn't really lie; we have to reread that verse. What Jacob is really saying is, "I am"—*period*: "I am." And then, "Esau is your firstborn."

AP: Making it into two separate thoughts. So basically, they inserted some punctuation that makes him not a liar.

DL: *Technically* not a liar. But then what's the message? What's the lesson learned when we repeat this Rabbinic interpretation? If this becomes part of how we're educating our kids—which often is the case, at least within traditional circles—then the cost of defending Jacob's honor is teaching that it's okay to lie and cheat as long as you're not technically telling a lie.

AP: So you acknowledge that he's a liar. Is that the end of the story for you? Or is there an "And yet . . ." coming?

DL: Yes: *And yet* . . . I don't think the Torah itself is condoning Jacob's behavior. If you continue to read the story, you see that Jacob comes to suffer a great deal.

AP: How so?

DL: Well, as you pointed out, he is later deceived the same way he deceived others. He runs away from Esau and goes to the house of Laban, his uncle, where he falls in love with Rachel, Laban's younger daughter. Then, on his wedding night, Laban tricks Jacob, and Jacob winds up marrying Leah, the older daughter, instead. The message seems to be clear: because you, Jacob, the younger son, pretended to be Esau, the older son, in order to claim his birthright, now you will get your just desserts and have the younger daughter you love switched for the older one. As a result, Jacob winds up married to a woman he doesn't love and has to tend Laban's sheep for seven more years.

AP: So that's his punishment.

DL: Yes. It's like karma; if you put evil out there, it will come back to you. The Rabbis teach that God rewards and punishes "measure for measure." So at least the Torah is not condoning this type of immoral behavior.

AP: If you lie, you will be lied to.

DL: Correct. I think, in terms of my circles, the traditional community needs to call out this problem or else we are continuing to say that immoral behavior is okay. And you have to say—clearly—that Jacob was wrong, and he was punished. I think—and this is true more in general about sacred texts—we in the Orthodox community are often so ready to defend the text or the morality of the actors that we wind up condoning wrong behavior. We have to acknowledge what Jacob did was wrong, see that he got punished, and allow for the fact that our patriarch is imperfect. I think being forthright about Jacob's sin is worth it in order to not perpetuate bad behavior.

AP: But Jacob still got rewarded. He got the birthright. I'm not sure punishment is the takeaway here.

DL: I hear that. You're right, it hasn't really been resolved. But I think it starts by acknowledging the problem and not trying to explain it away. So bottom line, Abby, what's your final thought? Is Jacob nobody special?

AP: Obviously he's special, but the ends don't justify the means in my book. The Torah seems to be saying, "Look beneath the surface, and don't simply accept what's presented to you." It's another example of our Torah challenging us to see the human truth of our protagonists, to think critically about them and say, "There are parts of this person that I admire and parts that I reject."

DL: The only thing I would add is that I, personally, need to couple my criticisms with a sense of reverence. Jacob is one of our patriarchs. Part of my traditional orientation is that he must be revered, while at the same time, I believe it's necessary to address the problems and critique his behavior.

AP: I revere your reverence, Dov.

Toldot to Vayetzei

Fearful of Esau's murderous rage after Jacob stole his blessing, Rebekah, their mother, tells Jacob to flee the land of Canaan and to go to his uncle Laban's house in Haran until Esau's anger subsides. Isaac also charges him to go to Laban's land to choose a wife from one of Laban's daughters.

At one point during his journey, Jacob lies down to sleep and dreams of a ladder extending above his head toward the heavens. As angels ascend and descend the ladder, God appears above Jacob and promises to protect him, assuring that he and his descendants will inherit the land of Canaan. When Jacob wakes, he is filled with awe, realizing that above him are the very "gates of Heaven." He marks the spot with a stone, promising to establish that place as a house for God.

Upon arriving in Haran, Jacob sees Rachel, Laban's younger daughter and immediately falls in love with her. He agrees to tend to Laban's flock for seven years for the right to marry Rachel, but he is tricked on the wedding night into marrying Leah, the older daughter, instead. He is then also given Rachel as a wife on the condition that he tend Laban's sheep for yet another seven years.

VAYETZEI

וַיֵּצֵא

AP: We are now in Genesis 29 and talking about the sisters, Leah and Rachel.

DL: The parsha is Vayetzei, which means, "He went from the land." Jacob is running away from his brother, Esau, who wants to kill him for stealing what was meant to be his blessing. Jacob arrives at Laban's home—

AP: Laban is his uncle.

DL: Yes, and there he meets his two wives.

AP: But he doesn't know they're going to be his wives yet.

DL: Right, exactly.

AP: You're jumping the gun here. If you were writing a movie, you would have ruined the arc. Maybe we should first set up Rachel and Leah and who they are. They're sisters—Laban's daughters—and one of them is described as beautiful while the other is not.

DL: It doesn't say Leah isn't pretty; it says her eyes were soft. We tend to assume she was less pretty than Rachel.

AP: In my translation, Genesis 29:17 says, "Leah had weak eyes; Rachel was shapely and beautiful."

DL: So, by contrasting the two, the implication is that Leah was not pretty.

AP: Why are you resisting that contrast?

DL: I just don't think it *explicitly* says that Leah was not attractive, but I think that's the right read.

AP: What strikes me about this parsha and these two sisters is that they end up at war with each other over one man, and it feels like the worst kind of lesson, which is that ultimately, the popular, prettier girl wins.

DL: Yes, I think that's totally correct. You know, I'm sure, about this modern test about Hollywood movies, how they're all about men, and whether women have more than a few minutes—

AP: The Bechdel Test.

DL: That's the one. It asks whether there's more than a few minutes of dialogue between two women that's *not about a man*. I think our parsha would totally fail that test because, while there's a focus on the sisters, it's all about fighting over Jacob and his attention.

AP: Very true. Let's go to Genesis 29:31: "And the Lord saw that Leah was hated, and he opened her womb; but Rachel was barren." So God helps Leah gain an advantage by making her fertile, but Rachel, with all of her physical advantages is suffering from infertility.

DL: Yes, and I think that speaks not only to Jacob's affections but to a woman's worth in that society and to her perception of her own value. This story parallels another story about Hannah and Peninnah, which we read in the Book of Samuel on Rosh Hashanah. Peninnah has many children, and Hannah, who is barren, is distraught. Her husband, Elkanah, says to her, "Don't let not having children trouble you. I love you and am totally devoted to you; aren't I better than many children?" It doesn't help, she's still bereft. Ultimately, it ends with—

AP: Hannah giving birth.

DL: Yes, Hannah prays to God and gives birth to Samuel who becomes a great prophet. But, to me, one of the messages is how much having children was prized, not only by society—

AP: It was also self-defining.

DL: Precisely. "If I can't have children, what is my worth as a woman, even if my husband is devoted to me?"

AP: It struck me while reading this that Leah and Rachel are using fertility as a way to win, to be victorious in some way. To go back to what you were saying about self-worth, verse 30:1 says, "Rachel envied her sister, and she said unto Jacob, "Give me children or else I'll die." I remember Hannah had the same desperation. I think there's an implication that a woman's life is tied to her ability to give life.

DL: I think that's completely correct. And I don't know how much we've escaped that at this point in our society. I'm curious about your perspective. How much do you think that still defines a woman's sense of self-worth?

AP: I think it's still pretty dominant. There are all kinds of ways women define their self-worth that go beyond fertility, but I think it cuts to the core of a woman's identity not to be able to conceive if she wants to. Part of that is some kind of maternal drive, but I do think there's also something extremely powerful about the cycle of life. To be denied that is, in a way, more viscerally difficult than people can appreciate unless they've been there. At my synagogue, Central Synagogue, Rabbi Angela Buchdahl asked a congregant to offer some personal remarks about infertility on Rosh Hashanah morning, as an introduction to the Hannah story, which, as you mentioned, is always read aloud. You could have heard a pin drop in the sanctuary, and it was exactly about this issue: all our Jewish structures and *simchas* [joyous events] are heavily geared toward family and the tumult of many children, cousins, aunts, and uncles. If you're excluded from that, you are, in a way, cut out of Jewish life.

DL: That is something we try to sensitize our rabbinical students to. I remember one student and his wife got up at their son's *bris* and talked about their challenges with infertility and what their path felt like until they were able to have a child. Another spoke at his son's *bris* and said, "I want to acknowledge that there might be some here who are struggling to have a child." We need to surface this issue much more.

I want to turn back to the sister discussion and what is redeeming about this story. This is the one place where we focus on our foremothers—the one story about sisters in the Torah—and it's all petty rivalry, catfights, and attention-seeking. Do we find anything redeeming? We've seen Jacob and Esau fighting, but they eventually reconcile. But here, we're left with this image of our foremothers.

AP: I find it pretty simplistic. Whoever the authors are—divine or human—they are really missing the truth of what I've experienced and witnessed when it comes to a sisterly relationship. It is not centered on competition. I know that rivalry exists for some, but it isn't a given, and I say that as an identical twin. Suggesting it's a battle is not just reductive, it's kind of dehumanizing; it gives the sisters no layers of humanity and character other than this, which is, "I want him to sleep with *me*; I want to produce children for *him*." It's all about pleasing this man, getting this man, not about *their* relationship, *their* interactions, or their history at all.

DL: These sisters were put in a very difficult situation. They were married to the same man. One was beautiful and loved, and the other was fertile. It was a recipe for disaster; I'm not sure how any of us would fare in that situation. But it is the only story that we have in the Torah about their relationship as sisters. The Rabbis' commentary gives more compassionate color to the story we referenced earlier about switching the brides in the middle of the night. It balances this jealous and competitive sisterly dynamic with one of empathy and self-sacrifice. It has to do with a story that takes place before either sister was married to Jacob. The Torah tells us that on the night Jacob was supposed to marry Rachel, he was tricked the same way he tricked his brother. Laban gave him Leah instead of Rachel, and he wound up sleeping with her on the wedding night instead.

AP: They slip Leah in, in the middle of the night, and she's wearing a veil or something.

DL: The Rabbis ask—wait a minute, how did that happen? How did Jacob not know who he was sleeping with? So, they say Jacob anticipated that Laban would try something like this, and he and Rachel had these secret hand signals between them—it was going to be dark after all, and this would be Jacob's way of knowing whether it was really her. But then, on the wedding night, when Laban was about to send Leah into Jacob's tent, Rachel was so concerned that her sister would be publicly shamed—imagine Jacob kicking her out of the tent; it would be a whole big public scandal—that she *revealed* the secret signal to Leah so Leah could pretend to be Rachel on the wedding night. That is shocking, if you think about it. They're competing their entire life for their husband's attention and love, but Rachel wants to spare her sister humiliation and allows her to marry Jacob.

AP: She's protecting Leah by sacrificing her claim to Jacob.

DL: Right, essentially saying, "I'm willing to give up the man I love to spare you." Rachel didn't know that she was ultimately going to marry Jacob after Leah did. That's a strong counterbalance, and it's why you need the Rabbis.

AP: They're always trying to correct or mitigate bad behavior.

DL: True. But it's not just the Rabbis. A softer image of Rachel emerges from the book of Jeremiah. There, the prophet has a vision of Rachel as the one who weeps for the people a thousand years later when they are exiled from the Land of Israel after the Temple is destroyed. She is the one who cares not just for her own children, but for all the Jewish people. It ties back to the story of Rebekah watering the camels and that generosity of spirit. There are times we're caught in circumstances where the worst part of our character comes out, but that's not who we truly are.

AP: I would also like to talk about the word "unloved" used to describe Leah in this parsha. I don't know what that is in the Hebrew, but I think it's such a powerful—

DL: The Hebrew is harsher. The Hebrew is "hated."

AP: Really?

DL: Yes.

AP: Wow. It's hard to fathom why Leah is *hated* and unloved. What an isolating and desperate condition that is.

DL: That is so true. Each sister must have carried so much pain and loneliness. One because she was unloved—hated, even—and the other because she was unable to bear children, which was central to her sense of self-worth. Leah and Rachel were both caught in an impossible situation, and I think if we can appreciate that, we can view their relationship in a more sympathetic light.

Vayetzei to Vayishlach

Jacob's family life begins with Rachel and Leah, and he has many children: eleven boys and one girl. Leah gives birth to six sons and a daughter, and each of the wives' maidservants give birth to two of Jacob's sons, but Rachel herself is infertile. Finally, Rachel becomes pregnant and gives birth to Joseph.

At this point, Jacob is ready to return to Canaan, but Laban begs him to stay. Jacob agrees on the condition that he receive a portion of Laban's flock, which he then multiplies by employing skillful breeding tactics. Sensing his newfound wealth has angered Laban, and with the prodding of an angel who appears to him in a dream, Jacob seeks his wives' permission to return to Canaan, gathers his family, and flees his uncle's home. Laban chases them down with violent intent, but God intervenes, and the two men reconcile and part peacefully.

Jacob's fear of the inevitable confrontation with his brother grows as he enters Canaan and receives a report that Esau is approaching with 400 men, likely for the purpose of waging war against Jacob. Jacob immediately takes defensive measures, splitting his family into two groups and sending gifts ahead to Esau. Left alone at a crossing of the river, Jacob grapples with an angel and emerges with a limp, but not before having extracted a blessing that he will be called "Israel," which means one who wrestles with God.

The next morning, the brothers' two camps meet, and to Jacob's great relief, Esau greets him with a loving embrace. After a brief reconciliation, the brothers go their separate ways—Esau to Se'ir and Jacob to the city of Shechem.

VAYISHLACH

וַיִּשְׁלַח

AP: This week, we are taking on one of the darkest chapters in the Torah. In the middle of Genesis comes "The Rape of Dinah." Cue the dark music.

DL: Yes, it's in the parsha of Vayishlach, and Dinah is a daughter we almost didn't even know Jacob had. And there's a whole story about her.

AP: Here are the verses from Genesis 34:1:

> And Dinah, the daughter of Leah, whom she had born unto Jacob, went out to see the daughters of the land. And Shechem, the son of Hamor, the Hivite, the Prince of the land, saw her. And he took her and lay with her and humbled her.

Or, as the Hebrew suggests—

DL: He afflicted her.

AP: Yes, he afflicted her. "And his soul did cleave unto Dinah, the daughter of Jacob, and he loved the damsel and spoke comfortingly unto the damsel, and Shechem"—again, her rapist—"spoke unto his father, Hamor, saying, 'Get me this damsel to wife.'"

DL: When was the last time you used the word "damsel," Abby?

AP: Very funny, Dov. Continuing on: "Now Jacob heard that he [Shechem] had defiled Dinah, his daughter. And his sons were with his cattle in the field. And Jacob held his peace until they came." So Jacob stays quiet until he can talk to his sons about her rape. Before we find out what Dinah's brothers did, let's do a deep dive into the text and try to understand what's happened here. Dinah went out. Where?

DL: Into the town. She wanted to see the people of the land.

AP: It's not her town.

DL: No, it's not her town—it's the Hivites' town, not the Jewish people's—and she wants to mingle. The prince of the town sees her, and he takes her . . . rapes her. That is why the word "afflict" is used in this context.

AP: But then he falls in love with her.

DL: Yes, and he asks Jacob, her father, for her hand in marriage.

AP: So romantic.

DL: The part you didn't read is that Jacob's sons tell Shechem if he wants to marry their sister, he and all the male townspeople must circumcise themselves.

AP: Wait, stop. So Shechem wants to marry Dinah?

DL: Yes.

AP: And Dinah's brothers say, "If you really want to marry our sister, you have to circumcise all your people."

DL: Correct.

AP: That's a pretty high price.

DL: Yes, it is. And Shechem convinces them to pay it, and the men do so. And then, while they're recovering from their circumcision, two of Dinah's brothers, Simeon and Levi, go in with their swords and slaughter the whole town, take their sister, and leave. That's the story.

AP: A bloody end.

DL: Yes.

AP: What we want to talk about today is: Why do we never hear from Dinah?

DL: That's a very good question.

AP: She has no words. No dialogue.

DL: No voice.

AP: And yet, in modern readings, people do see some agency on her part—that in some ways, she wasn't given her due in this story.

DL: That's because in the traditional reading, she is not only a victim of rape, but the men defending her honor are doing it without her participation. She's not consulted. She's always acted upon—whether being defended or attacked. She's a victim in multiple ways. Traditionally, the Rabbis even blame her a little bit for this. They ask, "Why was Dinah mingling with the daughters of the land?"

AP: The equivalent today of: "Why did you go out dressed like that?"

DL: Exactly, or, "She must have been asking for it." Rashi, the eleventh-century French commentator and a preeminent commentator of the Bible, says, "What was she doing going out and mingling with the women? Why does it say she's a daughter of Leah and not the daughter of Jacob?" The insinuation is that she's learning from her mother, and she doesn't stay at home like a good Jewish woman should.

AP: In other words, she deserved it.

DL: Or that she brought it on herself. To some degree, that's what is being implied.

AP: But in the last twenty years, we've seen a more feminist take on Dinah, which is to say her silence mirrors the silence of so many women who didn't have agency. And maybe her relationship with Shechem was consensual, but her father and brothers couldn't deal with it, so they called it a rape because Dinah had no right to choose to be with somebody who wasn't Hebrew and who wasn't chosen for her.

DL: What you're saying is that this story might have looked very different through Dinah's eyes, and what we're reading in the Torah is the story through the eyes of Jacob and his sons. They see this as a rape—they have no other way of explaining it. But through Dinah's eyes, it could have been a completely different story.

AP: What I struggle with is—can modern commentators just alter the perspective and possibilities like that?

DL: I guess it depends how convincing it is. Can you tell me who interprets the story this way, about Dinah loving Shechem?

AP: One example is Anita Diamant in *The Red Tent*, a bestseller. She reframes the Dinah story and makes her a real character who's able to make her own decisions. But I have seen rabbis really resist the idea that you could reinvent this story. I guess my question to you is, do you think we can decide that Dinah has a voice when she clearly has none on the page? Or is the text maybe giving us an opening to read Dinah in a more complicated, more human way? For instance, it says in Genesis 34:3, "Shechem loved her, and spoke to her heart." Does that not suggest they might have had a relationship?

DL: Is there an opening for that interpretation? Sure. I still think the literal reading of the text indicates he raped her. But I also think it's a good Jewish tradition to give alternative readings of the text, even ones that don't necessarily align with the literal reading. That's what we call midrash—when the Rabbis imagine other stories that are going on. Sometimes, they do it to fill gaps within the text, but other times they do it in ways that go against the text's simple meaning. One of the things that bothers me about this new interpretation that gives Dinah agency is less about whether it's the literal meaning of the text, but—

AP: That it dismisses the rape.

DL: Yes. I feel like we've just made her a victim again. If she really was raped, and now we're trying to redefine it by saying, "Oh, you weren't raped. You wanted it. It was consensual—"

AP: "You enjoyed it."

DL: Exactly.

AP: It's a dangerous feminist reading. It ends up being an anti-feminist feminist reading.

DL: But the flipside is that you can imagine a series of events, which through the eyes of Jacob and his sons amounted to rape, but through Dinah's eyes—whose voice we never hear because we don't hear women's voices in the Torah—it may have been a very different story. There's real power to that. Does that resonate with you—that it winds up dismissing the fact that she was raped?

AP: I'm uncomfortable with the idea that we might minimize an assault, a sexual assault, by saying it was a "romantic encounter."

DL: That's also my concern.

AP: So yes, I struggle with it. But I also want to be open enough to say that we're missing a lot of data here, and maybe it's partly because men wrote it. There is something to be said for what may be unsaid between the lines.

DL: All right, Abby. What's your one-sentence takeaway? What do you get out of this story?

AP: That the confusion in the text is possibly intentional, and what we've learned from the Torah is that sometimes you're left with a little discomfort about what the truth really is or may be. What about you, Dov? What's your takeaway?

DL: That no matter how far we think we've advanced as a society, problems that were with us thousands of years ago are still with us today.

AP: Dinah was the first "Me Too."

DL: Yes, exactly. My other takeaway is that we must remember how radically different a story can be based on the perspective and bias of the person telling it.

AP: I think we should add that, for anyone who has been sexually assaulted, this could be a very hard parsha to parse.

Vayishlach to Vayeshev

God commands Jacob to return to the site where God appeared to him while he was fleeing Esau. Jacob takes his family and builds an altar, as God instructed, first purging any idols in their possession. God reappears to Jacob, blesses him with a new name—Israel—and tells him that he and his descendants will inherit the land of Canaan, which God had sworn and promised to Abraham and Isaac.

Jacob then travels with his household from Beit El to Efrat. En route, Rachel dies while giving birth to a second son, Benjamin. Sometime later, Isaac dies as well and is buried by his two sons.

Jacob shows favoritism to Joseph, his youngest son, and makes him a multicolored cloak, breeding enmity and resentment among his brothers. This is further exacerbated by Joseph regularly talking ill of them to their father. Joseph then dreams that he and his brothers were out in the fields and that the brothers' sheaves of wheat all bowed down to him, followed by a similar dream of the sun, moon, and stars bowing down to him. Joseph's father rebukes him for his hubris, and his brothers' hatred of him deepens.

One day, when Joseph's brothers are away tending the sheep, Jacob sends Joseph to go find his brothers to see how they are faring. This puts in motion a series of events that leads to Joseph being sold by traders and taken down to Egypt.

VAYESHEV

וַיֵּשֶׁב

DL: The parsha of Vayeshev is a story some people might have heard of: *Joseph and the Technicolor Dreamcoat*. Oh no, that's the musical!

AP: I know every lyric. I could sing it all right now.

DL: I do not doubt it, Abby. Please don't.

AP: Just to translate Vayeshev before we dive into the story, it means, "And he dwelt," which refers to Jacob settling in Hebron with his twelve sons.

DL: Right, but we are going to focus on Jacob's son Reuben, how he tried to save his brother Joseph, and whether good intentions matter.

AP: We are in Genesis, Chapter 37. I'm starting with Verse 19. This is when the brothers are all together and they see the dreamer—that's Joseph—coming.

> And they said, one to another, "Behold, the dreamer cometh. Come now, therefore, and let us slay him and cast him into some pit. And we will say some evil beast hath devoured him, and we shall see what will become of his dreams." And Reuben [Joseph's eldest brother] heard it, and he delivered him out of their hands and said, "Let us not kill him." And Reuben said unto them, "Shed no blood, but cast him into this pit that is in the wilderness and lay no hand upon him," that he might rid him out of their hands to deliver him to his father again.

Reuben is basically saying to his brothers, "Don't do this, we want to bring Joseph back to our dad, Jacob. Don't lay a hand on him."

DL: And that word you read, "rid" as in "that he might rid him out of their hands," it's actually in order to *save* him.

AP: But his brothers don't listen.

DL: They do listen!

AP: Well, they still throw Joseph into the pit! So Reuben's not effective in stopping the larger malfeasance here.

DL: Yes, because Reuben goes off somewhere and then—

AP: He just walks off.

DL: The text doesn't say where he went.

AP: He's simply offstage for a little bit.

DL: He later comes back and finds out his brothers sold Joseph to these Midianites, who wound up bringing him down to Egypt.

AP: So Joseph is gone, and Reuben failed.

DL: Yes, Reuben failed to return Joseph to his father.

AP: The late Jonathan Sacks, former Chief Rabbi of Great Britain and a beautiful writer, has a take that I love about Reuben, written in 2008 and titled "Reuben: The Might-Have-Been":

> He is a person of good intentions. He cares. He thinks. He is not led by the crowd or by his darker instincts, he penetrates to the moral core of a situation. That is the first thing we notice about him. The second, however, is that somehow his interventions backfire. They fail to achieve their effect.

What I like about that, what resonates for me, is that yes, Reuben had a good impulse, but he didn't see it through. And ultimately, I think that is something I relate to. I feel it for myself, and I've seen it in others. We care, but we don't affect the situation in a significant enough way to improve it.

DL: Yes, I mean, where's the follow-through? Where did Reuben go? Where'd he walk off to? Does Jonathan Sacks say his follow-through is the problem?

AP: Sacks says he lacks confidence. He says, "He begins well but does not drive the deed to closure." How many of us don't drive to closure? I mean this, for me, is the lesson: You can't just care; you have to finish the job.

DL: That resonates with me too. I see in other stories about Reuben that he also has good intentions, but he doesn't succeed. I see him as someone who can be rash and not just someone who doesn't follow through—

AP: He's impulsive.

DL: Yes, impulsive. He has an immediate response to the situation but doesn't step back enough to develop an effective strategy. You can't follow through if you don't have a plan.

AP: Maybe, though, there is still something admirable in doing what you can in the moment.

DL: I'm with you. The only reason Joseph survived was because Reuben stepped up when he did. So, before we criticize his lack of follow-through, the fact that he jumped in and stood up to his brothers saved Joseph's life. What's your takeaway?

AP: Mine in one line would be: it's not enough to have empathy. You also need courage. I don't think Reuben had courage enough to get it done.

DL: Wait, can we talk about that? What do you mean he didn't have courage? He didn't have follow-through. He didn't have a strategy. But he did stand up to his brothers. You really don't think that took courage?

AP: He took a baby step. To me, that's not—

DL: What's the difference? Where is the line between courage and foolhardiness? What would you have had him do? Stand up to ten brothers who are against him, then totally fail?

AP: He walked away from his brother in a pit, Dov.

DL: So it's that he left Joseph behind? Okay. That I hear. For me, the lesson is that it's best to have a plan, but sometimes, even in the absence of one, we have to take action, because otherwise, it might be too late. Reuben saw that something had to be done, but he knew if he confronted his brothers too forcefully, he wouldn't succeed, so he came up with this idea on the spot. And guess what? Joseph survived. So, my takeaway is to have the courage to intervene in a bad situation even if nobody else does.

Vayeshev to Miketz

Joseph's brother Judah convinces the brothers to not let Joseph die at the bottom of the pit, but rather to sell him into slavery to a passing caravan of Ishmaelites. They do so, and Joseph is brought down to Egypt and sold to Potiphar, an officer in Pharaoh's court. The brothers then dip Joseph's favored cloak in the blood of a goat and bring it back to their father, Jacob, who is deceived by their ruse and believes Joseph has been devoured by a wild animal. Jacob descends into a deep and seemingly permanent state of grief.

Judah moves away from his brothers, weds, and has three sons. The first marries a woman by the name of Tamar and dies young, without a child. His brother then marries Tamar, and he, too, dies suddenly. Tamar is now expected to marry Judah's youngest son, but Judah is hesitant. Desperate for children, Tamar takes matters into her own hands, disguising herself as a prostitute and seduces Judah, becoming pregnant. Judah owns up to his actions and acknowledges that he is the father. Tamar gives birth to twin boys named Perez and Zerah.

Meanwhile, Joseph is in Egypt, enslaved to Potiphar. He quickly rises in the ranks of the household's slaves, but when he rebuffs the advances of Potiphar's wife, he is framed by her for attempted rape and thrown in jail. There, he meets two of Pharaoh's ministers whom he impresses by correctly interpreting their cryptic dreams.

MIKETZ

מִקֵּץ

AP: We're in Miketz. Genesis 41.

DL: Miketz is translated as "at the end of" because this parsha's events happen two full years after Joseph interpreted the dreams of his fellow jail mates.

AP: Right. We didn't talk about Joseph's jail time in our discussion of the previous parsha, but Joseph was unjustly thrown in the lockup.

DL: And while there, he met Pharaoh's wine steward and baker and predicted what was going to happen to them based on their dreams.

AP: They'd had scary, weird dreams, and Joseph managed to interpret them so accurately that they came to believe he was a seer or prophet.

DL: Correct. What he predicted came true: one of the two men would be executed, and one would be elevated. The one who was elevated—the cupbearer—was supposed to tell Pharaoh that Joseph had been imprisoned unjustly, but he either forgot or intentionally chose not to.

AP: But then Pharaoh starts having his own strange dreams, and he is desperate to understand them, at which point the cupbearer remembers and tells Pharaoh about Joseph. But let's talk about Pharaoh's dreams for a minute. Talk to me about the cows.

DL: Pharaoh dreamed that seven healthy cows rose out of the Nile, and he said, "I've never seen such beautiful, healthy cows in all of the land of Egypt." Immediately afterward, seven emaciated cows rise up out of the Nile and consume the seven healthy cows.

AP: And then the same thing happened with grain.

DL: Stalks of wheat, yes. Seven emaciated, wind-blasted stalks of wheat swallowed up the healthy ones and remained just as emaciated as before.

AP: Joseph is summoned by Pharaoh to interpret the dreams, and he explains them by saying, "You are going to have seven years of a bumper crop followed by seven years of famine, and you need to prepare for it." And Pharaoh basically says, "You're brilliant. You've got the job."

DL: Yes, Pharaoh makes Joseph his second in command. He says, "Everything that will take place in the land of Egypt will take place on your orders. Nobody is greater than you in the entire land of Egypt, other than me." So, Joseph is now head honcho number two.

AP: Let's pause there, because while it's amazing that it works out well and Joseph's predictions are right, when someone tells me about their dreams, I just tune out. I don't put a lot of stock in them. Dreams are your subconscious, and I just don't understand why they were trusted back then.

DL: If you read the verses, God is consistently referenced. Joseph says to Pharaoh, "Dreams are from God; God will help me interpret them for you." And then after he does so, Pharaoh says, "Can we find another man such as this? A man in whom the spirit of God resides" (Gen. 41:38). So, in the story, there is a clear sense that God is communicating through these dreams.

AP: There is a line in verse 41:32 that says, "As for Pharaoh having had the same dream twice, it means that the matter has been determined by God, and that God will soon carry it out." Is there something about the repetition of this dream that shows God had a hand in it?

DL: That certainly is a part of it. In the Torah, when God wants to communicate with someone, God will often appear in that person's dreams. Which is not exactly the same, I suppose, as saying that disturbing, unusual dreams are a message from God. Look, amazing things happen in our dreams that don't happen in real life—we see people who are dead; we see images we would never see while awake; we can even fly. There's a sense of something magical about dreams, so you can certainly understand how people could have believed—and how plenty still believe—that they are otherworldly, a means through which God communicated with us.

AP: Pharaoh goes on to say, "See, I put you in charge of all of the land of Egypt." What are Joseph's qualifications for this job?

DL: Joseph is so filled with the spirit of God that he will be wise and successful in whatever he does.

AP: But Pharaoh and Joseph don't share the same religion.

DL: That's a good point. I think Pharaoh would say, "Whoever your god is—"

AP: "You are connected to the divine in some way."

DL: Right. "Dreams come from your god, and you are connected to that god, and hey, it seems like it works, so you're the man to go with." That's what I think it is. We've seen this before in the Joseph story. When he is in the house of Potiphar, the captain of Pharaoh's guard, the text says Potiphar told Joseph, "I see that God is with you in whatever you do."

AP: All right, but what about you, Dov? When you dream, do you feel like God is telling you something?

DL: No, I certainly don't.

AP: Do you think it's a predictor of something or a prophecy?

DL: No. Sometimes dreams agitate me or get under my skin. But even the Talmud says that most dreams are chaff—there's only a little bit of wheat there, only a little bit of truth. It also says that what we dream at night has a lot to do with what we were thinking about during the day. And get this: the Talmud also says that dreams follow the interpretation—regardless of who interprets the dream, the interpretation will determine how the dream will play out in real life. Which means a dream can be a self-fulfilling prophecy; if you believe a dream means something, it's more likely that it will come true in your life.

AP: That sounds very Oprah.

DL: Think about palm readers nowadays, the crystal ball. If you buy into that—and I think a lot of the ancient world did buy into that—

AP: Sure. People wanted to make sense of the chaos of dreams because they're not usually linear, and all sorts of weird things are happening, which aren't necessarily realistic—like thin cows eating fat cows.

DL: Precisely. There's a whole other world that doesn't make sense to you. There's no modern science, so you don't know why it rains or why the sun rises or why there is lightning or anything. You don't understand what dreams are, but they are intriguing and mysterious, and you'd want someone to explain them to you.

AP: Okay. Let's revisit Joseph's brothers. Joseph is in charge in Egypt, and his brothers are back in the land of Canaan and starving because we are now in the seven years of famine. They're already in a time of scarcity and hunger when they come to Joseph for help, right?

DL: Yes.

AP: And they are basically beggars at that point.

DL: Yes. They have money to offer, but Joseph has total control over them. He's got the food that they need because he'd convinced Pharaoh to prepare for the famine.

AP: So all the leverage is his.

DL: It's a seller's market.

AP: And what does he do? He basically plays with them, right?

DL: He manipulates them and claims they are all spies. But the key moment is when the text says he recognized his brothers, but they did not recognize him.

AP: Here is the quote from 42:7 in Genesis: "When Joseph saw his brothers, he recognized them; but he acted like a stranger towards them and spoke harshly towards them. He asked them, 'Where do you come from?' And they said, 'From the land of Canaan, to procure food.'" He acts like he doesn't know them, and he is forcing them to articulate their need. He was abused by them, they threw him in the pit, and now, instead of taking the high road—

DL: He doesn't. He could have come clean right at that moment. Genesis 42:8 reiterates: "Joseph knew his brothers, but they did not know him." Why do you think he is doing this to his brothers? Do you think it's revenge, or is it something more than that?

AP: It seems like retribution: "You did this terrible thing to me, and I'm going to make you suffer a bit before I help you."

DL: I think it could be something else. Remember the dream Joseph had before his brothers sold him into slavery? The wheat, sun, moon, and eleven stars—that he believed to be his brothers—all bowed down to him. Just like before, when Joseph saw himself as a vehicle of God to interpret dreams, now he sees himself as a vehicle of God to make his own dream come true.

AP: So, this was God's plan, and Joseph has to actualize it.

DL: Exactly. Joseph is going to manipulate the situation, so his brothers bow down to him and everything he saw before is realized.

AP: That sounds a little bit like a rationalization to me. Joseph is on a power trip—his brothers are coming to him, desperate and starving, and he could lend a hand here instead of humiliating them. He *chooses* to humiliate them.

DL: Let me be clear here. I don't think we should inflict suffering on others because we believe we are fulfilling God's plan. That is very dangerous thinking indeed. What I'm asking is, what is Joseph's motivation? Does he think he is exacting revenge on his brothers, or in his mind, is he making the dreams come true? I think that's why he manipulates them to bring his other brother Benjamin down to Egypt, as we hear when the story continues. It's part of getting *all* the brothers to bow down to him, which is what he saw in his dream. And he also wants to see if they are going to treat Benjamin the same way they treated *him*, as the younger, favored brother. I see those things playing a much bigger role for Joseph than retaliation or causing his brothers to suffer.

AP: Maybe it's also a warning to readers: if you are going to do an evil thing, ultimately you are going to pay a price, and you will be called to account. This is that moment of truth for the brothers. Is it not a cautionary tale?

DL: I think it is. Listen to what they say to one another when they are about to go back to their father, Jacob, in Canaan: "We are truly guilty regarding our brother, for we saw the anguish of his soul, when he pleaded with us, and we would not hear; therefore, these travails have come upon us" (Gen. 42:21).

AP: The crime catches up to you. It stays with you.

DL: Right. I've been pushing the idea that Joseph is trying to make his dreams come true; you are saying it's payback. Maybe both are true. We think we can disentangle our motives, but it's easier said than done. Sometimes we believe we are doing what God wants of us, but how much of that is doing what we want for ourselves, for less-than-ideal motives? Does that resonate?

AP: I think it's the perfect note to end on: entangled motives.

DL: And we can end by saying we were both right.

Miketz to Vayigash

After having accused his brothers of being spies, Joseph allows them to return to Canaan with grain for their household but keeps Simeon behind, imprisoned. He tells the brothers that they may only return if they do so along with their younger brother, Benjamin, who can verify that they are not spies. The brothers return to Canaan and to their father, Jacob, who initially refuses to permit Benjamin to go back to Egypt, fearful that he, too, will die or go missing, just as happened first to Joseph.

The famine, however, becomes so severe that Jacob is forced to relent and send his sons—Benjamin included—back to Egypt to purchase more food. Judah swears to be personally responsible for his younger brother's protection. Upon arrival in Egypt, Joseph—still unrecognizable to his brothers—invites them all into his home, where he struggles to hold back tears upon meeting Benjamin. Joseph dines with the brothers and sends them back to their father with sacks full of grain, but not before secretly ordering that his goblet be hidden in Benjamin's sack. He then sends his servant to chase the brothers down, recover the "stolen" goblet, and bring them all back to Joseph's house. When Joseph insists on taking Benjamin prisoner for the "theft," Judah acts on his vow and begs Joseph to imprison him instead.

Vayigash

וַיִּגַּשׁ

AP: Today, we'll be discussing Vayigash, which means . . . .

DL: "He approached."

AP: Or, "he drew near."

DL: The "he" in Vayigash is Judah, one of Joseph's brothers. But why is he drawing near? And to whom? Abby, can you set the scene for us?

AP: The brothers come to Joseph because of the famine. They're desperate, and they have come to Egypt for food. Joseph plays with them, he tests them, and he secretly puts a goblet into the youngest brother, Benjamin's, sack, then accuses him of stealing it. The brothers all panic, and Judah "draws near" to implore Joseph to have compassion for Benjamin. He says, "Please, let him return to his father. Let me take his place!"

DL: Joseph is trying to find out what they are willing to sacrifice to save their younger brother—the favored brother. Remember, years before, they sold Joseph into slavery because of their jealousy of him.

AP: Not only did they *not* save him, they almost left him for dead.

DL: Exactly. So are they going to leave Benjamin behind as they did Joseph, or are they going to protect him?

AP: Finally, Joseph reveals himself. Cue the drumroll! You can just imagine the scene as he rips off his disguise. By the way, I don't really find it credible that they didn't recognize Joseph sooner. What do you think? I guess it's possible since it's been years since they've last seen him.

DL: It's been years, Joseph is dressed in a very different way, and there's no reason for them to think he'd be there. It's just as likely they would have thought him dead. The Rabbis note that Joseph left home at seventeen years old, and now he is a much older man with a beard. He'd be too hard to recognize. I buy it.

AP: Okay. I'll suspend disbelief. So Joseph reveals himself and says, "It's me, your brother," and then there's this amazing reunion scene. Joseph cries. It says in verse 45:2: "His sobs were so loud that the Egyptians could hear, and so the news reached Pharaoh's palace." He cried so loud Pharaoh could hear it.

DL: I think Joseph wept, and news of it came to Pharaoh's house. It doesn't mean Pharaoh literally heard his weeping.

AP: The bottom line is, Joseph is very emotional.

DL: I'd say so.

AP: And he is *publicly* emotional. One minute, Joseph is the man running the show and playing with his brother's emotions, and now he breaks open. I think it's moving.

DL: It does say earlier that when Joseph was manipulating the brothers, he wept in private.

AP: I happen to have that verse handy, Genesis 42:24: "He turned away from them and wept." So, we already have a clue about how fragile he is and how on-the-surface this pain is. It's the first time he has seen his brothers since their betrayal, so the reunion is hard for him. In 45:15 it goes on, "He kissed all his brothers and wept upon them; only then were his brothers able to talk to him." Maybe this is a contemporary read on my part, but it feels like everyone has dropped their pretenses at this point. And yet, the brothers don't cry. What do you make of that? Why is Joseph the only one weeping?

DL: It's difficult to say for sure, but Joseph has had a good twenty years to think about the way he was rejected and unloved by his brothers. He'd been stewing on that and probably wondered why his father never came looking for him. He's lived with twenty years of resentment and rejection. The brothers have surely been living with guilt for what they did to Joseph, but guilt is not the same as abandonment. What do you think?

AP: I think he could have used a good therapist.

DL: But do you think he has greater emotion stewing? His brothers definitely have guilt over what they have done.

AP: This is one of the more human parshas that we have read so far. On the one hand, Joseph survived the mistreatment by his brothers and even capitalized on it—look at how successful he has become. But it was not the road he would have chosen, and that history is present in this reunion. He's not just the manipulator and the viceroy; he's still the brother they turned their backs on and left stranded.

DL: I'm still curious why you think the brothers didn't cry.

AP: I can only assume they were shocked. Tears wouldn't be my first response in this situation either. They would likely be trying to process everything. The scenario is so surreal, it's almost impossible to comprehend, even today.

DL: I find that interesting. Joseph knows what is happening all along, so he's had time to work through his emotions; the brothers, however, are stunned. There's something similar later in the parsha during an encounter between Joseph and his father, Jacob. Joseph is again the one who cries, and his father does not. This is when Jacob finally comes with all of his family to Egypt. Jacob knows Joseph is alive, which is why he is making the trip. Genesis 46:29 says,

> And Joseph made ready his chariot and went up to meet his father, Israel [Jacob], to Goshen; and presented himself unto him and fell on his neck and wept on his neck a good while. And Israel said unto Joseph, "Now I can die, since I have seen your face because you are still alive."

So, Jacob is saying, "Now that I know you're alive, I can die in peace." But he does not cry. Only Joseph does. What do you make of the fact that Jacob did not cry?

AP: I think for Jacob, there's more relief that he is not going to die without having seen his son again. In a way, their reunion is giving him permission to depart the world because he is, once again, complete. There had been this hole in his life—he had lost his son—but now this gives him closure; he knows Joseph is alive.

DL: Do you think Joseph is crying tears of joy or of sadness? Is he joyful for the reunion, or is he crying over all the lost years?

AP: I don't think it's that simple. I don't think it is joy or sorrow—it's relief; but I also think there's a lot of trauma that has been locked up and repressed for two decades, finally unleashed.

DL: But you don't think any of those emotions would have been brought up for Jacob?

AP: Look, Jacob was the one who tricked his father to get his brother's birthright.

DL: That's what you think is going on here?

AP: I don't know. I just feel like we need to look at people's fundamental character. Jacob is not above discounting familial ties.

DL: Well, Jacob did cry a great deal when he thought Joseph died.

AP: So, he is all cried out?

DL: Yes, maybe, whereas Joseph has tried to avoid thinking about the family who betrayed him. Joseph names one of his sons Manasseh, which means, "Because God made me forget all my toil and all my father's house" (Gen. 41:51). He has been avoiding his emotions, whereas Jacob has dealt with his interior life plenty.

AP: Do you remember the song "It's All Right to Cry" from the seventies' children's album, *Free to Be You and Me*?

DL: I don't remember that, but I do remember reading a great op-ed in the *New York Times* about Mr. Rogers—I don't know if you saw this—but he specifically tried not to distract kids from negative emotions; instead, he validated them. It was quite an insightful piece.

AP: On that note, I look forward to your tears.

DL: And I will say, "It's all right to cry."

Vayigash to Vayechi

Now reunited with his father, Jacob, Joseph's mind turns to how he can best provide for his family in Egypt. He brings his father and five of his brothers before Pharaoh and asks to settle them in the fertile land of Goshen. Pharaoh agrees and receives a blessing from Jacob. As the famine remains severe, Joseph distributes grain to the people of Egypt. In exchange, Joseph acquires all their land and livestock, thereby consolidating wealth into Pharaoh's hands.

When Jacob realizes his death is imminent, he gathers his family. First, he blesses Joseph's two sons, Ephraim and Manasseh, declaring that Ephraim will be granted a higher status than his older brother. Jacob goes on to give a detailed, personalized blessing to each of his twelve sons before taking his final breaths.

VAYECHI

וַיְחִי

AP: This week, Dov, we're asking whether human beings can ever be a substitute for God. Just a small question.

DL: Oh yeah. Just a teeny tiny one.

AP: We're zeroing in on the parsha at the end of Genesis called Vayechi, which means . . .?

DL: "And he lived," which, of course, refers to Jacob's death.

AP: Because Jacob lived, and now he's dying. It's like a eulogy of sorts.

DL: Correct.

AP: Tell us what happens in this part of the story.

DL: When Jacob dies, his sons worry that Joseph may still hold a grudge against them for throwing him in a pit and abandoning him for dead. So, the brothers want to "remind" Joseph—I did air quotes there around "remind"—

AP: Why the air quotes?

DL: Because they might have been fabricating what I'm about to tell you, which is that Jacob left instructions for Joseph to forgive them.

AP: In other words, "Dad exonerated us for throwing you in a pit and walking away, and you should forgive us, too."

DL: Exactly.

AP: I'm going to read the verses. It starts with Genesis 50:15, "When Joseph's brothers saw that their father was dead, they said, 'What if Joseph still bears a grudge against us and pays us back for all the wrong that we did him!'" The "wrong" they're referring to is the pit episode, correct?

DL: Yes.

AP: So they sent this message to Joseph: "Before his death, your father left this instruction . . . ." By "father," they mean Jacob here, right?

DL: Correct.

AP: Jacob's reported instructions continue, as relayed by his sons in 50:17: "So shall you say to Joseph, 'Forgive, I urge you, the offense and guilt of your brothers who treated you so harshly. Therefore, please forgive the offense of the servants of the God of your father's [house].'" Joseph was in tears as they spoke to him. He is emotionally moved again, right?

DL: Yes.

AP: It goes on to say, "And his brothers went to him themselves, they flung themselves before him"—when people fling themselves, they're prostrating—

DL: They're showing that they're subject to him, that they see themselves as in his power.

AP: "And they said, 'We are prepared to be your slaves.' But Joseph said to them, 'Have no fear! Am I a substitute for God? Besides, although you intended me harm, God intended it for good, so as to bring about the present result—the survival of many people.'" Let's unpack that, Dov.

DL: What do you think is meant by, "The present result—the survival of many people"?

AP: That Joseph saved many of Egypt's people from a famine. That was the ultimate "good" that "God intended," even though Joseph had to suffer first to get there.

DL: The brothers wanted to kill Joseph initially, but instead, they cast him into the pit and sold him. Ultimately, however, it led to something positive. Joseph went down to Egypt, he started interpreting dreams, and came to the notice of Pharaoh.

AP: And Pharaoh hired him.

DL: Pharaoh designated him as viceroy. Pharaoh's dreams had predicted a famine, so Joseph saw to it that wheat was stockpiled for the future. Not only did that lead to the survival of the people in Egypt, it also led to the survival of Jacob and the entire Israelite family.

AP: When the verse says, "God intended it for good," it means the attack the brothers perpetrated on Joseph and their disregard for his life was ultimately part of a greater plan.

DL: It was all part of how God wanted to save them in a time of famine.

AP: So, when Joseph says he's not a substitute for God, he means he's not in a position to forgive his brothers, or *not* to forgive them.

DL: True. It also means he's not in a position to exact punishment on God's behalf.

AP: But it seems to me that Joseph *was* a surrogate for God. Joseph was harmed, he survived, he interpreted dreams, he got power because of his gift for reading Pharaoh's dreams, and he ultimately saved this population from starvation. He was executing God's blueprint.

DL: Joseph is saying that it was all God's guiding hand, and he did not see himself in a position to make the types of choices that God would. He didn't take the rights and privileges of God upon himself.

AP: Or the hubris of it.

DL: Exactly.

AP: He's saying, "I'm not a replacement for God; I am merely God's instrument."

DL: Right. But I think the line between those two is a pretty thin one, and it's easy to cross over it without realizing you're doing it. I would ask: was it really a good thing that he said, "I'm not in God's place"? I mean, if somebody wrongs us, should we say, "Don't worry about it because it was all part of God's plan"? Whatever happened to human responsibility? And then there is the question you raised—if we see God as operating through us, what does that do to our accountability for our choices? Seeing ourselves as God's instrument could give us license to do horrific things.

AP: That's why I'm struggling with the idea that this is the way God works in the world. This story tells us, essentially, that God has a master chessboard, and we are pawns on it. Or that we're playing roles we don't even know we're playing in order to achieve God's desired result. Sometimes that involves us suffering along the way, but that is not for us to know or to question or change. Which means, as you said, it's also easy to say our actions aren't our fault because someone else's hands are on the controls.

DL: Right, it sort of frees us or others from responsibility. I see another problem with the way Joseph responded because he didn't really allay his brothers' fears and anxieties. They wanted his forgiveness, and instead he says, "Who am I to judge?" That's not the forgiveness they were looking for.

AP: It's kind of like my late Jewish grandma, Esther, used to say: "Who am I to judge how rarely you visit me? I'm not God."

DL: Exactly.

AP: Then, the ultimate question is: should we see ourselves as able to forgive those who wrong us the way Joseph forgives his brothers? Do we have the right to absolve each other?

DL: I think that's the right question to ask. The problem is that Joseph is saying, "I'm not here to judge what you've done." That's not the same as saying, "I forgive you."

AP: He does forgive them in the sense that he doesn't punish them or hold it against them later.

DL: Yes, okay.

AP: Am I wrong?

DL: No, you're not wrong, but I still don't think it's the forgiveness his brothers were looking for. Deep down, people know when they've done wrong and want to be told that they're absolved. Joseph saying, "I'm not holding you responsible for your actions," is not the same as forgiveness. He's not going to seek revenge, but I still would not call this forgiveness.

AP: That sort of throws me back to Yom Kippur, when we are directed—in a way that I think is profound and particularly challenging—to seek pardon from each other. If I have harmed someone, I owe them an apology face-to-face; that's not atonement that I can seek from God—I have to ask it of the person I've wronged. Is that same mandate not operating here on some level?

DL: That's an excellent point. This scene poignantly portrays what it means to lay yourself bare before a person to ask them for forgiveness for how you have wronged them.

I'd like to end with one final reflection, a positive takeaway for us in terms of our own personal religious lives. If we can try to see God operating through us and through other people, then we'll see God more in this world. In my experience, for Christians, this is very much part of their religious view and discourse. I don't think it is as much for Jews, but it can lead us to be kinder to others if we think that whatever happens, it's all part of God's plan.

What I want to caution against is when we *impose* it on other people. There's this horrific thing people say when somebody has suffered a tragedy, which is, "Oh, it's all part of God's plan; God never gives us anything that we can't handle." If a person really aligns with that belief, it can be very comforting; but if a person isn't feeling that way, *saying* it can make it seem like we're minimizing their pain. We should never impose that perspective on others.

AP: Maybe the idea of God's plan offers some people an internal sense of reassurance, that there's a greater design, and if I'm suffering *now*, it is for a greater end later.

DL: It's wonderful if you believe that. But please don't tell other people that's why they're suffering. And don't tell other people, they're not responsible for their actions because God's at the wheel. We *are* responsible for our actions.

AP: Good rabbinic advice, Dov.

Vayechi to Shemot

After mourning their father, Joseph and his brothers go up to Canaan—accompanied by a royal delegation—to fulfill Jacob's dying wish to be buried in the Cave of Machpelah. Sometime after, Joseph dies as well, and per his father's example, insists that his own remains eventually be taken back to Canaan.

Generations later, the Israelite inhabitants of Egypt—originally just seventy members of Jacob's household—have become numerous and strong, arousing the suspicion of a new Pharaoh who did not know Joseph. Fearful the growing minority could rise up against him, this Pharaoh enslaves the Israelites, forcing them to perform backbreaking manual labor. When their numbers continue to increase, Pharaoh commands the Israelites' midwives to murder every male Israelite newborn. They boldly refuse.

EXODUS

שְׁמוֹת

Shemot

שְׁמוֹת

AP: We've wrapped up Genesis and are now starting the Book of Exodus—Shemot. This is one of the more well-known of the Five Books. Shemot is also the name of the first parsha.

DL: Shemot means "Names," referring to the names of the sons of Jacob who come down to Egypt. When Jacob's family grows to become the Israelite people, the descendants of each son becomes a separate tribe within the nation. So, their names are also the names of the Twelve Tribes of Israel.

AP: You and I have decided to talk about what makes great leadership as it relates to the Twelve Tribes. And why was Moses, of all people, tapped to free the Israelites? Let's zero in on the three times that Moses intervenes to right a wrong. It's kind of mind-boggling to me that this was the only job requirement—just three good deeds, and he becomes the savior of the Jewish people. So, take it away, Dov, tell us about Moses's résumé.

DL: This story is presented right before God appears to Moses in the burning bush.

AP: All three things happen before the burning bush?

DL: Yes, and in quick succession. From Exodus 2:11–17:

> And it came to pass in those days when Moses was grown, that he went out to his brothers and looked on their burdens. And he spied an Egyptian beating a Hebrew, one of his brothers. And he looked this way and that way and saw that there was no man. He slew the Egyptian and hid him in the sand.

AP: Which means no one was watching.

DL: Exactly. There were no witnesses, so he could kill the Egyptian and get away with it. That's the first intervention. Now for number two—in Exodus 2.13:

> And when he went down on the second day, behold, two men of the Hebrews were struggling together. And he said to the one who did the wrong, "Why are you striking your fellow?" And he said, "Who made you a prince and judge over us? Do you intend to kill me as you killed the Egyptian?" And Moses feared and said, "Certainly, this thing is known."

AP: So two Jews are fighting together, and they know Moses killed somebody the day before.

DL: Apparently, word got out. But this is Moses's second intervention—trying to protect the innocent who's being struck.

AP: But it's Hebrew against Hebrew.

DL: Right. Hebrew against Hebrew. "And when Pharaoh heard this matter, he sought to slay Moses; but Moses fled from the face of Pharaoh and dwelt in the land of Midian."

AP: Which brings us to the third intervention . . . .

DL: Yes—Exodus 2:16:

> And the priest of Midian had seven daughters, and they came and drew water and filled the troughs to water their father's flock. And the shepherds came and drove them away. But Moses stood up and helped them and watered their flock.

Actually, the Hebrew word for "help them"—*vayoshian*—can also mean "*redeemed* them." It's a sign that Moses will be the future redeemer.

AP: Who are these bad shepherds coming to drive away the daughters of the priest of Midian?

DL: We have no idea. They don't ever appear again.

AP: I thought shepherds were kind and gentle.

DL: What can I tell you? They wanted the water for themselves.

AP: Selfish shepherds.

DL: These verses illustrate a progression: from protecting your own against an outside oppressor . . . to intervening to defend the innocent party between two of your own people . . . to defending those with whom you have no connection. I believe the Torah is telling us that to be the savior and leader of your people, your *first* obligation has to be to them. Moses protects and fights for his brothers, but what makes that anything more than self-interest or tribalism? The next message is that you must be a person of principle; you have to stand for justice and protect the innocent, whether that means intervening between two of your own people or those you have no connection to. It's like that line from Hillel the sage in *Chapters of Our Fathers*, who said, "If I'm not for myself, who is for me? But if I'm only for myself, what am I?" So, it starts with your own, but it also has to be more than that. It's reasonable to think the Torah is telling us that these three instances are why Moses was chosen.

AP: I like the idea of going from the particular to the universal. But as for Moses showing courage, in all three of those examples, I'm struck by the fact that he didn't seem particularly bold. When Moses kills the Egyptian, the Torah says he looks this way and that before he acts, as if to make sure he won't get caught before he saves the slave. And in the second instance, he runs away after he breaks up the fight. It makes me think maybe the best and most courageous leaders lack courage at first, that the most effective saviors are ones who hesitate or fear that they're not up to the task. And maybe we can see ourselves in Moses, because who among us hasn't glanced over our shoulders before doing what we think is right, if only to make sure we don't get in trouble or ruffle someone's feathers? Do you agree?

DL: Hmm. I don't fully agree with that. I think there are two things going on here. One is distinguishing between bravery and stupidity or foolhardiness. You can't help people if you get yourself killed in the process. I think Moses "looking this way and that" might be the prudent move to make. I think what you're talking about is hesitating to take on leadership. That does happen at the burning bush, when God tries to send Moses to free the Israelite slaves and Moses says, "Who am I? Send anybody but me." There, I agree with you. If somebody's too eager to lead, you have to wonder what else might be going on with them. An ego or power trip? That's, I think, the lesson of reluctant leadership. But, in saving the Hebrew slave, I believe what we are seeing is reasonable caution more than a hesitation to lead.

AP: Do you think the three times Moses intervenes are just his instinctual response to help those in trouble? Does he have a genuinely altruistic disposition, or do you think he's checking off boxes? "These are my people; I'm going to help. This is a stranger; I'm going to help."

DL: My take is that when Moses sees injustice, he can't tolerate it. He cannot help but stand up and defend the person being oppressed. But I do think he feels a deep connection to his people. He leaves the comfort of Pharaoh's palace to go see his fellow Hebrews, to see their travails as mistreated slaves. It's important that this story of caring for *his* people comes first. The Torah is saying: if you want to be a Jewish leader, the first and most important thing is to care deeply for the people. Even if you are in a place of privilege, their pain must be your pain, their suffering must be your suffering.

AP: That really speaks to me. Let's go back to Moses's reluctance at the burning bush. What you're saying is that he is compelled to act in the face of injustice, but despite that, he's hesitant to be the leader who is going to correct the wrongs.

DL: Yes.

AP: That reminds me of the Purim story. When Esther says to her cousin Mordecai, "I won't be able to save the Jewish people from this edict of extermination, from the horrible Haman—"

DL: Booooo!

AP: Mordecai says, "Maybe you were put on earth for exactly this moment." In other words, "You may not want this job or feel like you're up to it, but maybe that's exactly why you're here, whether it's comfortable for you or not."

DL: Right. I think, as you said about Moses, we want people of principle who have to be persuaded to take on a leadership role, not the people who are overeager to take the position. But sometimes you have to step up. Another line in *Chapters of Our Fathers* is, "Where there is no man, strive to be a man." And that's symbolic of this story of Moses deciding to intervene, because it's an alternate way of reading the verse: "Moses looked here and there and saw there was no man." Moses saw nobody else was stepping up and realized *he* had to step up.

AP: Like if not you, who?

DL: Exactly.

AP: Let's wind this up by focusing on that one line in the third of the three examples you gave of Moses's qualifications for leadership, in Exodus 2:17, because it strikes me. When Moses is helping the daughters who are being driven away by the bad shepherds, it says, "Moses stood up and helped them and watered their flock." It's such a simple line, but it speaks volumes to me about the kind of leader we hold up as our best. Moses didn't just rescue the daughters; he went beyond what he needed to do and watered their sheep. That reminds me of Rebekah watering the camels and tells me that we sometimes need to go beyond that big, grand gesture and make sure we do the small one. You know, sometimes we swoop in to help, such as sending money after the California wildfires recently, but we don't always circle back six months later to see whether people are still living in temporary shelters.

DL: You are so right. Sometimes I think that one teaching of this story is the need for follow-through. I mean, did Moses's smiting of the Egyptian solve any problem? It certainly didn't do anything to address the systemic problems of slavery. Reflecting on this story, we should realize that leading is about more than taking immediate action; it has to also be about the next steps, what comes after.

What you're pointing out is something different. A leader must also be caring and nurturing. Leading isn't just about abstract causes or justice writ large. It's about people. There's a famous *midrash* that speaks to this: "Moses was shepherding his father-in-law's sheep one day, when one of them bolted—"

AP: Bolted as in "ran"?

DL: Yes, it ran away. "Moses followed the runaway animal until it reached a body of water where it stopped for a drink." This is a translation from the Hebrew:

> Moses compassionately said to the sheep, "If only I had known that you thirsted for water. You must be exhausted from running."

> Saying this, he scooped up the animal, placed it on his shoulders, and headed back to his flock. God said, "If this is how he cares for the sheep of man, he is definitely fit to shepherd my flock."

To me this *midrash* is making an essential point about what it means to be a leader. I find sometimes there are people who fight for causes—they're ideologues, and they're people of principle, but they have a hard time connecting and caring for individual human beings. The *midrash* is saying it starts with people, and it ends with people. This story about watering the flocks captures the person who cares for every individual and for every sheep in the herd.

AP: Amen.

Shemot to Va'era

Moses runs away from Egypt after having killed the Egyptian overlord and arrives in Midian, where he meets his wife, Tzipporah. One day, while tending the flock of his father-in-law, Jethro, he sees a bush that is burning with fire yet not being consumed by it. He draws close to get a better look, and God appears to him and says that God has heard the outcry of the Israelite people, and the time has come to free them from servitude. Moses will be the one to take them out of Egypt and bring them to their ancestral land of Canaan—a land "flowing with milk and honey."

Moses resists God's assignment, asking that God choose anyone else other than him for the job. God insists and gives Moses signs to show the people that he has been sent by God. Moses is told that he is to appear before Pharaoh and demand that Pharaoh allow the people to go serve God in the wilderness for three days. God tells Moses that his brother, Aaron, will join him in his role and serve as his mouthpiece to Pharaoh.

Moses returns with his family to Egypt and delivers his message to the Israelites and shows them God's signs. The people believe in the future redemption and give thanks to God. Moses and Aaron then appear before Pharaoh, who rejects their request to liberate their people. He commands his officers to increase the workload on the Israelites, requiring them to gather the straw needed for making bricks. The people are beaten for their failure to make quota, and they turn on Moses and Aaron, saying the two of them have only made their lives worse. Moses calls out to God, and God tells Moses that the future redemption is imminent.

VA'ERA

וָאֵרָא

AP: Here we are in Va'era.

DL: Which means, "And I appeared."

AP: And who appeared?

DL: God. After Moses complains to God that things have only gotten worse since he appeared before Pharaoh, God responds and says, I, God, have appeared to the forefathers—Abraham, Isaac, and Jacob—but I have yet to fulfill the promise to give them the land of Canaan. Now, through you, I will bring the Israelites out of Egypt and make true my promises."

AP: How is Moses going to bring them out of Egypt?

DL: By using the plagues to pressure Pharaoh.

AP: The ten plagues! We all remember dripping wine on our plates and never licking our pinky. Before we get to the plagues, Dov, let's talk about Pharaoh facing off with Aaron and Moses, as if to say, "You think you've got tricks? *I've* got tricks." In verse 7:9, God says, "When Pharaoh speaks to you"—you being Moses and Aaron—"and says, 'Produce your marvel,' you shall say to Aaron, 'Take your rod and cast it down before Pharaoh.' It shall turn into a serpent." So basically, God is saying, "I will transform Aaron's rod into a snake, and Pharaoh will be scared and accept that God is here and powerful."

DL: Right.

AP: It continues in 7:10:

> So Moses and Aaron came before Pharaoh just as the Lord had commanded: Aaron cast down his rod in the presence of Pharaoh and his courtiers, and it turned into a serpent. Then Pharaoh, for his part, summoned the wise men and the sorcerers; and the

> Egyptian magicians, in turn, did the same with their spells: each cast down his rod, and they turned into serpents. But Aaron's rod swallowed their rods.

It's like, "Whose rod is more powerful?"

DL: On one level it's just, "Is this really a god that I should listen to, or is it just a magic trick?"

AP: It seems trivial to me. Why are they doing magic tricks? God has real power, why does God need to make it visible, tangible?

DL: You mean why start with the small?

AP: Yes—why waste time turning a rod into a snake?

DL: To give Pharaoh a chance to listen before he gets whacked over the head with the plagues.

AP: Does God really think that Pharaoh is going to let the Israelites go because of this snake magic?

DL: I suppose not. But there is also this question of a contest. God sends prophets and Pharaoh sends magicians—who is the real power, who is the real king, who is the real god?

AP: Well, the question of whose power is greater gets answered very quickly when the plagues start. Pharaoh does not bend, and ultimately God sends in the big guns.

DL: Can we stop there for a moment? What do you think is the purpose of the plagues, Abby? How would you end this sentence: "God brought ten plagues to Egypt in order to . . . ."

AP: Terrify the people.

DL: So they would pressure Pharaoh to free the Israelites?

AP: Yes: "Let them go already; we can't endure these plagues!"

DL: But then why does God harden Pharaoh's heart so that Pharaoh continues to refuse, which will allow God to bring even more plagues?

AP: Let's first point out that God does that more than once. Every time it feels like a plague might be the breaking point for Pharaoh, suddenly his heart is hardened, and he changes his mind and says, "I will not let them go."

DL: Exactly.

AP: That confuses me, and I bring this conundrum to my seder table year after year. If God is hardening Pharaoh's heart, that ultimately means

God has a hand in Pharaoh's intransigence. So, is Pharaoh really culpable?

DL: Yes, there is the question of culpability. That's an issue that has vexed many Jewish thinkers. Some say Pharaoh is culpable, not for refusing to let them go, but for enslaving the people in the first place. Others point out that God only started hardening Pharaoh's heart after he said "no" the first few times all on his own, and it is for those initial refusals that he is being punished. But what I also want to know is this: if, by hardening Pharaoh's heart, God is forestalling him from freeing the Israelites, why is God sending these plagues? *One* of the plagues might have persuaded Pharaoh to relent if God had left Pharaoh's heart alone.

AP: I think it's because this is God's show; the deliverance of the Israelites needs to have a major buildup for it to be remembered in the way God wants it remembered. The Exodus is going to be the seminal event of our people, so it can't just be a snake from a rod; it can't be just frogs or hail.

DL: Yes, I think so too. The purpose is to make an impression on us. It will be the most foundational moment for our culture, so we need to remember the story of the ten plagues. We would never have had the movie *The Ten Commandments* were it not for all these plagues.

AP: And if it were just one or two plagues, it wouldn't have been nearly as momentous.

DL: So, the intensity of the plagues is not really about forcing the Egyptians to free us. It's about making this our foundational narrative. I agree with that completely. Do you think it may also be there to punish the Egyptians for having enslaved us?

AP: Absolutely. Are you asking me if I'm focusing too much on the theater of the plagues and glossing over the huge fact that Pharaoh and his army did horrible things and deserve to pay a stiff price? I'm not. Ultimately, the Egyptians are going to suffer the worst of what they did to Hebrew families—through the killings of their firstborn.

DL: Got it. So Pharaoh's punishment for hundreds of years of enslaving the Israelites is the ten plagues. And God hardens his heart because God wants him to get his due punishment.

AP: Because otherwise he won't get *enough* punishment.

DL: Yes.

AP: It also feels like the drama of increasing plagues is the point.

DL: Okay. Let's go back to that: the drama is the point.

AP: It feels like this has to be—

DL: An event that is seared in our memory. And the Bible says that is the case. I can read a verse that underscores that idea.

AP: Sure.

DL: This is from the next parsha—Bo—Exodus 10:2. God tells Moses: "And that thou may tell in the ears of thy child and thy child's child what things I have wrought in Egypt, and my signs which I have done among them, that you may know that I am the Lord." In other words, "The reason I am bringing all of these plagues is so this becomes a living memory for you—as a people—to pass down from generation to generation."

AP: It also becomes a story that is going to be told and retold. And a story needs chapters.

DL: Right. So, we're saying the plagues have a couple of functions: they are a punishment for the Egyptians, a way to pressure them to free the Israelites, and they are also intended to heighten the drama of the story.

AP: So we'll have a big story to tell.

DL: And, I would add, not just a big story to tell, but a way to learn the messages of faith that God is the true god. God is all-powerful. I wonder, too, if that ties into the beginning of our discussion, which was the contest between God and Pharaoh. We are more likely to listen to human rulers and human authorities than the divine one. And this contest is meant to say, "You must learn who the real God is, who the real king is." Maybe that is the message of the plagues: "*I* am where the real power resides."

AP: God runs the show.

DL: Exactly. God runs the show. Don't be distracted by the power of humans. God has the real power, and that is the message you must pass down through the generations.

Va'era to Bo

Pharaoh remains unmoved by God's display of superiority over the Egyptian sorcerers and refuses to accede to Moses's demand to let the people go. God tells Moses to have Aaron smite the Nile with his staff, and Aaron does so, turning the Nile and all the water in Egypt to blood. Pharaoh's magicians are able to perform a somewhat similar feat, and Pharoah still refuses to free the people.

Eight more plagues follow: infestations of frogs, lice, wild animals, cattle disease, boils, fiery hail, locusts, and utter darkness, in which terrible destruction is brought unto the Egyptians and from which the Israelites are spared. After each plague, Pharaoh initially shows willingness to free the Israelites, at least to some degree, but as soon as the horror of the plague has passed, his intransigence returns, and he reneges on his agreement.

God then tells Moses that there is one more plague that will befall the Egyptians, after which, Pharaoh will release the Israelites in earnest. This plague will be the most extreme by far: in the middle of the night, God will kill the firstborn child of each Egyptian household and every firstborn animal. Only then will the Egyptians understand God's supreme power and beg the Israelites to leave the land. Moses is then told to instruct the people to ask their Egyptian neighbors for clothes and gold and silver, and the Egyptians comply willingly.

Moses is now commanded to establish the month of redemption—what is now call Nissan—as the first month of the calendar; to slaughter a lamb on the fourteenth day of this month and to place its blood on the doorframe; and to eat the roasted meat of this Paschal lamb with matzah and bitter herbs. The people are told that when God passes through Egypt to smite the firstborn, God will see the blood on the doorposts and pass over the houses of the Israelites.

Bo

בֹּא

AP: Tell us what Bo means, Dov.

DL: "Come" or "Go"; in this case, "Go unto Pharaoh." Moses and Aaron are going to appeal to Pharaoh. They are wrapping up the ten plagues and bringing the Israelites out of Egypt.

AP: And we all know the final plague. No matter how much Jewish education we received in our childhoods, nobody forgets the deaths of the firstborn.

DL: Especially if you are a firstborn child. I have to tell you that, throughout my kids' childhood, every Passover night when we would recite the ten plagues, both of my boys would refuse to recite the last one because they took a moral objection to it. They said, "How is it fair that all of these innocent Egyptian babies are slaughtered?" I didn't have a good answer for them.

AP: How would you answer today?

DL: I still don't have a response that is truly satisfying on a moral plane. One thing I could say is that the Torah often deals with collective justice or punishment, where the community suffers for the sins of the individuals. I think that's part of what's going on here, although I would be the first to admit that this goes against our ideas of individual justice.

In an earlier verse, God says, "Israel [the Jewish people] is my firstborn, and if you refuse to let my firstborn go, I will slay *your* firstborn." So, on a symbolic level, if you think about the Egyptian nation not freeing God's firstborn, and their firstborn being slayed, there is a nice tit-for-tat there.

AP: I'd be careful about characterizing it as "nice."

DL: Fair point. It's still a strong metaphor. But on a human level, you have a lot of innocent babies dying while having done nothing wrong.

AP: It's very hard to reconcile. In Exodus 12:29, just to remind everyone how bleak it is, "In the middle of the night, the Lord struck down all the firstborn in the land of Egypt"—this is obviously the Egyptian firstborn, not Israelite—"from the firstborn of Pharaoh who sat on the throne to the firstborn of the captive who was in the dungeon, and all the firstborn of the cattle." I didn't remember that the cows were struck down.

DL: Comparatively they don't get a lot of play.

AP: Skipping ahead, "Pharaoh arose in the night, with all of his courtiers and all the Egyptians—because there was a loud cry in Egypt; for there was no house where there was not someone dead." That's—

DL: Tragic. Horrific.

AP: Don't you think we have to at least take a moment and look at how scorched-earth this punishment is? This is as awful as it gets, killing these innocent kids.

DL: Totally. And honestly, I don't have any good explanation for that. I should add that the same way my boys have a problem with this, they have a problem every time in the Torah that God is punishing the Israelites and setting forth lethal plagues for sins *they* committed. The plague of the firstborn is particularly harsh because there are all these innocent babies, but there seems to be a lot of collective punishment going on in the Torah. I can't pretend to justify it.

AP: What do you really believe, though? When you look at what the Egyptians did to the Israelites—how many years of oppression?

DL: A verse says it was four hundred years.

AP: There's a lot of revenge stored up there, which is justifiable. So, in your heart of hearts, how does this sit with you?

DL: It's not justifiable at all, in my opinion, because it does not explain punishing innocent babies. There are ways you can make people suffer without killing the innocent. I can afflict the guilty with boils and blisters and tremendous suffering and agony; they are the guilty party. But you don't punish the guilty by killing their firstborn sons.

AP: Except it worked.

DL: It worked to free the Israelites, but the Egyptians would have freed them sooner had God not hardened Pharaoh's heart.

AP: You don't think we needed the last plague to be set free?

DL: I don't. There were other ways God could have forced Pharoah to free the Israelites.

Look, I'd rather live with a good question—*how is it fair that the innocent were killed in this plague?*—than to accept a bad answer. This isn't something that can be nicely wrapped up in a bow. I think it's okay to say, "This is a real moral dilemma for me, and I'm not going to try to give an answer that I know won't justify suffering of innocents. Instead, I'm going to struggle with it and let it bother me . . . ." I feel that's the better approach.

AP: That's just a shortcut.

DL: You'd rather have a bad answer? What's your answer, Abby?

AP: When we take our pinkies and drop ten drops of wine on our plates as we recite these plagues, is it not the case that these are our symbolic tears for the loss of Egyptian life?

DL: Yes. That is traditionally how it's understood, that even when punishment is justified, we should still cry over the loss of life. But that assumes the punishment *is* justified, that those who died were deserving. It doesn't address the *injustice* of the innocent being punished.

I don't think we have ever fully confronted it. I'd rather leave it as an open question and continue to grapple with it.

AP: Do you do those drops of wine at your seder?

DL: I do.

AP: What do you think you are doing them for?

DL: What you're really asking is whether I am willing to reinterpret this ritual as marking the loss of innocent life—and I could. That is an interesting approach. But it still does not answer the question of whether we needed this last horrible plague to be freed; it is just saying, "I am going to acknowledge—"

AP: "I am going to be conscious of the price that was paid for our freedom."

DL: Right.

AP: Okay, let's move to the matzah. Here's one thing that always confused me: The people were told to eat matzah while they were still in Egypt—*before* they were on the run and didn't have time for the bread to leaven. God foresaw that wc would need a seder and a symbol to mark this Exodus story forever.

DL: This is such a good point. We were given the *mitzvah* of matzah well in advance of the Exodus itself.

AP: I have the verse here; it is 12:14:

> This day shall be to you one of remembrance: you shall celebrate it as a festival to the Lord throughout the ages; you shall celebrate it as an institution for all time. Seven days you shall eat unleavened bread; on the very first day you shall remove leaven from your houses, for whoever eats leavened bread from the first day to the seventh shall be cut off from Israel.

So, is God commanding us to eat matzah to commemorate something that hasn't happened yet?

DL: One way of understanding this is that the matzah may, on one level, not have anything to do with the story of hastening out of the land. It could have other meanings.

AP: Like what?

DL: There is evidence that, in the ancient world, this was a time to celebrate the first harvest, and maybe there was a traditional eating of matzah associated with this agricultural period, which had nothing to do with the Exodus. I know that sounds strange.

AP: It's a bit of an anticlimax, honestly. Was matzah on the menu any other time in the Torah?

DL: Yes, actually, in Genesis 19:3. Way back when the angels came to Lot to save him from the Sodomite mob. I don't think we ever covered this story; it happens after the angels visit Abraham, and it says Lot fed matzah to the visiting angels. So it could be that this was the time of year when matzah was the traditional food. I don't know if that explains why it should be the focus of the story, but that's one idea. A more satisfying explanation is that matzah is not only a symbol of freedom but also of slavery.

AP: Yes, it says so in the Haggadah.

DL: Right at the beginning: "This is the poor person's bread that our ancestors ate in the land of Egypt."

AP: "This is the bread of affliction."

DL: Correct. It's not just symbolizing the freedom and the hurrying out of Egypt. It's a thin bread that doesn't rise—it's meant to feed poor people and fill up your stomach. So maybe at this stage of the story, it symbolizes oppression, and only when they left did that symbol of oppression transform into a symbol of freedom.

AP: I really like that. I think that's a completely Jewish idea. There are so many times where the suffering of our ancestors turns into reinvention and redemption.

DL: We were once discussing what it means to remember the Exodus story, and you said we are supposed to recall that we suffered, and I said, "Why are we supposed to remember that we suffered? We are supposed to remember that we were freed." It seems to me you're saying it's really important that those two ideas should be part of the same story. The same symbol can be about freedom one year and about slavery the next, and sometimes it's about both of them together.

AP: That's the way life is—we are both the experience of our suffering and our survival of the suffering. Hopefully we don't suffer to *this* extent, but we carry our struggles with us.

DL: That's a great insight, Abby.

AP: Rabbi David Ingber once gave a teaching on the brokenness of the matzah and how brokenness is a marker of maturity, growing up—how we all have to break in order to find our wholeness. We do carry our brokenness, and in the same way the matzah is a reminder of how hard things were, it's also a reminder that we were saved, and that we got the chance to live again, to start again.

DL: I like that idea, because the story we tell is also not whole, not a prepackaged narrative where we are just reciting the words given to us. Instead, we take a few verses and break them up into little pieces, extrapolate and interpret every word. That gets to your point about brokenness: if it was such a perfect narrative from beginning to end, and if we just read the words, it would go in one ear and out the other. But by breaking it up into pieces and finding the cracks . . . . What was that line from Leonard Cohen? "There is a crack in everything; that's how the light gets in." I think that's part of how we tell the Passover story.

AP: Here's to brokenness—and matzah every morning.

DL: Oh God.

Bo to Beshalach

God does as promised and passes through Egypt at midnight, smiting the firstborn of all Egyptians while passing over the homes of the Israelites. Pharoah and the Egyptian people arise in the middle of the night, demanding that the Israelites leave their land immediately. The Israelites depart Egypt the next morning, leaving so hastily that their bread does not have time to rise.

God gives Moses instructions for the future: When the people enter the Promised Land, they must bring a Paschal sacrifice each year and commemorate the departure from Egypt by eating matzah and avoiding leavened bread for seven days each spring. Furthermore, each firstborn animal must be offered as a sacrifice to God.

God leads the Israelites through the desert with a pillar of cloud during the day and a pillar of fire at night, and they arrive at the Red Sea. God then hardens Pharaoh's heart once more, and Pharoah, now regretting having freed the people, gathers his army and chases after the Israelites, reaching them at the Red Sea. The people, seeing Pharoah's army in hot pursuit, cry out to Moses, who turns to God for help. God tells Moses to lift his staff up over the sea, and Moses does so, causing the sea to part. The Israelites walk through the sea on dry land and emerge safely on the other side. The Egyptian army follows, at which point Moses again lifts up his staff, and the sea closes up over them, causing them all to perish.

Beshalach

בְּשַׁלַּח

AP: We're talking today about justifiable revenge. I know this is one of your favorite subjects, Dov. We're looking at the parsha of Beshalach, which means?

DL: "When he let go," which refers to Pharaoh finally relenting and "letting go" of the Israelite slaves—letting them leave.

AP: After all the, "Yes, I'll let them go now; no, I won't; yes, I will . . . ."

DL: God has sent the ten plagues, culminating in the slaying of the firstborn. And now, finally, Pharaoh lets them go, and they travel out of Egypt.

AP: But then he changes his mind yet again and sends his army chasing after them.

DL: Yes.

AP: So, we're going to discuss whether it's okay that our people celebrate when Pharaoh's army drowns behind them. Moses raises his staff, the waters of the Red Sea part, and the Israelites pass through safely. Then God closes the sea back up and drowns Pharaoh's army, which is chasing the Israelites, their former slaves. Let's share some verses to anchor us where we are in Exodus.

DL: This is from Chapter 14. I'll just read two verses: "The Egyptians came in pursuit after them into the sea, all of Pharaoh's horses, chariots, and horsemen." And then it says, "God caused the sea to close." It ends by saying, "The waters turned back and covered the chariots and the horsemen, Pharaoh's entire army that followed them into the sea; not one of them remained."

AP: "Not one of them remained." That's pretty stark revenge right there. And I'm kind of fine with it.

DL: Really?

AP: These aren't noncombatants. These are Pharaoh's slave drivers and oppressors. They're chasing the Israelites who'd been enslaved for *400 years*. They've finally released them, and now they're doubling back and going after them. I feel like, hey, you get what you deserve. It's enough already.

DL: Well, first of all, I'm not sure the slave drivers are the same as the soldiers who've been sent to bring Moses and his people back. And I also think it's really important to ask whether we think every soldier bears the guilt of the wars declared by their leaders.

AP: Are you saying they're not all combatants?

DL: They're combatants, yes, but how much does that mean that they, personally, are guilty of all the sins of Pharaoh and the country? But beyond that, I think that even if we believe this punishment is justified—and I would say "punishment" here, by the way, as opposed to "revenge"—that it's still one thing for God to mete it out and another thing for the people to rejoice in it. This is the parsha that includes the "Song of the Sea." I think you probably know the Debbie Friedman song—

AP: "And the women dancing with their timbrels!" Do you want me to sing it?

DL: Uhh . . . .

AP: I'd need some slivovitz for that anyway, which is a family tradition on Pesach in our family. "Miriam's Song" is so joyful, and you're about to tell me there should not be joy . . . .

DL: If the Israelites just sang, "Thank you, God, for saving us," that would be great. But I'm going to read some of the parsha's verses. I don't think most people are aware of the content of the song.

AP: This is going to be like finding out there is no Tooth Fairy. We're going to be shocked by what we're singing, aren't we?

DL: Probably. Here we go—starting at Exodus 15:1:

> I will sing unto the Lord, for He has triumphed gloriously. The horse and his rider hath he thrown into the sea . . . Pharaoh's chariots . . . and his host he cast into the sea . . . The depths have covered them. They sank into the bottom as a stone. Thy right hand, O Lord, is glorious in power: thy right hand, O Lord, hath dashed

> in pieces the enemy . . . Thou hast overthrown them that rose up against thee: thou sendest forth thy wrath, which consumed them as stubble . . . .

AP: Wow, talk about dancing on someone's grave. You're right. It's hard to square the mass drowning with the mirth of the dancing and singing.

DL: Yes, so I mean—

AP: I feel chastened, disillusioned.

DL: Well, I do think that we should sing and celebrate when God saves us. But what challenges me is delighting in the punishment and downfall of our enemies. There's actually a verse in Proverbs, which says, "In the downfall of thine enemies, you shall not rejoice."

AP: Didn't God get angry and exclaim, "How can you be dancing?"

DL: That's a famous *midrash*. The angels wanted to rejoice and sing when the Egyptians were drowning. And God said, "My handiwork is drowning in the sea, and you think you can burst into song?"

AP: I thought it was "My creation" or "My people" or "My children" are drowning . . . .

DL: I think the actual words are, *ma'asei yadei tovim bi'yam*, which translates to something like "the acts of My hand." In other words, "My handiwork."

AP: But basically, God is saying, "My creation is drowning, and you're—"

DL: "And you're singing," yes. But I want to acknowledge the point you're making about the feelings of those who have been oppressed. The *midrash* says God is scolding the *angels* for singing. They are outsiders to this whole drama. They shouldn't be singing when people, even oppressors, are dying. But the *midrash* doesn't have a problem with the Israelites singing. *They* were the ones who were oppressed. Their joy for being avenged is understandable.

In the end, the *midrash* is trying to capture our attention around the redemption and the feelings of gratitude and perhaps even joy at the downfall of one's enemies, but, alongside that, the tragedy of human life being lost. How do we hold on to both of those at the same time?

AP: It also reminds us very starkly that God doesn't separate Jews from non-Jews in this instance. God is saying, "The Egyptians are my creations too," right? And "You shouldn't celebrate death," essentially.

DL: Correct, the Egyptians are human beings. It's interesting because when we do this ritual at the seder, where we dip our finger in the wine, and we let a drop of wine fall on the plate for each one of the ten plagues, the common explanation for that practice is that we are shedding a tear and feeling the suffering of Egyptians as we mention each plague.

AP: But, in particular, the tenth plague, no? We are crying for the babies and their blood.

DL: I tend to think about it more generally, but, yes, it can be seen as highlighting the tenth plague, as we discussed in last week's parsha. The interesting thing, though, is that scholars have researched it and found that the seder ritual originated in the time of the Crusades. It actually was a way of saying, "You think these ten plagues are bad? They're just a drop in the ocean of what you—our non-Jewish enemies—are going to get when God finally metes out justice for the evil you've done to us."

AP: So, it's not just that these are tears of compassion, but they're also a warning or a threat. Like, "That was just the tip of the iceberg."

DL: Look, for an oppressed people to have something that gives them hope that they're not always going to suffer, coupled with some sense of justice that the people who did these evil things to them will be punished, is really key. Nowadays, we tend to speak from a position of privilege. For many years, we have not felt that type of oppression,* so we've been able to focus on God telling the angels not to sing and that the wine is symbolic of our tears.*

AP: But I think even today we want to know that we can—not necessarily get revenge—but see justice done when we've been wronged. No one's lost sight of that sense of balancing the scales after generations of persecution.

DL: I think there's a difference between exacting justice and when we personally want to act out on our passions. That's why we have courts, judges, police, and a system of laws—so justice can be done. But we

* It's a sad truth that Dov would speak very differently—post October 7, 2023—about the absence of oppression for the Jewish people. But Torah takes a snapshot of the climate when it's read, and we chose to leave his sentiments intact—as a marker of how powerfully the world (and one's perspective) can change in an awful instant.

have to separate "justice" from "revenge." Even in that context, it's important to remember that the Talmud says, when a Jewish court is executing someone, it has to treat him with full human dignity. We must remember that the verse, "Love your brother as yourself," applies even to a person who we're in the process of executing. So, we really need to find a way to honor both justice and the dignity and preciousness of human life.

AP: This reminds me of a controversial prayer in the Haggadah, which I learned as an adult because it wasn't one we said at my childhood seder table: "Pour out thy wrath," where we urge God to punish our enemies.

DL: Exactly. *Sh'foch Ha'matcha*.

AP: That's not a prayer that is necessarily intuitive for a seder where you're talking about welcoming the stranger.

DL: I understand that at your seder you are talking about welcoming the stranger, but more traditional Jews are talking about how we were saved after oppression. At our seders, we tend to focus not on welcoming the stranger, but on the idea, throughout history, there have always been those who have hated us and tried to destroy us, and God, in the end, will punish them for their evildoings. I think it's a question of interpretation.

AP: That's a darker doomsday seder, Dov. As we wrap this parsha up, I'm left with the hope that we push ourselves within our community, but also outside it—to talk more honestly about the balance between self-defense and vengeance. There's tension between the urge to fight back and the admonition not to revel in reprisal or bloodshed.

DL: I agree. We have to be able to hold these contradictory ideals at the same time, and that can be a tall order.

Beshalach to Yitro

Low on food and deep in the desert, some of the Israelites wonder aloud whether it was worth it to leave Egypt. In response, God brings them a flock of quail for meat in the evening and then, in the morning, rains down a miraculous bread-like food called manna. Moses instructs each Israelite to take only as much as he or she needs each day. On the sixth day of the week, everyone must collect a double portion of manna in order to have enough left over for Shabbat, when gathering food is prohibited. Some people, however, do not heed Moses's orders and go out to gather the manna on the Sabbath, provoking God's anger.

The Israelites continue on to Rephidim and are thirsting for water. Again, God miraculously intervenes, instructing Moses to strike a rock—from which water bursts forth.

After surviving an attack by the enemy nation of Amalek, the Israelites are joined by Moses's father-in-law Jethro, who hears of God's miracles and the exodus of the people from Egypt. Jethro encourages Moses to set up a judicial system in which Moses delegates some of his authority and responsibilities, and Moses does so.

Finally, in the third month after the parting of the Red Sea, the Israelites arrive at Mount Sinai where, through Moses, God tells them that they will be God's chosen people and partners to God's covenant: if the Israelites heed God's teachings, God will treasure the Israelites and make them into a holy nation. The people are told to prepare themselves for the giving of the Torah and to keep their distance from the mountain. Moses ascends Mount Sinai, and God descends upon the mountain. Amidst the thunder and lightning, and with smoke rising to the heavens, God proclaims the Ten Commandments to the people.

YITRO

יִתְרוֹ

AP: We've got a big one to discuss.

DL: The Ten Commandments!

AP: We need a thunder sound effect.

DL: I'm ready. Let's do it.

AP: We're going to discuss something today that could sound sacrilegious: are they the *right* Ten Commandments? First, let's review what the Ten are, even though we know that all our listeners have them memorized and inscribed on their hearts.

DL: I'm going to reframe the question a bit and say, "Are they the same Ten Commandments *I* would have picked?"

AP: That's a little solipsistic, Dov.

DL: Not really. I just prefer not to frame the question as whether the Torah—and thus God—was *right* or not. Let's get started. Number one, "I am the Lord your God."

AP: We're not going to stop at each one, but can you explain why that is a commandment? Because it confuses people.

DL: Well, there's some debate about that. Some understand this to be a commandment to believe in God, and others argue that it's a preamble, not a commandment. The Torah doesn't call them the Ten Commandments; it calls them the Ten Utterances, but that's a whole other conversation.

AP: So, this is the first utterance: "I am the Lord your God."

DL: Number two: "Don't have other gods or make idols." Number three: "Do not take the Lord's name in vain." Number four: "Keep the Sabbath." Number five: "Honor your parents." Number six: "Do not commit murder." Number seven: "Do not commit adultery." Number eight: "Do not steal." Number nine: "Do not bear false witness." And number ten: "Do not covet."

AP: I just want to point out that you did that from memory. Impressive. I've heard rabbis teach that half of these commandments apply to our relationship with God and half to our relationship with other people.

DL: That's the standard explanation, but I have a different way of looking at it: the First Commandment is the preamble, and then I divide it into thirds. The first three are about our relationship to God: "Don't have other gods," "Don't take God's name in vain," and "Keep the Sabbath." The next three are about our relationship to people: "Honor your parents," "Don't commit murder," and "Don't commit adultery." The last three have to do with our relationship to property: "Don't steal," "Don't bear false witness"—which is usually related to monetary matters—and "Don't covet." If we read it the other way, number five—honoring your parents—isn't really about our relationship with God. Although, the Rabbis try to finesse that by saying our relationship to our parents models our relationship to God and vice versa.

AP: Why does God identify Him- or Herself as, "The one who took you out of the land of Egypt"? Why is that the foremost qualification that God chooses instead of, "Don't forget, I was the creator of heaven and earth; I created human beings; I created the world you're in." Why emphasize "the one who took you out of Egypt?"

DL: You're asking a question that was asked almost 1,000 years ago by Judah Halevi. And it's a classic Jewish philosophical question.

AP: Talk about Judah Halevi.

DL: He was a Jewish poet, philosopher, and the author of a work of Jewish religious thought called the *Kuzari*. He said the focus on God taking us out of Egypt is because that defines our relationship with God. We did not come to know God through intellectual, philosophical speculation but through history and direct experience. It is this God whom we know and this God with whom we have a relationship. The Jewish God is a God of history. And it is through history that our relationship has been forged.

AP: So, it's ultimately about our collaboration with God—that we did the Exodus together.

DL: It's like a couple saying, "All the things we've experienced together define us. We're in this together." It's about that bond, that partnership, and that relationship.

AP: And leaving Egypt was a peak moment, because it defined our freedom. It's a way of saying, "You gave us instruction and we followed it. You were with us through the parting of the sea and the desert with the fire and cloud. You took care of us, and we were together in this difficult liberation."

DL: Yes, I really like that, because so much of the Torah is about the centrality of relationship. I would also say it's because, if God is involved in our history and took us out of Egypt, God is not up in the heavens but *alongside us.* That's why God can command us; that's why God cares how we act in this world—because God is in our lives.

AP: Then doesn't that link to Sinai? Because when God sent the law down, it was not a mandate but an invitation. Ultimately, it was our choice to accept the law or not.

DL: Yes, absolutely. We had to willingly accept it.

AP: In that sense, the relationship—the covenant—was played out in a very intense way.

DL: You're 100 percent correct. I think that word, "covenant," is key. We talk about the Ten *Command*ments, but to command is unilateral; it's one-directional. But the Torah frames it as, "a covenant with God," which is bilateral.

AP: It's a mutual contract, a partnership.

DL: Exactly.

AP: Okay. Let's get beyond the opening commandments. It feels like the next ones are obvious—"Don't murder," for example, is a no-brainer. But some of the others are a little bit less intuitive, like, "Don't covet." I mean, how can one be commanded not to *feel*—jealousy, in particular?

DL: That is a really good question. And why does this make it into the top ten? The Rabbis say that coveting is not just jealousy or envy or desire. It's specifically a desire to try to take and possess something that belongs to another. It's like a gateway sin to stealing. In a way, that was the very first sin of humanity: Adam and Eve's eating from the fruit of the forbidden tree. Something was off-limits, they desired it, so they took it and ate it. This one sin can be seen as the core of a lot of evil in this world, such as stealing and adultery and so on.

AP: That's very true. We know covetousness leads to other bad things. If you want what someone else has, you might kill for it; you might even go to war to take it. In other words, it's a seed that often leads to worse offenses.

DL: Exactly. So, let me ask you a question. Is there one of these commandments that would not be on your top ten list?

AP: Taking the Lord's name in vain.

DL: Why that one?

AP: It just seems like a waste of a commandment. These are the Big Ten, and you're going to waste one of those precious directives on something people shouldn't *say*?

DL: I think the message is that everything is rooted in our relationship with God, as we discussed earlier. If we have awe for and fear of God, and if saying God's name is something that carries weight, then we're going to be very careful about keeping God's commandments. It's like how, in *Harry Potter*, you're not supposed to say Voldemort's name; throughout the whole series, everybody avoids saying the name. That creates a tremendous sense of weight and, in that case, fear—it gets into your consciousness. If we didn't go around saying, "Oh God," and "for God's sake," then every time we *did* say God's name, it would mean a lot more. We might even live our lives differently.

AP: Do you think it would make us more faithful or more pious just because we didn't utter it?

DL: Let me be clear, *halacha* interprets "Do not take the Lord's name in vain" as: Do not take a false or unnecessary oath in God's name. Saying God's name in normal speech is fine and can be a very good thing—it can bring God into our lives, create discourse, and increase our God-consciousness. But if you just throw God's name around casually, or curse with it, then I get why that's a problem.

Okay, Abigail, if we removed taking the Lord's name in vain from the Ten Commandments, what would you include instead?

AP: If I were going to add a commandment—not that anybody but you is asking me—it would be to not desecrate the earth. It should matter that God created something that's not only beautiful and precious but also miraculous and life-sustaining. God should be saying to us, "Don't ruin what I gave you."

DL: There is a *midrash* that states exactly that almost word-for-word. It says that after God created the world, Adam and Eve were shown everything God had made, and God said, "Look at this beautiful world I have created and have given to you. Take great care not to waste it." And you're right—why *isn't* that one of the Ten Commandments? And not just that, why isn't it a more explicit *mitzvah* in the Torah that is part of our ethos? I think perhaps one of the reasons is that, in the past, it didn't *have* to be specified so much.

AP: What didn't have to be specified?

DL: The mandate to protect the world. Until the Industrial Revolution, I don't think the world was at grave risk.

AP: We shouldn't even have to spell it out.

DL: In a way, it *was* said in the Genesis story. God says to Adam, "I've given you dominion over the world. Watch the garden; protect the garden," and at that time, the risk wasn't as great. But now that the life of the planet is in peril, we all would like that to be a much weightier directive than it is.

AP: What about bearing false witness? How often are we witnesses? I'm not sure why this is relevant for the Big Ten?

DL: That's a question of how you define what it means to "bear false witness." In the narrow sense, it means to go to court and testify on someone's behalf and to make something up. Maybe a person is paying you to testify so that they can win their court case. But I think that's pretty narrow. Do you have a way of understanding it in a broader way?

AP: You once explained that "false witness" is basically lying. And, without getting too close to the line of politics, that, to me, is very relevant for this moment. What does it mean to testify falsely or to speak falsely in the public setting, which, to me, seems to do grave damage? We're seeing the impact of that now—that it can cause people to doubt facts that we used to take for granted as truth.

DL: I just want to add that, according to Jewish tradition, it's okay to tell a white lie. It's not an absolute that we can never speak an untruth. But saying or perpetuating falsehoods that really hurt people, that's the type of thing we're talking about here.

Let me ask you this, Abby: all of these commandments seem to be universal, right? Is that a good explanation for why these are the top ten? Because there isn't anything particularistic to Judaism here. We don't have the idea of keeping kosher; we don't have circumcision; we don't have the Jewish holidays . . . . One way of thinking about these ten is that they provide a kind of universal ethics.

AP: Except for the Sabbath.

DL: Well, that's true. But, you know, it's also true that the Sabbath was created before the Jews. The Sabbath was the seventh day of Creation. God sanctifies it. That's before there was a Jewish people. And certainly, Western religions all have a Sabbath—Christians on Sunday and Muslims on Friday. Is there a way you can relate to Sabbath as a universal?

AP: What's universal about the Sabbath directive to me is that God isn't just insisting that we rest; God's commanding us to allow our workers to rest, whether it's your subordinates or your colleagues. It's a commandment not to *enslave*, and it goes back to the idea that we were once slaves. We are remembering, "I am God who took you out of slavery." The Sabbath is universal in that there has to be a time when everyone gets a break.

DL: I totally agree with that. When the Ten Commandments are repeated in the book of Deuteronomy—

AP: That's the last book of Torah.

DL: Yes. There, the verses are explicit: "Remember, keep the Sabbath. Remember, you were a slave. God took you out of Egypt. Therefore, you must give rest to your slaves and servants, to your animals." Blu Greenberg once told me that she was on a UN commission about universal human rights—

AP: Before you go on, let's explain who Blu Greenberg is.

DL: A leading Orthodox Jewish feminist. Everything else is commentary.

AP: True. She's an amazing thinker and leader.

DL: She pointed this out to me: from the commandment of the Sabbath, we can learn that there is a universal right to rest, that we do not have to work seven days a week. We should never enslave others, and we should never be enslaved ourselves. In a nutshell: don't be a slave to your job, and every human being has a right to rest.

AP: I'm going to give *you* a rest now, Dov. Have a restful Shabbat.

DL: You too, Abby. Shabbat shalom.

Yitro to Mishpatim

Having laid out in the Ten Commandments the core principles by which the Israelites must live, God gives Moses and the people detailed laws and *mitzvot* for creating a just, ethical, and God-oriented society. These *mitzvot* first address slavery: while the institution is permitted, strict conditions govern it. For example, an Israelite may enslave another Israelite for up to six years but must free him in the seventh year unless the slave explicitly demands to remain with his owner. Next come prohibitions and penalties for various kinds of violence: murder, manslaughter, and assault—notably introducing the concept of "an eye for an eye."

This is followed by laws regarding torts and damages, the responsibilities of people given objects for safekeeping, returning lost objects, and helping a donkey that is struggling under its load. There are also prohibitions against eating unslaughtered meat, taking an oath in vain, giving false testimony, and taking a bribe, among many others.

Mishpatim

מִשְׁפָּטִים

DL: After the amazing event of God giving us the Torah and the Ten Commandments on Mount Sinai, now we have a long list of detailed laws: Mishpatim.

AP: Why don't you summarize them; I know you know them cold.

DL: There are so, so many. One set of laws is about what type of liability you have if you dig a hole and somebody's ox falls into it or if you make a fire and it spreads.

AP: Or if your animal goes crazy in a field and ruins someone's crops.

DL: Exactly, the oxen falling into the well are basic laws about torts and responsibility, which still apply today. If you are dealing with a car or with pollution, those things are ready applications of this.

AP: Today, we're going to focus on this line that we hear so much: "You shall not wrong a stranger or oppress him, for you were strangers in the land of Egypt." This is from Exodus 22:20, but the idea of not oppressing a stranger appears thirty-six times in the Torah. That is something that is often highlighted by the Rabbis, because nothing else appears as often. As we get started, though, I want to zero in on the word, "stranger." Let's first define it as it is in the Torah. Dov?

DL: It is someone who is not a citizen of the land. The Hebrew word is *ger*. Abraham describes himself as a *ger*—a "stranger"—when he is trying to buy the burial plot that becomes Sarah's resting place. What he is saying is, "I don't have rights to this land; I am not a citizen." In the strictest sense, "stranger" is not accurate; "non-citizen" or "sojourner" is really a much closer definition.

AP: But it has been used, or extrapolated, to mean the "other" or someone who is outside the group.

DL: Right. Somebody who is a non-citizen is vulnerable and can be taken advantage of or marginalized. It gets expanded to everyone who is an outsider.

AP: But there is a directive not to oppress, which seems to insist on compassion for others. Am I wrong about that? "You shall not wrong the *ger* because *you* were once the *ger*." So there is this idea of, "Remember what it felt like to be persecuted, and don't do it to someone else."

DL: I completely agree, and the command to show compassion appears in a different verse, which says, "You shall love the *ger*, the stranger." The next verse then states that you shall not oppress the orphan and the widow. A major theme of the Torah is having compassion for those less fortunate.

AP: Let's talk about your personal thoughts in the context of today. When you read this verse and look at the debate about immigration, it seems to apply pretty directly.

DL: Totally. One qualification I'll make is that this verse does not specify what your immigration policy has to be. You can have a limited immigration policy—you don't have to welcome everyone. But once somebody is in our land, we have a responsibility to them. And even if we don't live up to the ideal that there should be one law that applies equally to everyone—stranger and citizen alike—we can all make sure to not fall below the minimum standard of, "You shall not oppress the stranger."

AP: When I look at the people who oppose a policy of more compassion—whether it be an Evangelical Christian or an Orthodox Jew—I don't see how you square that with Exodus 22:20.

DL: I'll tell you how, at least from a *halachic* point of view. It is because the Rabbis interpret "stranger," not as a person on the outside but as somebody who came from the outside and is now on the inside. They say the word *ger* refers to the proselyte—someone who converted to Judaism from another religion. Part of the reason for this interpretation of the word *ger* is that the Rabbis were living in a time when the Jewish people didn't have a land over which they were sovereign; they only had a religion. So for them, "sojourner" or "stranger" can't mean a non-citizen living in your land. The closest thing it could have meant at the time was a person who came to your religion from the outside—a person who is Jewish by choice, not Jewish by birth.

AP: So the *ger* is not really a full stranger because he or she is a Jew.

DL: Exactly, and this Rabbinic reading results in the *halachic* understanding that the obligation to the stranger does not extend beyond the Jewish people.

AP: Wait, you're saying that every one of those thirty-six times the word "stranger" appears in the Torah, they are talking about a convert?

DL: From the *halachic* point of view, yes.

AP: This is a bit of a shock.

DL: I know, I know.

AP: Then how does it become a moral value? A Jewish value?

DL: Sadly, for some it isn't, which is deeply disturbing.

AP: For some Jews it isn't?

DL: Correct.

AP: So, for some observant Jews, this idea of loving and welcoming the stranger excludes anyone who isn't a Jew?

DL: Right. They would say, "This is intended only for the Jew who converted."

AP: That's a *shanda*—a shame, a disgrace.

DL: Yes, it is.

AP: Don't get me wrong, I'm not saying we shouldn't welcome the convert, but this charge of compassion should apply beyond just Jews.

DL: I absolutely agree with you. Look, there is the question of what *halacha* commands and what our Jewish values demand. *Halacha* might not demand that we act outside of the community—I wish it did—but I think our Jewish values unquestionably do. Sadly, not everyone agrees.

AP: Is there any *halacha* that *does* demand empathy for the non-Jew?

DL: Well . . . .

AP: It's that difficult to come up with?

DL: Yes, I'm afraid so.

AP: This explanation is not good for the Jews. You're telling me that it's hard to find any text in *halacha* that says you should be good to the non-Jew, to those who are not in our family?

DL: It is hard. But I need to give this some historical context. The Rabbis of the Talmud—and the rabbis for centuries afterward—were living in a time when the Jews were an oppressed minority, often suffering mercilessly at the hands of non-Jews. It's not so hard to see why they understood our obligations to the "other" to be focused specifically on our fellow Jews.

As for texts that speak about caring for non-Jews, there's one that says you are not allowed to cheat or steal from a non-Jew, but that's not exactly the same as having compassion for them. There are also Rabbinic teachings based on the principle of *Darchei Shalom*, the principle of "Ways of Peace," that says that if you are going to take care of the Jews in your community, you also have to take care of the non-Jews. You have to visit their sick, bury their dead, give them *tzedakah* [charity], and take *tzedakah* from them if they want to support the Jewish community.

AP: Where is that?

DL: That is a text that appears in the Talmud—*Tractate Gittin*. Some people read it as self-interest—"We have to be good to them so they don't do bad things to us." But I think the much better read of it is that we all recognize that we are intertwined, and therefore, if we want to live together in ways of peace, we have to take care of one another.

AP: Got it. I am going to put you on the spot—*both* of us on the spot—here.

DL: You know I'm going to turn this question back onto you.

AP: Well, if we are honest about it, we are all wronging a stranger every day. Can you give an example or a way in which you think about trying to avoid that, trying to be mindful of it?

DL: I admit I have not been active at all in terms of the immigration issue. Some of my students have really been politically active; they have gone out there and participated in rallies. I have made myself more aware of the problem but not to the point of actually doing something about it. That really is something I haven't done correctly. What about you, Abby?

AP: You stole mine in the sense that, it's a sin of omission rather than commission. I read about the plights of immigrants, and I feel helpless. But that reaction is an excuse. To feel like you are impotent is a poor excuse for inaction. There is something all of us can do. I am very compassionate but without figuring out a way to make a difference.

DL: That is a very good point about compassion, because that gets back not just to acting, but to *loving* the stranger. And teaching ourselves how to act on those feelings and at least do something—I think that will make a real difference. Can you think of something that you want to do . . . tomorrow?

AP: I think loving the stranger is hard. This is what I am struggling with: our families and ancestors were absolutely marginalized when they were new immigrants, but those of us who are their descendants have absolutely no emotional memory of what that felt like. What I need to do is to get inside the experience of being a person who has come late to the majority, or late to the city, or late to the classroom, or late to the boardroom. There is a consciousness I lack—the feeling of being the outsider, coming in afresh. There are all these assumptions that come with being new to the group, where it *appears* equal and welcoming because we are all sitting at the same table. But they are carrying something extra and harder. I should go out of my way to get inside what that feels like, and then act differently. This might be the person from whom you buy your morning coffee, or the person you are sitting next to in a meeting.

DL: That makes me think of something that has been occurring regularly at our rabbinical school, which is that we open on Monday morning with a circle—you know, reflecting and reviewing—and one person is usually late because he finishes his prayers after everyone else. When he comes, we are all ready to open up the circle, to make space for him. But when this happens, he gets very upset. He says, "I don't want you to have to make space for me; I want to be included in the first place." Since then, we have been leaving an empty chair for him. What would be best is if we all waited for him to finish his prayers, but sometimes that is not exactly possible.

AP: Let's finish with a commitment to open the circle or to leave a chair.

DL: Amen to that, Abby.

Mishpatim to Terumah

THE LIST OF God's instructions for society continues. The Israelites are commanded to act objectively and honestly in matters of interpersonal judgment and not to oppress a stranger, "for you yourselves were strangers in the land of Egypt." God reiterates the commandment to rest on the seventh day of the week and introduces the related practice of Shmita, wherein the Israelites' land must lie fallow every seventh year.

All Israelite males must gather before God for three yearly festivals that will come to be known as Passover, Shavuot, and Sukkot. Lastly, God promises to protect the Israelites as they enter the Promised Land and drive out its inhabitants.

Moses relays all these laws to the people and writes them down. He has the people formally enter into a covenant with God to be bound by the Ten Commandments and the laws of Mishpatim. Following God's word, Moses ascends the mountain to receive the tablets on which the Ten Commandments are inscribed. Moses remains on the mountain for forty days and forty nights.

Terumah

תְּרוּמָה

AP: This is the parsha of Terumah, which means "gift" or "offering." What's being offered, Dov?

DL: The Israelites are offering up their gold, silver, and copper to help construct the Tabernacle, which will be a portable temple that will travel with the Jewish people in the desert.

AP: We've left Sinai with the law, and now we need something in which to carry it. This must be a vessel appropriate to transport God's Word.

DL: Yes, and kept inside the Tabernacle was the Ark of the Covenant, as in *Raiders of the Lost Ark*.

AP: I could sing the theme music, but I'll spare you.

DL: Thank you. So that was the vessel, a box, essentially—gold on the inside and outside—that was used for carrying the tablets. There's a Jewish commentator, Nachmanides, in the thirteenth-century—

AP: We should make it clear this is not Maimonides.

DL: No, not Maimonides.

AP: *Nachmanides.*

DL: Nachmanides.

AP: Get the "*Nach.*"

DL: The Nach! Anyway, he says the Ark was the center of the Tabernacle.

AP: As opposed to what?

DL: As opposed to the altar and the sacrifices. It was really about the tablets representing God's presence. It was like a portable Mount Sinai. So even when they left Mount Sinai, God would still be in their midst.

AP: I love the idea that we're carrying God with us. Those who have read this parsha know that it is heavy on minutiae; it's a dump truck of detail. One could get overwhelmed. There are a million specific requirements and all this ornamentation and opulence—every element of this Tabernacle is laid out. Let's read a sample from the verses; this is Exodus 25:3–9:

> And this is the offering which ye shall take of them: gold and silver and brass; and blue and purple and scarlet and fine linen and goats' hair; and ram skins dyed red and seal skins, and acacia wood; oil for the lights, spices for the anointing oil and for the sweet incense; onyx stones, and stones to be set for the ephod and for the breastplate. And let them make me a sanctuary that I may dwell among them.

It's quite a laundry list.

DL: It was definitely an ornate temple. I understand why we need it and why it has to be different from normal structures so as not to feel like a normal building—it needed to have a special architecture. The Temple in Jerusalem was situated high up on the Temple Mount, and when Jews would build a synagogue in a town, they would also build it on an elevated location; it points us upward and gives a sense of connecting to God.

AP: It was supposed to be the highest spot in town, right?

DL: Right. All of that I accept—the symbolism and the power. But what bothers me is the opulence: the gold, the silver. It feels like we're elevating material wealth—which may be a concession to what we as human beings value. But shouldn't the Temple be focusing us on what really matters—on the spiritual?

AP: Maybe it's less about opulence for opulence's sake and more about how an ornate space can have a physical impact that's spiritual. I feel moved when I'm sitting in Central Synagogue, which you know is spectacular if you've ever been there—*have* you been there?

DL: Yes, I've been there a few times.

AP: It would be inexcusable if you hadn't.

DL: You'll have to invite me to visit again, Abby.

AP: It has Moorish Revival architecture, and it was built in the late nineteenth century. There's a combination of grandeur and serenity there, and it fills me up. So yes, I do see how a physical place can pack an emotional or spiritual punch. What about you, Dov? It feels like an obvious question for a rabbi, but it's not self-evident. Do you feel God in synagogue, and did the Tabernacle concept in this parsha end up succeeding—if you were to evaluate it personally?

DL: In all honesty, on a very personal religious basis, no. It's really hard for me to feel connected in a synagogue most of the time.

AP: That's quite a revelation. It might surprise people who know you.

DL: Well, I don't think I'm alone. I think many people find it challenging, and more people nowadays are looking for spiritual Jewish experiences outside of synagogue.

AP: You don't believe we need physical synagogues?

DL: Oh, I do. It makes me very much feel like part of a community. But if you're asking me about feeling connected, it can often be hard for me to find God in a space like that. When I do find God . . . wait, let me take that back. It's not harder in a synagogue than it is somewhere else, but the space itself doesn't often make it any *easier*. What enables me to feel more connected is what's going on around me. If other people are praying with intention, the energy can be elevating and uplifting and can make me feel connected. Sometimes, maybe ironically, a small, simple space with a low ceiling where there's a community praying intensely—that really does it for me.

AP: But you've also said to me that you sometimes feel God the most outdoors. Talk about that a bit.

DL: Yes, being out in nature is when I feel God's grandeur and beauty the most. I find more of a connectedness to the natural world and to a sense of something larger than myself. How about you? Do you experience God in the synagogue?

AP: I do, but I also have a sense of God's presence at many unexpected moments. Like you, it's sometimes in the synagogue, but it's often outside of it—with my children, with my husband, with a close friend, or sometimes when I'm grappling with something hard. There's this quote I keep from the Kotzker Rebbe, the eighteenth-century Hasidic rabbi. I don't know where I first read it, but I held on to it. He says, "God dwells wherever we are ready to let God in." That resonates for me. If we're open to an unexpected sense of the divine, I think we do stumble upon it more than we thought we might.

DL: I can totally understand that, and it's a great quote. Let me tell you a story. There was a Lithuanian rabbi, stern and intellectual, the opposite of Hasidim, who are more focused on the spiritual. This rabbi went to the *yeshiva* where his son was learning to check up on him, but he couldn't find him—not in the study hall where he was supposed to be, not anywhere. Finally, he finds his son outside in the forest. The father says, "What are you doing in the forest?" The son says, "I came here to pray and be close to God." The rabbi says, "But God is everywhere. God is in the study hall just as much as God is in the forest. God is the same everywhere." And the son replies, "Yes, father, *God* is the same everywhere . . . but I am not."

AP: Oh, that's wonderful. So, *we* change. Or, better put, it's where we are that affects what we feel or how we experience God.

DL: Yes.

AP: I love that. I want to finish by drilling down on one line in the parsha that we started with, because it strikes me as the crux of the matter. It's the line that says, "And let them make me a sanctuary that I may dwell among them." That's Exodus 25:8. God says the point of the sanctuary, the Temple, is for us to be together with the divine, not just worshiping God, but spending time with God. The quote is "That I may dwell among," not *above* them. That reminds me that though God many times seems to require our praise, our gratitude, or even our supplication, God is ultimately our companion; the sanctuary was envisioned for us to be side-by-side.

DL: That idea of companionship and community—with God and with others—is so on target. God dwells among *us*, the people, the collective. For many people, the synagogue is not simply about praying. It's about connecting with others and being part of the community. When our central institution is a synagogue, it means we define our community as a religious one, a Jewish one.

AP: It's true. I didn't grow up as a regular member of one synagogue, but when I finally joined one as an adult—Central Synagogue—it did change everything. Because suddenly I felt like I had, not just a Jewish home, but a Jewish family. Some of the closest friendships that my kids, my husband, and I have made have been forged there.

We feel connected, not just to each other, but to a larger project and story.

DL: Right, and I think that idea of a "project" is a great one. Because it's not just the space and the coming together but also having an activity or activities that you do together. And that's also a central part of this parsha. It's all the hustle and bustle, the gathering of the gold and the silver—

AP: To build it.

DL: Yes. To build it. The act of gathering everything and putting all the materials together. When we do these large communal projects, such as building a synagogue—something for a larger purpose—it brings us closer, and it defines us as a community and helps to set our priorities to pursue that thing that transcends all of us.

AP: After Central Synagogue had that tragic fire in 1998, it was amazing to see how it took a village to put the sanctuary back together. Not just to raise money for it, but hundreds pitched in—the kids even stenciled the walls. Now congregants can walk into that place and know their mark is there; their sign of contribution is evident.

DL: One of the opening verses of this parsha says, "You shall *make* me a temple." We should focus on the *making* and how fundamental that is to finding God.

AP: That's a nice place to end this parsha. Thanks, Dov.

DL: Thank you, Abby.

Terumah to Tetzaveh

God continues to outline detailed instructions for both the overall design of the Tabernacle and for the aesthetic specifications of its various components. The core structure of the Tabernacle is to be composed of acacia wood boards held in place by silver sockets. Those boards will support colorful cloths covered by the dyed skins of various animals. Surrounding the Tabernacle will be a courtyard made of linen curtains supported by bronze pillars, where an altar for animal sacrifices will be situated. In the Tabernacle itself, there would be special golden vessels: a menorah, which was to be lit every evening; a table, on which fresh bread was placed weekly; and an altar on which incense was offered twice daily. In the innermost chamber of the Tabernacle was an area delineated by a curtain, designated as the "Holy of Holies," which would house the Ark of the Covenant, inside of which would sit the tablets on which the Ten Commandments are inscribed.

TETZAVEH

תְּצַוֶּה

AP: Translate Tetzaveh for us, please, Dov.

DL: Tetzaveh means, "You shall command."

AP: And who is being commanded?

DL: The Children of Israel are being commanded to take pure oil for the lighting of the menorah in the Temple.

AP: This parsha is a deep dive into the vestments of the priests, correct?

DL: Yes, correct.

AP: Which means the costumes and the pomp and the uniform: gold, purple, crimson yarns, twisted linen, shoulder pieces, engravings. This text goes on and on.

DL: Everything you just listed is really about the High Priest. The other priests wore very simple white garments. Their uniforms would not have the pomp and circumstance that defines the garments of the High Priest.

AP: Let's fill our audience in on what it's like to be a priest, because that's not a term we use anymore.

DL: The term "priest" feels very Christian. The priests in the Torah—the *kohanim*—were descendants of Aaron, brother of Moses. They served in the Temple, and they were the ones who brought the sacrifices.

AP: Yet, they cannot stand at a gravesite.

DL: Right. Among the prohibitions that apply to them is one that states they are not allowed to come in contact with or within a certain proximity to a corpse. There is a beautiful explanation from nineteenth-century rabbi Samson Raphael Hirsch: unlike priests in other religions who were needed at the time of death and exerted enormous control at that moment because they would determine if the person about to die would get into heaven, in Judaism, priests were required to be physically distant at the time of death, which limited potential abuse of their religious authority.

On a more basic level, they had to remain ritually pure so they would always be ready to serve in the Temple. This put restrictions on them, but it also gave them special status.

AP: This parsha made me think of the Ron Chernow biography of George Washington, which is amazing. Washington spent so much time on his uniforms—designing them, choosing the fabric, and the color of the velvet. He was a general running an army, then later he was president, and I found myself thinking, *George, why are you spending so much time on your clothes?* But it occurs to me that's like this—the power of the costume and what it confers in terms of authority.

DL: When I became president of Yeshivat Chovevei Torah, my wife told me, I had to get all new suits.

AP: And you've been looking sharp ever since.

DL: Oh, thank you. Sometimes, maybe. The Talmud says that a Torah scholar cannot go out with a stain on his garments. There is a certain reverence for what you represent and what people see when you present yourself, which I think goes beyond uniform.

AP: What about the idea that there is hierarchy conveyed by this costume? The fact that the priests have different clothing is saying that they are set apart and in some sense superior.

DL: I wonder if the uniform of the regular priests conveys superiority. The regular priestly garments are pretty plain and simple. It does set them apart, no question, but I think the regular priests were supposed to be like matching furniture in the Temple, not to have individuality. They are the workmen of the Temple. You bring your sacrifice and give it to one of the priests—it doesn't matter which one—and it gets put on the altar. I wouldn't say the regular priests are superior, but certainly the High Priest is.

AP: In terms of more modern times and the question of what we wear as Jews: I have talked to some young people about this—that in a sense, you are making a choice to affirm or announce your difference when you wear a public marker like a *kippah*, *tzitzit*, or a Jewish star. That is a conscious decision that one makes—particularly now, when there is more risk in certain cities or settings. Even to sit in a *sukkah* on a campus is to announce something about yourself. That is part of what struck me in this parsha: there are visible things that signal our difference, which maybe weren't a choice back then, but today they are. I was just at a speech given by historian Deborah Lipstadt, and she talked about how she is now wearing a *Magen David* around her neck, not because she wants to highlight the victimization that has reared its ugly head again, but to publicly signal her identity wherever she goes. It may not be a vestment, but in some way, it's a statement of identity and solidarity.

DL: I am thinking as you're talking that it's not only signaling to the outside world but also informing our self-definition and how we think about ourselves. When you wear a special garment, it's with you all the time—it's on your body—so in a real way, it becomes an extension of you. Can you see how that might change our own sense of self?

AP: Absolutely. In fact, you just raised an issue that carries into the verse I want to highlight: Exodus 28:29. It says, "Aaron shall carry the names of the sons of Israel on the breastplate of judgment over his heart, when he enters the sanctuary, for remembrance before the Lord at all times." Aaron must *wear* the names of his forebears. There is something about that physical symbolism of the ancestors—of wearing your inheritance—that is extremely powerful to me and resonant for those of us who choose to accept the ancestral DNA we've been handed. What are your thoughts about what it means to carry your inheritance visibly?

DL: That's something I feel I do every day in my learning and teaching Torah. Every time I open a Talmud, I am connecting back to the Rabbis of 2,000 years ago in the land of Israel. Or 1,500 years ago in Babylon, where we were exiled. And then I read the commentaries from the Rabbis who lived 1,000 years ago in France, Germany, or Spain. I travel to the countries where Jews have lived through the centuries. I connect with that inheritance every day.

AP: Is there a piece of clothing or an object that you carry or own that ties you especially to your ancestors?

DL: Personally, no. But my son wears tefillin that was passed down from his great-grandfather. It is very meaningful to him to connect with all those past generations when he puts on his tefillin every morning. How about you, Abby?

AP: My uncle Bernie used to officiate the seder at his house in Larchmont, and when that role was passed to my mother and then to me, I inherited his *kittel*, the white robe he wore at the head of the table. That is very powerful to me because I remember my uncle wearing it. I have not had the courage to wear it yet—it just doesn't feel like I've earned it—but I am proud to own it.

DL: That's beautiful. Just like Aaron, you will be carrying the names of your forebears when you finally decide to wear that *kittel.*

AP: I'd like to think that's true.

Tetzaveh to Ki Tisa

After laying out thorough directions for the Tabernacle's construction and the *kohanim's* vestments, God addresses more particular matters such as the consecration of the *kohanim*, the details of the daily animal and incense offerings, and the specifications of the altar, anointing oil, and hand-washing basin. When the instructions for the Tabernacle have been delivered in full, God identifies two men—Betzalel and Oholiab—whom God has endowed with artisanal skills and puts them in charge of the building process. God commands the people regarding the sanctity of the Sabbath, and with that final edict, gives Moses the two tablets.

Ki Tisa

כִּי תִשָּׂא

DL: Ki Tisa is commonly referred to as the "golden calf parsha." We're going to focus on what it means to create or worship false idols.

AP: Let's remind everyone that the golden calf was built by the Israelites while Moses was up on Mount Sinai receiving the Ten Commandments. Here's what the parsha says—in Exodus 32:1:

> When the people saw that Moses was so long in coming down from the mountain, the people gathered against Aaron [Moses's brother] and said to him, "Come, make us a God who shall go before us, for that man Moses, who brought us from the land of Egypt, we do not know what has happened to him." Aaron said to them, "Take off the gold rings that are in the ears of your wives, your sons, and your daughters and bring them to me." And all the people took off the gold rings that were in their ears and brought them to Aaron. This he took from them and cast in a mold and made it into a molten calf, and they exclaimed, "This is your God, O Israel, who brought you out of the land of Egypt!"

So, this violates the Second Commandment: "You shall have no other gods besides me."

DL: That's it.

AP: Is that the whole sin, violating Commandment Two?

DL: Yes, but it's not just, "Okay, *technically*, you did something wrong." We have to understand the size and the weight of this. The Second Commandment says in Exodus 20:3, "You shall have no other gods before me," and then in 20:5, "for I the Lord thy God am a jealous God." What does that mean, "a jealous God"? It means that when we give our worship and our fealty to another god, it's like committing adultery; it's an act of betrayal. A committed relationship means sticking together through the hard times, not stepping out of the marriage and being unfaithful as soon as there's a little trouble at home. Betrayal is a profound theological sin; it's the abandonment of God.

AP: And they did it pretty quickly.

DL: Yup.

AP: People often look at the golden calf as a metaphor for worshiping the wrong things. But, in a way, I feel like that metaphor is a little hackneyed by now, maybe because I've heard it so much in sermons. But there is something to consider: what false idols replace the right kind of worship or the right kind of adoration?

DL: I want to talk about something similar. I don't think the calf was really another god, in the sense that the people believed it had divine powers. I think its purpose was to physically represent God in some way. But that also corrupts the idea of God. It makes the infinite finite. And if you worship God through this or any other representation, you've put something *between* you and God.

AP: But is the idol a barrier between you and God, or is it a replacement for God?

DL: It *is* a barrier, and it means you're thinking about and idolizing this physical object. It was meant as a means of connecting, but it instead distorts what God is and therefore distorts the relationship. Does that resonate with you in any way? If we ask the question not as, "What do we give ultimate meaning to?" but rather, "Do we ever make or allow something to stand between us and God?"

AP: I think a million things get in the way of a connection with God or with spirituality, and I'm not sure I could even list all the barriers I, in my own life, set up. But I find it challenging just to believe we're entitled to a personal dialogue with God.

DL: I think it's exactly that, because it's so hard to think that I can talk directly to God. And that's exactly what the Israelites were feeling: "Where's this God?" So we try to create *things* that will take God's place. In my community, I think one thing that sometimes takes the place of developing a spiritual relationship with God is a hyper-focus on *halachic* detail—religious law—which, don't get me wrong, is very important. I mean, it's how I live my life, but when all of our conversation is about *halacha* and only *halacha*, we're often not asking the questions we need to be asking. And we're often not thinking about God.

AP: Let's turn to the coda of this story, which seems to be conveniently excised or omitted in most retellings. Moses not only burns the golden calf and forces his followers to drink the resulting gold dust, but he also encourages the slaughter of 3,000 of his Israelite family as punishment for their lack of faith. They built this false idol, and thus they should die. I thought Moses had prevailed upon God. I thought he had begged and convinced God to forgive his people for the sin of the golden calf.

DL: Yes, he stopped God from *collective* punishment. He stopped God from wiping out the entire people and convinced him to spare those who were innocent, or at least those who were bystanders and not active participants.

AP: So this wasn't like Noah and the flood that wiped out all humanity.

DL: Exactly. Sometimes when the Torah deals with idolatry, you'll see this idea of collective punishment, but here Moses stopped it. He was still going to punish those who were guilty, so when he came down from the mountain, he gathered the Levites—one of the Twelve Tribes—the tribe that Moses and Aaron are from. And he said, "Whoever is for God come to me," and they went through the camp and drew their swords and slaughtered 3,000 people—presumably, all those who worshiped the calf. The Rabbis try to tame this a little bit. They say Moses and Aaron held court cases, and witnesses came and testified against the people who had transgressed. The Rabbis often try to bring things into a legal construct—

AP: In the Talmud, you mean, in the commentary. But there's no evidence of that here.

DL: No. There's no evidence of that in the Torah text.

AP: That's a pretty bloody ending to Revelation. So not everyone who made it to Sinai lived to travel forth from the mountain. Is that right?

DL: That is true.

AP: Some escaped years of slavery, only to die at the hands of their own people.

DL: Yes.

AP: That's harsh.

DL: Yes, but it was a small percentage—3,000 out of 600,000.

AP: Yeah, *just* 3,000 people.

DL: How do you deal with this violent punishment, Abby? The golden calf offense was a theological sin. The Israelites were not doing something immoral against another human being—they were sinning only against God. So, do you think that makes this harsh punishment more or less justifiable?

AP: It's hard for me to feel like it's anything but patently unfair. You have these Israelites who are just getting used to monotheism . . . of course they're going to get it wrong at first. And it's understandable that they would be doubters of God after what they'd been through in Egypt for the previous 400 years. What do you think?

DL: From the Torah's perspective, theological sins are at least as bad as interpersonal ones. But personally, I agree that it's hard to justify such a harsh punishment for something that was done only against God. God is able to forgive. It's not like human beings were hurt in the process. That said, it's somewhat easier to understand the disproportionate penalty when we remember that this was, as you said, the beginning of their formation as a nation, the first establishment of their relationship with God. So, on the one hand, we could expect them to get it wrong. But on the other hand, one could argue that it was critically important that, at this stage, the message of absolute fidelity be sent out loud and clear, that just-freed slaves needed a strong penalty to absorb the urgency of monotheism. I don't necessarily agree with that viewpoint, but it is one way of understanding the harsh punishments meted out here.

One of the most radical teachings of Judaism was not just that there's a single God as opposed to many, but was also that God cannot and should not ever be represented physically. That's really hard—to connect to something that's completely out of your experience and understanding. Without Moses physically there among them, they worried they were unprotected and alone and maybe felt they needed something tangible to worship. And it had to be made clear that, no matter how strongly they felt that way, it was *not* okay.

AP: It seems to me they had PTSD from centuries of slavery. The Israelites didn't know how to trust a new leader who promised a better land and no more oppression. And who can blame them? They didn't know whether or not to believe in a God that was invisible to them, so they built a God that they could see.

DL: I think that's it exactly.

Ki Tisa to Vayakhel–Pekudei

After having been informed at the mountaintop of the people's sin of making the golden calf, Moses prays to God to forgive the people and to not destroy them. God relents and Moses descends from the mountain, breaks the tablets, and calls on the Levites to kill the perpetrators.

Deeply disappointed at the "stiff-necked" people's turn toward idolatry, God informs Moses that, though the Israelites will still journey to the Promised Land, they will be led by a messenger rather than by God. Moses beseeches God to dwell in their midst and makes an unprecedented request: to see God's face and learn of God's ways. God responds that no one can see God's face and live, but that God will nevertheless pass before Moses and reveal God's glory to him.

Moses is commanded to carve two new stone tablets to replace the ones he shattered and to return to the top of Mount Sinai. Moses does so, after which God descends in a cloud, passes before Moses, and—pronouncing God's holy name—proclaims the Thirteen Divine Attributes of God, among them: compassionate, gracious, slow to anger, abundant in kindness, and true.

After reaffirming God's covenant with the Israelites and highlighting a number of the obligations it demands, God instructs Moses to spend forty days and forty nights on the mountaintop inscribing the Ten Commandments—the terms of the covenant—on the tablets. When Moses finally descends from the mountain, his face is aglow with beams of light, and it becomes necessary for him to put on a veil, which he would remove when talking with the people or with God.

VAYAKHEL–PEKUDEI

וַיַּקְהֵל–פְקוּדֵי

DL: This is a double parsha.

AP: Which is what, exactly?

DL: There are fifty-four *parshiyot* [Torah portions] in total, which are more than the normal number of weeks in a year, so based on the Jewish calendar, some of them get doubled up from time to time.

AP: Got it.

DL: So these are parshas Vayakhel and Pekudei. The first parsha, Vayakhel, means "He gathered." This is where Moses gathers the people to instruct them about building the Tabernacle. The second parsha, Pekudei, means something like "The Enumeration."

AP: And what is being enumerated?

DL: All the materials and components of the Tabernacle, which they now were ready to build.

AP: And to remind everyone, the Tabernacle is the portable sanctuary they're carrying to the Promised Land.

DL: Correct. After the giving of the Ten Commandments and the Torah at Mount Sinai and all the laws that followed, the next major thing that the Israelites were commanded to do was to build a sanctuary.

AP: We've talked about this before, and something we both find interesting is how many times it's repeated in these multiple verses that those who are coming to help build the Tabernacle should be moved to contribute. Let's look at Exodus 35:21: "And everyone who excelled in ability and everyone whose spirit was moved came." Then later: "Men and women, all whose hearts moved them, all who would make an elevation offering of gold . . . ." Then in 35:29: "Thus the Israelites, all the men and women whose hearts moved them to bring anything for the work . . . ." This idea of being "moved" is repeated over and over, and we know that nothing in the Torah is repeated by accident. So, what is moving them?

DL: I think the point here is that their involvement is voluntary and not demanded of them. Why do you think building the Tabernacle was discretionary? "Whoever volunteers, whoever's heart moves them to help"?

AP: In the desert, no one is *required* to participate in the building of the Tabernacle.

DL: Right. The Torah tells us elsewhere that everybody was required to give a small amount of money, but beyond that, it's totally up to them. Some people gave gold and silver, but other people gave of their talents and of their skills. What do you think about my earlier question: How do we respond differently when given an opportunity to contribute as opposed to being required to do so?

AP: That's ultimately what I'm watching every day from people of every religion—they feel moved. The spirit moves you to participate when you see that something needs to be done. That might be filling bags with blankets and cans of soup after a hurricane, or it might be writing a check because you see something across the world that upsets you and you want to help. There are many ways it can take shape, but it does resonate with me that something has moved people to do it; you have to be stirred to participate.

DL: That's also the challenge of leaving something up to volunteers and not requiring it: people might *not* be moved. In an earlier discussion, you and I talked about how we might not feel moved enough to do something on behalf of immigrants. The surprise here is that it says, "Every man and woman . . . ." This was such a big project and people were so inspired that everyone was moved to participate.

AP: And all the artisans working on the sanctuary tell Moses there are already too many contributions—in Exodus 36:5: "The people are bringing more than is needed for all the tasks entailed in the work that the Lord has commanded to be done." So Moses actually halts participation: "Moses thereupon had this proclamation made before the camp: 'Let no man or woman make further effort toward gifts for the sanctuary!' So the people stopped bringing." I don't know of any Jewish organization that would ask people to stop giving!

DL: I wonder, if you are doing something you love and you feel great about it, would you be able to stop when you are asked to?

AP: There is also an interesting lesson here. The last part of that verse—that their efforts had been more than enough—the concept of being "finished" is rarely the message of volunteering. It's usually a bottomless task, and our obligation, as we're often told, is not to complete the work, but neither can we desist from it. So, it's interesting to me that this verse has completion. It kind of says, *Dayenu* [it would have been enough].

DL: So much of volunteer work is service-oriented, and you're right, that work is never done. Here, though, it was a building project. Do you think people would volunteer more readily if it were for a project that they knew would be completed at some point and there wasn't always a sense of there being no point because it's going on and on?

AP: That's interesting, and I think the answer is yes. It's not that you're done because you run out of time but because you actually accomplish something.

DL: Here's another question. How do you think the experience of volunteering is different from that of being obligated? You mentioned before that you are moved to volunteer, but how would you feel if you were doing a task—say, stuffing envelopes—solely because it's your job? How do you think it's different?

AP: There's a huge difference. I thought about this a lot when I was privileged to serve as president of Central Synagogue, and one of my duties was giving the Yom Kippur appeal. I felt entirely moved to ask because I knew others were moved to give. I think that's what this parsha reflects. It's not necessarily that you want to feel good about yourself; you believe in the institution that you are supporting. If you didn't believe in it, you wouldn't write the check.

DL: Sometimes in fundraising appeals, they ask that everybody give something, to try to achieve 100 percent participation to create a sense that we're all part of it, even if we can't give a lot. That's a central theme that comes through in this parsha. Everybody could have been commanded to give a certain amount so they would be sure to have enough, but instead it was left to volunteerism. What benefit was served by that?

AP: I think as volunteers, we all do it with more heart. But I do believe that if we had mandatory community service in every school, it would say something about our country. We would be conveying in the strongest terms that service is as core a tenet of citizenship as anything else we teach or require. People don't want to help in a way that doesn't feel specific to what they can bring to the table. They are usually much more energized when they feel like they have a talent to contribute. Yes, we can all lick envelopes—well, I guess you don't have to lick them anymore—but it's different when someone says, "Because you have experience or expertise, I know you are able to help in this way." What about you, Dov? How does it feel when you are asked to do something versus doing it just because you are moved?

DL: That's a good question. When asked what I have done in terms of volunteering, immediately my mind goes to, "Have I read to the blind? Have I spent time in a homeless shelter?" I haven't. So, I'm left worrying whether I really do *any* volunteering. And then I realize I've been teaching the *Daf Yomi*—the daily page of Talmud—at my synagogue, for free, for the past ten years. Preparing and giving that class is two hours of my time a day. That's my unique talent, and it feels really good.

Uh-oh. You're giving me a look, and now I wonder if you think giving a class for people in the synagogue is not the same as volunteering.

AP: It's not that I don't think that's a huge contribution—it is a huge contribution. But I don't think it's challenging you to move out of your comfort zone, to help someone who is not as close to your community.

DL: You think building the Tabernacle was forcing people to move out of their comfort zone in this parsha?

AP: I'm not sure.

DL: When we think about volunteering, we sometimes specifically think about taking care of the less advantaged, but that's not always the case.

AP: That's fair.

DL: Earlier, I thought you were saying something very similar about your volunteering as president of Central Synagogue.

AP: I was, but I also co-created and participate in a weekly program where we go into a public high school and mentor kids who are applying to college, because there are 400 kids in the senior class but only two college counselors. It takes us into a school and has us working with kids we would otherwise not be spending time with. And it's challenging in the sense that there is a different vocabulary in terms of how they approach a task with deadlines and with parents who are usually working two jobs or who haven't necessarily gone to college. We remind ourselves not to act as parental substitutes but as supporters to help these kids over the finish line and to hit their application deadlines on time. To me, that's different from what I do within the walls of Central Synagogue because it's on the students' turf, not mine.

DL: Well, you've inspired me to try to find other ways to volunteer, Abby. But I'm still going to give the *Daf Yomi.*

AP: Shabbat shalom.

DL: Shabbat shalom.

Vayakhel–Pekudei to Vayikra

The Torah continues to narrate, in meticulous detail, the process of building the Tabernacle and crafting its components. Under the direction of Betzalel, artisans put together the Ark and its adornments, the table and utensils that sit on it, a solid gold menorah, two altars (one for incense and one for sacrifices), and the *kohanim's* garments. When Moses sees that the work is complete, God commands him to prepare the Tabernacle for use by consecrating its various elements, placing everything in its designated location, and anointing the *kohanim*. After this is done, the cloud of God's presence fills the Tabernacle.

LEVITICUS

וַיִּקְרָא

Vayikra

וַיִּקְרָא

DL: This first parsha in Leviticus gives us a whole litany of animal sacrifices. Chapter and verse about the types of sacrifices a person can bring: what animals can be used; male or female; cow, goat, or sheep; how they're supposed to be slaughtered; how they're washed, cut up, and put on the altar.

AP: We've decided to focus our discussion on how the idea of animal sacrifice feels so foreign in the modern era. It sounds a bit like you're feeding God or filling God up in some way.

DL: Wait, back up there. In my opinion, this is not about *feeding* God. That was a pagan idea, of which you can hear some echoes in the text—like the sacrifices being called the "bread of the Lord"—but it never says God eats or consumes the sacrifices or that they are intended to feed God.

AP: Aren't we killing an animal and offering it up to God?

DL: Yes, but that doesn't mean God is consuming it. The most anthropomorphic the Torah gets about God is when it says—back in Genesis 8:21—that "God smelled the pleasing odor" of the sacrifice, or here in Leviticus 1:13, when it describes the burnt offering to be "of pleasing odor to God," which, again, could echo a more pagan idea.

AP: So, God smells but doesn't eat.

DL: And Rambam says—

AP: Rambam is Maimonides, whom we've mentioned before. He was a Jewish philosopher and Torah scholar in the twelfth century.

DL: Yes, Maimonides, thank you. He observed that smelling is something you can do at a distance. The Torah often uses human terms to talk about God, like God's "outstretched arm," but these are metaphors. Maimonides points out that the Torah never says that God touches or eats something; that would be too humanlike, too pagan. It would put God in direct contact with us. But it *does* say that God sees or hears or smells; these are things that God can do while in heaven, as it were.

So, when the Torah says the sacrifices are a pleasing odor to God, I interpret that metaphorically. It's a way of saying God is pleased with our actions. It's not God who needs the sacrifices; *we* need them—or needed them—as a way to connect.

AP: Okay, we needed them. Why? Were we proving our fidelity to God by killing God's creatures and wasting the burned meat because we're offering it up to nobody?

DL: To some degree, it's about giving up something of value. These animals were of great value—

AP: And we're offering them up.

DL: That's powerful, yes. When we sacrifice something, we recognize God has given us material success. And a way of showing thanks is to take some of that wealth and give it back to God.

AP: But couldn't that wealth have been used in more productive ways? You could give it to the poor. You could use it to do good deeds. This meat went to waste.

DL: I totally agree, so it was clearly about a lot more than that. The act of sacrifice is deeply impactful, symbolically, to the worshipper—

AP: To the person making the sacrifice.

DL: Correct. The Hebrew word for sacrifice is *korban.* The root of that word is *karev,* which means "to draw close."

AP: We remember *korban* from the seder plate.

DL: Right, because the lamb shank reminds us of the *Korban Pesach*, the Paschal sacrifice. When you give this thing up that you helped to produce—something you feel connected to—and you place it on the altar and it burns and the smoke rises up to Heaven, in some ways, that symbolizes your attempt to reach out and give to and connect with God.

AP: It sounds like it moves you.

DL: It does. Can you be wistful for something you never had? I'm wistful for the opportunity to do something that concrete.

AP: Are you wistful for animal sacrifices?

DL: No, but I long for an experience that will allow me to have that type of a connection. With grain sacrifices that was partially true.

AP: Grains, such as barley and wheat.

DL: Right. You invest your time and energy into it, you harvest, and you're connected to it. But it's truer with animal sacrifices. The animal is alive, it feels more like us, closer to us. We can see it as a type of substitute for ourselves.

AP: You've also mentioned to me that animal sacrifices took the place of *child* sacrifices, horrific as that was. That used to happen, which echoes the Binding of Isaac—the Akedah—when the ram in that story was offered to God instead of Isaac: "Go kill the ram, Abraham. You don't have to kill your son."

DL: Exactly.

AP: Now animals were offered to God instead of kids.

DL: Right, and the prevalence of child sacrifice in the ancient world shows just how pervasive this religious instinct was.

AP: To be willing to *give that much*, essentially.

DL: Yes, to give of yourself, to give something of incredible value. If you can't give your life, you're going to give your child's life; if you can't give your child's life, you're going to give an animal's life. The takeaway of the Akedah, as I read it, is that when the angel tells Abraham not to sacrifice Isaac, this is the Torah's way of saying that human sacrifice stops here. Then animals become the way of creating that connection to God.

AP: The animals stand in for the intensity of what you're giving up. Maimonides seemed to think that animal sacrifices were lazy. That it was just a way for Jews to understand faith because they were rookies at it.

DL: A concession.

AP: The quote from his *Guide for the Perplexed*, is, "Change was very difficult for the Jewish people." Meaning they were not used to channeling worship this way.

DL: They weren't used to worshiping God in the *true* way, without animals.

AP: "And therefore," the quote continues, "God gave them animal sacrifices, because that is the type of service they were used to, not because it was the best type. God wanted to turn their sacrificial service of idols to the service of the One God." God's teaching them monotheism with baby steps.

DL: Right.

AP: The Jewish people were accustomed to worshiping idols. They didn't switch easily to worshiping one God whom they couldn't see or touch. Animals made faith more literal. Is that a good way of looking at it?

DL: It is. Exactly. "Continue with the same worship you're used to, but now just directed to the true God. We're not going to advance you yet to stage two, where you'll attain the higher forms of worship." Maimonides likes to frame this as an ancient, pagan-like impulse that no longer exists. Maybe that was true for him because he was a total intellectual and could live a life of the mind. But I think most of us also need to also live a life of the body. We're human, we're physical beings, and we need tangible ways to connect. This is true even today—not necessarily the need to do it through this type of sacrifice, but when we're able to do something more physical in our worship, we are able to feel more connected to God.

AP: That's interesting. I'm not much of an animal person, particularly. I admit I've never had a pet other than the class hamsters I got to take home for one weekend in second grade . . . and I actually misplaced them and panicked. I know I'm not the best person to talk about human-to-animal relationships, but with regard to the whole sacrifice model, it seems grisly and excessive to me. I can't imagine that God really needed such a bloody display.

DL: I agree with that. It's not actually God who needs this. There's a section in Psalms 50 that notes this explicitly. It says, "Do I eat the flesh of bulls or drink the blood of goats?" (Psalm 50:13–14). That is God speaking. "Offer unto God thanksgiving and pay your vows to the Most High. Call upon Me in time of trouble; I will rescue you, and you shall honor Me." What God is saying is, "What do I need your sacrifices for?"

AP: In other words, "I don't need all that. I don't need to drink the blood of goats."

DL: Right.

AP: But that might be a critique of Temple worship in favor of prayer. Like, "Give me your prayers instead."

DL: That's true. At the end of the day, I don't believe God needs burnt offerings from us. God was prescribing sacrifices to give us a visceral form of worship when internal worship or words alone might be too amorphous, elusive. You mentioned something before about the taking of the animal life, and I want to respond to the critique that I sometimes hear, which is, "Why would God want us to give up an animal life just to do this type of ritual?" And my response is, "Look, buddy, if you're a vegetarian, and you never take animal life—"

AP: "Buddy?" That's strong language.

DL: Ha ha. But my point is, if someone is a vegetarian, then that's a legitimate objection. But if you're a meat eater—and in the past, *everyone* was a meat eater—then hey, you take animal life to fill your belly. So why shouldn't we take animal life to do something that's meaningful for us and allows us a way of connecting to God?

AP: Okay, I'm not complaining about animal rights, though I believe in them. What I'm saying is I don't see how it's helpful, or particularly spiritual, even—to God or to human beings—to sacrifice animals. It seems primitive, repellent, wasteful. You read this stuff: "Animals were slaughtered, there was blood and guts everywhere." It's a very ugly, messy scene, and it seems very un-sacred to me.

DL: I totally get it; animal sacrifice does not work for us. The Rabbis say the priests would walk around the temple, ankle-deep in blood. There would be like two inches of blood on the floor.

AP: That's a nauseating image.

DL: Yes, it is. And they go further. They say—this is in the Talmud, Zevachim 35a—"It is a source of praise for the *kohanim* that they would walk in blood up to their ankles." To which I can only say, "Huh? What?" To us it all feels pretty icky. But when we pray nowadays, it's just too abstract. We might feel it more if we sway or sing or find other ways to be more embodied. Worship doesn't require blood and guts. I'm not advocating for that.

AP: I'm so relieved.

DL: I just want us to find ways to get more in touch with deeper religious feelings that we're sometimes too sterile or too fastidious to try. Sometimes I'm envious of Muslims who do a real prostration every time they pray. There was a time when Jews used to do that as well. Now, as you said, we feel we're too refined for that.

AP: That might be a New Year's resolution for me—more prostration.

DL: All right, then I'll see you on the floor.

Vayikra to Tzav

Through Moses, God dictates detailed laws to the people regarding different types of sacrifice. Burnt offerings are sacrifices of animals—cattle, goats, and sheep—that are offered fully to God and burnt on the altar. Meal offerings are made of raw, baked, or fried flour mixed with oil and are partially eaten by the *kohanim*. Peace offerings of animals are given to express gratitude to God and can be partially eaten both by the offeror's family and the *kohanim*. Sin offerings are made when a person sins unintentionally, and special sin offerings are delineated for when a political or religious leader or an entire community sins. Finally, guilt offerings are mandated for sins involving misuse of Temple funds and for taking a false oath in the misappropriation of someone else's property.

TZAV

צַו

DL: Ah, Leviticus—the third book that everyone loves. Not! It's the one with all the sacrifices.

AP: That's like the yoke on the back of a bar or bat mitzvah—getting the Leviticus parsha. We are in Tzav. Translate, Dov, *por favor*.

DL: Tsav means "command." God is telling Moses to command the *kohanim*—

AP: The priests.

DL: Yes, to command the priests to tend the altar so it's ready to be used the next morning.

AP: The altar is for sacrifices, which, as we discussed in the last parsha, are antiquated and repugnant ways to connect to the Divine.

DL: Well, I personally would not use the word "repugnant," but I get your point.

AP: We are going to zero in on verse 6:5 in Leviticus: "The fire on the altar shall be kept burning, not to go out: every morning the priest shall feed wood to it, lay out the burnt offering on it, and turn into smoke the fat parts of the offerings of well-being." And then a little bit later it says, "A perpetual fire shall be kept burning on the altar, not to go out."

That idea of eternal fire, a sense that there should always be this light, is something I want to talk about because—and maybe it's just this moment that we're in with the rise in antisemitism and the disquiet that our community has been feeling—there's a lot of language around endurance and survival and the number of times that people have tried to wipe us out. So that metaphor, whether intended or not, that this fire keeps burning—it's like a kind of stubborn optimism, an indefatigable, bright sign that we are alive and we continue. It just seems very resonant for this moment. What's your reaction to that? Am I getting too sentimental about resilience?

DL: No, not at all. I like your read of the eternal fire as a symbol of perseverance.

AP: "Eternal fire" reminds me of the *ner tamid*—the eternal light that we're supposed to always keep burning in every synagogue.

DL: The Hebrew echoes the parallel you're making. You mentioned the *ner tamid*, the eternal light, which comes from the section in the Torah where we are told to light the menorah in the Temple on a daily basis: *li'ha'alot ner tamid*, "to raise up an everlasting light" (Exod. 27:20). The Torah here in our parsha refers to the *esh tamid*—the fire that must burn constantly on the altar. I totally identify with that sense of perseverance and endurance, but when I think about what Judaism is about, that is a factor but not a central one.

AP: Our survival, our endurance?

DL: Right.

AP: That's not a central idea to you.

DL: No, not as much as many others. Maybe it's a core element if I think about the Jewish *people*, but if I think about *Judaism*, I think of other things, like learning Torah, doing *mitzvot*, and living an ethical, moral life, and doing all of these in the context of our larger relationship with God and within community. This, to me, is what our Jewish tradition is and what gives it life, not just the sense of endurance.

AP: What we're getting at, though, is one of the tensions that I hear a lot. Of course, those principles or maxims you mentioned are positive—the values that require you to go to the sick bed or to show up for the *shiva* or to worry about the stranger. But there is absolutely a huge focus on the fact that—and maybe I just hear it a lot because I'm invited to fundraisers for legacy institutions—*we have survived despite the odds*; that it's not only miraculous, it's also unlikely and therefore should be celebrated and protected. Are you suggesting that's not a part of Jewish identity for American Jews?

DL: No. I'm sure it is. But if we focus on that as central to our identity, then the message is, "You should give to the Federation in order to ensure that we continue to exist," which is, to me, a completely uninspiring message. Or, "In order to ensure our continuity, you should marry Jewish." To me, the better question is, "*Why* is it important for Jews to continue?" If you haven't articulated that, then what's the point? I'm not saying my view is the only legitimate one, but I, personally, am completely unmoved by being asked to give for the sake of our survival. I want to give because Judaism *means something*, not just because we are going to sustain the Jewish people. You know, like some old organizations that have lost a sense of mission and say, "Give to us because it's important that we still exist." Tell me *why* it's important that you exist!

AP: I hear that, and it speaks to me too. But it seems to me that the older generation, especially, is acutely aware of the fragility of endurance. Forget it being a fundraising talking point. It is a very real fear for the generation before us that it could all be lost, and that, yes, their kids and grandkids might not even *be* Jews. We are a tiny people who have been buffeted by history, and the persecution is a real thing—it shouldn't be the *only* reason why we would choose to be Jewish, but it is a pretty powerful aspect to the reality of our story.

DL: I hear that. But does our continuity inspire you? Does it move you to act in a particular way?

AP: I'm representing what I see more as an institutional message, but also one that is an undeniable throughline in the identity of American Jews, for better or for worse.

DL: I think for worse.

AP: You think *for worse*? I want to make sure I heard that. Say it again.

DL: I think for worse.

AP: Why? What damage does it do?

DL: The damage is that it doesn't do the job it's supposed to. "Existence just for the sake of existence" is not a reason to continue. We need to continue for some purpose; to me, it's an empty message.

AP: You are putting the focus on survival in disparaging terms: "Existence for existence's sake." What if it's for the sake of marking, marveling, and celebrating the fact that we are still here and that we've made huge contributions to society—to humanity as a whole, not just to Jews. It's a marking of the implausibility of our story given the cruel odds stacked against us.

DL: I hear that. And I've really been coming on too strong to make a point. There is no question that the belief in our endurance gives us tremendous strength, especially in times of hardship and tragedy. Consider *Zog nit keyn mol.*

AP: Which is . . .?

DL: You might know it as the Partisan Song. It was written in 1943 by Hirsch Glick in the Warsaw Ghetto, and it's something of an anthem of Holocaust survivors.

AP: Ah yes. I've heard it at Holocaust memorial ceremonies.

DL: And the Yiddish refrain of each stanza is "*Mir zaynen do*"—"We are still here!" There is a moving video of a gathering of Holocaust survivors by the Western Wall in Israel in 1981, where Menachem Begin spoke to the crowd and declared: "Where is the Emperor? Where is his might? Where is Rome?" And then he continued: "Jerusalem lives forever. *Mir zaynen do!* We are here!"

AP: You're saying that message echoes what I was getting at: the Jewish people have outlasted all these other civilizations, and that's something worth marking. So, you do agree with me, then?

DL: I believe that we as a people have endured against the most unimaginable odds, absolutely. And I believe that it is a sign of God's relationship with us. I know that this belief in our endurance has given and continues to give us strength and the courage to keep on moving forward, to persevere.

AP: But . . .?

DL: But I don't agree it's a central message about who we are as a people. It doesn't inspire me to be Jewish or to do Jewish. For me, the *ner tamid*, the eternal flame, or the *esh tamid*, the eternal fire, is a symbol about God's enduring presence among us. That is what inspires me.

AP: Can you see God's enduring presence made manifest in Judaism's perseverance throughout the ages?

DL: You know what, Abby, yes, I can. I think that really bridges the gap between us. An eternal, enduring people with an eternal, enduring relationship with God. That's the symbolism I want to keep with me.

AP: *Mir zaynen do!*

DL: Indeed.

Tzav to Shemini

More detail is laid out regarding the various sacrifices to instruct the *kohanim* in the specifics of how they are to be offered on the altar. The Torah here also emphasizes the prohibitions against eating blood and suet, which are the parts of the animal sacrifice that are placed on the altar.

God then instructs Moses in the steps he must take to consecrate the *kohanim* for service in the Tabernacle. The process includes the offering of sacrifices, bathing the *kohanim*, dressing them with the priestly garments, and anointing them with sanctified oil. This is repeated daily for seven days, during which, the *kohanim* stay in direct proximity to the Tent of Meeting, day and night.

This process culminates on the eighth day, when the *kohanim* officially begin their service in the Temple. Aaron and his sons make a series of sacrifices, after which Aaron lifts up his hands to bless the nation. God's presence appears to the people, and a fire descends from heaven that consumes the offerings. Awestruck, the Israelites fall on their faces and burst out in song.

SHEMINI

שְׁמִינִי

AP: We are in Shemini, which means "eighth"—

DL: Referring to the eighth day of the consecration process of the Temple.

AP: We'll be discussing the abrupt death of Aaron's sons, Nadab and Abihu. We're focusing on the theme of religious fervor and whether that's more harmful than admirable at the end of the day. Let's just remind everyone that Aaron is Moses's brother. We've seen him as Moses's support and his spokesman, and we've seen him help the Israelites build the golden calf.

DL: And he's a *kohen*—a priest—which means he and his sons are the ones who serve in the Temple. They're the ones who bring the sacrifices, and Aaron goes into the Holy of Holies on Yom Kippur.

AP: Isn't it true that the surname Kohen signifies a descendant of Aaron? And that includes the alternate spelling of "Cohen?"

DL: Yes, anybody who is a Kohen is a male descendent of Aaron or the sons, and someone with the last name Cohen is almost always of the *kohen* lineage. They even think they found the "*kohen* gene," and they can figure out if you're a *kohen* based on it.

AP: That's cool. I guess I missed out.

DL: It is cool. But back to the parsha: preceding the story of Nadab and Abihu, they had spent seven days sanctifying the Temple and consecrating Aaron and his sons to serve in it.

AP: It was a coronation, kind of like, "I hereby dub you a High Priest."

DL: And, "I hereby make you *holy* to serve as a High Priest and make the Temple a holy place."

AP: And this occurred on the eighth day?

DL: The eighth day is the culmination of the ceremonies. It's like, "The Temple is open for service."

AP: And Aaron appears before the people and heavenly fire comes down—

DL: Yes. It consumes the sacrifices that Aaron brings, and the people prostrate themselves and burst out in song.

AP: Do you want to sing it?

DL: It doesn't tell us what the lyrics or the melody was!

AP: Okay, so that's where our story begins. I'm reading Leviticus 10:1: "Now Aaron's sons, Nadab and Abihu,"—which are not names that most people remember from the Bible, right? Can you translate, Dov? Nadab means . . . .

DL: "Gift" or "generous."

AP: And Abihu?

DL: "God is my father." I should mention that Aaron has two other sons, Eleazar and Itamar, who are not part of this story. Nadab and Abihu are his oldest sons.

AP: The verse continues: "Each"—that's each of these two sons—"took his fire pan, put fire in it, and laid incense on it; and they offered before the Lord alien fire, which He had not enjoined upon them." Let's slow that down. What's an "alien fire"?

DL: "Alien" means, as the verse says, something that God had not commanded. God hadn't sanctioned or requested it. "Alien" is like a contaminant. The fire had no place in the temple to be brought to God. The Hebrew word here for "alien" or "foreign," is "*zar*." And that's also the word used for a non-priest who is barred from making an offering in the Temple. It is something that does not belong; it's against protocol.

AP: Okay, I'm continuing to read. This is Leviticus 10:2: "And fire came forth from the Lord and consumed them"—"them" being Aaron's sons.

DL: Right.

AP: "Thus, they died at the instance of the Lord." Pretty brutal. In lighting a fire for God, Aaron's sons burned to death in a fire sent by God.

DL: Yes. It's not tough love; this is tough death.

AP: I'll say. God doesn't even give the boys a second chance.

DL: Just to be clear, they weren't boys. They're Aaron's sons, but they're grown men.

AP: They're men, but they don't even get a warning. No one tells them, "You have to light the *right kind* of fire in the fire pan." They're just done—summary judgment. That doesn't feel very Godlike. It doesn't seem to be in the spirit of the God we've seen before this. You and I have talked about the God who gave the Israelites another chance after Mount Sinai, when God saw how stupidly and rashly they'd built the golden calf. He forgave them.

DL: Yes, but then again, maybe it *is* very Godlike. Remember, after the calf, God brought a plague upon the people, and this was even after the Levites had killed thousands who had worshiped the calf. God wanted to wipe out all the people, and it was only because Moses interceded that they were saved. Here, the response was so automatic that there wasn't a chance for anyone to intervene.

AP: You mean to say this is how God would have otherwise handled things if no one had interceded? To punish on the spot, without discussion?

DL: Yes. At times, that is what the Torah tells us God does. But I also think it's interesting that the verse says, "A fire went forth from God." It's almost like God didn't initiate it. It was like an automatic trigger response to what they had done.

AP: It is passive language, "A fire went forth . . . ." So perhaps God didn't bring it or instigate it?

DL: Right, it doesn't say, "God burned them with a fire."

AP: I've always understood this to be a clear punishment, yet it's not at all clear what the punishment is for. What did Nadab and Abihu really do wrong? They didn't violate the rules knowingly; they were rookies here.

DL: There are a lot of commands leading up to it, so maybe they should have known not to do anything that hadn't been commanded. But it's hard to understand what they did that was so bad. And the Rabbis try to find other ways to explain their sin.

AP: The Rabbis are always trying to find other ways to explain! That should be put on a T-shirt!

DL: The Rabbis are always trying to deal with difficulties in the text and fill in the lacunae. Anyway, the Rabbis say, "Maybe Aaron's sons were drunk when they offered the sacrifices."

AP: That's some weak sauce.

DL: You mean they *were* sauced.

AP: Very funny.

DL: In any case, there's no evidence that Aaron's sons were drunk. The lesson here is less about punishment and more about warning that when you get too close to God in a way you shouldn't, it can be dangerous, and you might die as a result. Remember *Raiders of the Lost Ark*—

AP: That's your second *Raiders* reference, Dov. You need to see more movies.

DL: Probably. But anyway, when they open up the Ark—remember, the fire angel comes out and kills everybody present? And in that scene, it's not just punishment; it's more like: "This is dangerous, and if you don't handle it properly, this is what's going to happen."

AP: You once mentioned that Rabbi Yitz Greenberg, who is a teacher of teachers to so many in your community, has a powerful metaphor that connects to this parsha. Tell us about that.

DL: He says that God's presence in the camp, in the Temple, is a source of enormous power. Imagine you have a power plant. It has enough energy, enough electricity, to light an entire city. But because of all that power, it must be handled very carefully. So, what do you do? All around it, you put signs that say, "Danger! High voltage." If a person ignores the signs and doesn't act with proper care, he's going to get electrocuted. Nobody is punishing him; that kind of power has to be treated with respect.

AP: I like that. I don't like that someone was electrocuted, but the analogy is wonderful. God's presence here is high voltage. If you had a sign that said, for example, "Authorized Personnel Only," it fits well with the idea that only the priests were authorized, and even they had to follow a very strict protocol. Aaron's sons should have known that. But it's still hard to connect this to our lives today.

DL: Well, here's a way I think the message is relevant. Consider the religious zealotry that led to 9/11 or the Crusades. Religious passion can be dangerous. It might be relatively harmless, or even positive, if it is directed only to how one worships God, but when it spills over to how one interacts with people, it can lead to death. Not because God is punishing someone, but because this person might harm those who don't abide by—or act in accordance with—*their* beliefs.

AP: Those whom that person considers to be a heretic.

DP: Exactly.

AP: So this parsha warns of religious zealotry.

DL: Or the danger of overdoing the pious gesture. But I want to say again that I think that religious passion can be a good thing. I feel that nowadays our religious lives are a little too sterile, too rote or ritualized. I'd like us to find a way to tap back into the religious fervor that Nadab and Abihu had—that feeling of awe and the desire to draw close to God.

AP: Then what's the lesson you would draw from their death?

DL: That religious passion has to operate within the bounds of morality. Within the bounds that God has commanded and set. And—I would add—within the bounds of humility.

AP: That's a message that I can get behind.

Shemini to Tazria

The dramatic narrative of the death of Aaron's sons immediately gives way to a directive that the *kohanim* may not be drunk when serving in the Temple or when teaching God's Torah to the people. This is followed by a long list of commandments identifying which animals the Israelites may eat—the "pure" ones—and those they may not eat—the "impure" ones (which will later come to be referred to as kosher and non-kosher animals, respectively). For mammals, those that may be eaten must both chew their cud and have split hooves. Fish must have fins and scales. Most birds may be eaten, with the Torah listing specific ones, primarily birds of prey, that may not. Most "swarming things"—insects, rodents, and reptiles—are forbidden.

The Torah then turns to discuss issues of ritual impurity, a state that would prevent a person from consuming sacrifices or entering into the Temple. One source of such impurity is people with certain bodily fluid emissions—such as a menstruating woman or a man who has had seminal emission—or a person with *tzara'at*, a skin disease. A woman who gives birth also enters a state of ritual impurity for a given period and must bring a sacrifice upon its completion. It is here that the Torah repeats the *mitzvah* that a boy must be circumcised on the eighth day.

Tazria

תַזְרִיעַ

DL: Tazria is about ritual impurity, menstrual bleeding, seminal emissions, skin diseases—

AP: Except we're not going to delve into that. At least I hope we're not, because as close as we've become as study buddies, I think I have to draw the line at discussing semen and menstruation with you.

DL: I'm okay with that, Abby.

AP: What does Tazria mean?

DL: Tazria means "Give forth seed," which is about a woman having a child. After a woman gives birth, she enters a state of ritual impurity. The Torah then lists other types of ritual impurity, beginning with *tzara'ath*, a type of skin disease.

AP: In reading the parsha this week, I kept coming back to the laws around skin disease, because they demand that a person be separated from the rest of the camp—essentially from the rest of the community. That highlights an ostracism that can come with illness—a banishment that strikes me as Judaism at its coldest. And even when a woman has given birth, it's like, "Stay back!" It's not a joyful occasion; no one wants to touch you. And when a woman has her period, it's, "Stay away!" Or, "You have an unsightly rash. See ya later!"

DL: Okay, wait a minute, that's an overgeneralization. In the Torah, for most people, if you have a ritual impurity, all that means is, "Don't enter into the sanctuary"—the *mishkan*—which later became the Temple. But normally, those people were just living their daily lives. They were in the camp, and no one was ostracizing them.

AP: They were ostracized while they were impure!

DL: Not from the community. They were only kept out of the Temple. It was only the *metzora*—the person with a skin disease—who was sent outside the camp and away from where everyone lived.

AP: Let's see what it says. We're in Leviticus, verses 13:1–13:59. "When a person has on the skin of his body a swelling, a rash or a discoloration"—this is when I start to get squeamish—"and it develops into a scaly affection on the skin of his body, it shall be reported to Aaron the priest, or to one of his sons, the priests." Want to read the next one?

DL: "If it is white discoloration on the skin of his body, which does not appear to be deeper than the skin, and the hair has not turned white, the priest shall isolate the affected person for seven days."

AP: And it goes on from there. It sounds like quarantine. Just to be clear: this skin condition, which is a visible skin eruption known as *tzara'ath,* is often referred to as leprosy, but that's not accurate, right?

DL: That's correct, it's not technically leprosy. *Tzara'ath* in the Torah, as we just read, is described as white-colored spots that are otherwise harmless. The Torah even says that they can appear on garments or on a person's house. Leprosy is a disease that affects only the body, not garments or a house, and it can cause paralysis—it's anything but harmless. The reason behind the misnomer is because the Septuagint, the ancient Greek translation of the Torah, translated the word *tzara'ath* as "*lepra*," which means "rough or scaly skin." And *lepra* became "leprosy" in the English translation. Nowadays, you will find more accurate translations that say "scaly affliction" or something like that.

AP: We've just blown the lid off another common Torah myth! The leprosy we learned about in Bible school is not actually leprosy, just like there's no apple mentioned in the Garden of Eden story in Genesis, and there's no rib mentioned when Adam and Eve are created.

DL: Yes, we're all about correcting fake news in this *chavrutah*.

AP: "Disillusionment 101." But it still sounds to me like we're designating someone a pariah because of an illness which he or she can't control, and that seems, honestly, cruel. It's antithetical to the Jewish commandment to visit the sick or to welcome the stranger. Doesn't this bother you?

DL: As I said before, Abby, this really is the exception. This is the one case—

AP: When you say my name, I know you're very serious.

DL: This is the one case where we cast out someone who is diseased or afflicted. And as you mentioned, there's a very big *mitzvah* and value in visiting the sick. The Rabbis even say that when you visit the sick, you take away some of their illness. Maybe you're risking your own health to some degree, but nevertheless, you are supposed to be there with those who are ill. But here, you're right, it's different. And the Rabbis say that *tzara'ath* was not a natural occurrence but was seen as a divine punishment—God's punishment for *lashon hara,* for "evil speech."

AP: But that's not made explicitly clear in the Bible. So where did the Rabbis get the idea that this rash is retribution for evil speech?

DL: Mostly from other stories in the Torah where someone gets this skin affliction. A good example is when siblings Miriam and Aaron gossip about Moses because he married a Cushite—an Ethiopian woman. Then it says that Miriam was "smitten with *tzara'ath*." That was directly after gossiping about her brother. Maybe it is also because of the issue you raised—the Rabbis are being sensitive to the question of, "Why are we isolating this person; what did they do to deserve that?"

AP: Therefore, our tradition teaches that gossip is cause for getting a skin rash and justification for being exiled.

DL: Our tradition teaches that evil speech is not just harmful to one person; it sows discord among many people. The gossiper must be exiled because he or she is harmful to the social order and well-being of the entire community. Another justification in the Talmud for seeing this as a punishment for *lashon hara*—evil speech—is that if someone is going to betray us by revealing our secrets to other people, God will punish them by making their blemishes physically manifest and obvious to all.

AP: So you can *see* it: this person is a gossiper; they're wearing it on their skin.

DL: Exactly.

AP: It's still upsetting to see that, instead of humanizing the infirm, we stigmatize them. Because, to me, it reinforces a kind of elitism that we only want healthy-looking people around us, and when we find people who are difficult to look at, we cast them out of our sight.

DL: It seems we're going back and forth on this, because, if you generalize, that's the sort of conclusion you would reach. But I see this as an outlier—there is no other instance when the Rabbis suggest that someone who is sick should be sent away for any amount of time. I also want to say that, before we judge the Torah, maybe we need to ask ourselves if we don't act in similar ways. In the past, even when people were seriously sick or dying, we had tight-knit communities and families, and they would be cared for in their homes with their family and loved ones around them. But now, we send people to hospitals and nursing homes. Obviously, they get a lot of care there, and maybe that's good for them, but sometimes I think it's also a way of putting them out of our sight.

AP: It makes it better because we do it also?

DL: No, it doesn't solve the problem in the Torah. But sometimes in a case like this, it's helpful for us to use the Torah as a mirror to society.

AP: Society today.

DL: Right. Society today. We wouldn't normally equate people going to hospitals and nursing homes as a type of exile. But if we're shocked when we see it in the Torah, we can easily find parallels in our society as well.

AP: And am I right that the Torah says the outcast isn't permanently gone? Miriam was invited back after her rash abated. The community waited for her; they didn't continue their journey through the desert until she could join them.

DL: That's absolutely correct. If we extrapolate that to today, we could ask, if people "leave our camp"—if they go into a hospital or an assisted-living facility or something of the like—how do we ensure that we continue to keep them among us and in our community and care for them? What are we doing to stay in touch and visit, to not go on with our lives as though they no longer exist?

AP: Maybe this parsha is reminding us to reach out to the outcasts. I don't know if you read Andrew Solomon's incredible book *Far from the Tree*. He interviewed family after family who faced ostracism because a child was born with autism, dwarfism, deafness . . . The parents defied the isolationism that their society imposed. They were insistent that their children stay involved and connected to the world.

DL: That is a wonderful book. I completely agree with the sentiment, and I really think we're on the same page here.

AP: That's more healing than calamine lotion.

DL: It is.

Tazria to Metzorah

THE *PARSHIYOT* OF Tazria and Metzorah both focus heavily on the skin disease called *tzara'ath*. They are often read together as a double parsha. Tazria closes with a discussion of the problems that occur when *tzara'ath* affects a person's clothing in the form of unexplained green or red spots. From here, the Torah moves on to discussing the process by which a person afflicted with *tzara'ath*—referred to in the Torah as the *metzorah*—who has been residing outside of the camp due to their impure status, can be purified and brought back into the camp.

METZORAH

מְצֹרָע

DL: *Metzorah* is translated as "leper" or a person with *tzara'ath*, which is the skin disease we discussed in the last chapter.

AP: Which is bizarrely apropos since we're in the midst of the COVID pandemic. I'm sure everyone will draw their own parallels as I read the verses. I'm going to read a few more than usual today because I think they speak for themselves. This is Leviticus 14:8:

> The one to be purified shall wash his clothes, shave off all his hair, and bathe in water—then he shall be clean. After that, he may enter the camp, but he must remain outside his tent seven days. On the seventh day, he shall shave off all his hair of head, beard, and eyebrows. When he has shaved off all his hair, he shall wash his clothes and bathe his body in water—then he shall be clean.

It is eerie that we are discussing this at a moment when someone who is "unclean" needs to be "cleansed" through quarantine before reentering the camp.

DL: You see this as paralleling recovery from the COVID virus.

AP: The directives in the parsha are so particular, specific, and that's what we are experiencing every day now: how to wash your hands thoroughly and sterilize your groceries; we've even been told how long the virus lives on a cardboard delivery box. This parsha is a stark reminder that—whether or not our ancestors knew what was coming—the fear of plagues and pandemics, infections, diseases, and even skin conditions never dies. Also, I'm struck by the minutiae of the sterilization process. But, Dov, do you think our tradition is ultimately valuing the *return* of the sick?

DL: Absolutely, and in that way, the washings in the parsha are different from those of our current reality. The washing we are doing for the coronavirus is about prevention, but in the case of the *metzorah*, it is about becoming clean again. But you really put your finger on what it means to come back. For me, this parsha is referring to someone who has been pushed out of the camp. In modern terms, that can be people in quarantine or those who have been in a hospital, mental institution, or prison. How do we reintegrate them back into society? How do we make them part of us again? The Torah creates this very detailed ritual, which sends the message: "You're now ready to come back to us," and there's a real power to that. We don't have those types of rituals now, and it can be hard if somebody has, for example, been in a mental health facility. Everyone is a little awkward when they return—nobody knows what to say, and there is no ritual of reentry.

AP: At the beginning of this pandemic, when it was first starting in China, I thought some of the measures they took were draconian and dehumanizing. It was extreme, an overreaction. However, now I think we are all bemoaning that we didn't take those exact measures sooner. Part of what this parsha says to me is that something that may seem over the top can often be the answer. When I heard about citizens of China being arrested for having a fever in public, I thought, *How can you do that to someone*? But now I think we should have cracked down months ago—not by arresting sick people, obviously, but by restricting their movement.

DL: Today, these restrictions mean keeping the sick quarantined at home, but in the Torah, it's sending someone out of the camp.

I'm going to read a few verses from the first half of the double parsha, the parsha of Tazria. This is from Leviticus 13:45. It says:

> The one with the *tzara'ath*, who has the spot, his clothes shall be rent, and his hair shall grow wild, and he should cover up his mouth; and "Impure! Impure!" he shall call out. All the days that the skin disease is on him, he is impure. He is impure and will dwell alone. Outside of the camp is where he dwells.

That's really what we are talking about. It may seem extreme, but the Rabbis saw it as a way of protecting others from the sin that the sick person represented. The idea of separation or isolation is sometimes harsh but necessary.

AP: I think we have learned that sometimes, to protect ourselves, we must sacrifice something. And it may appear callous. But, what may seem inhuman can actually be the most humane thing, which is to help protect and maybe save one another. It's counterintuitive, which is why we have struggled with it during this pandemic, and I believe it's why many Americans rebelled against it for so long. But it also orients us toward a better day when we'll come through this and be together again.

DL: What I look forward to on that better day is our reintegration. It's not only welcoming back the sick but also all of us who have been in quarantine or stuck in our homes. How do we find a way to recreate a connected society and our *human* connections? We are going to need some kind of ritual or process of reintegration so we can all become connected in a more powerful way.

AP: I look forward to that, Dov.

Metzorah to Acharei Mot

Upon concluding the lengthy section of laws concerning *tzara'ath*, which apply to houses as well as people and clothes, the Torah proceeds to set forth a series of commandments regarding the ways various bodily emissions may impact a person's ritual purity. These laws are directed at both men and women, and address both routine and unusual emissions. In many cases, a person's impure status can be transferred to others via both direct and indirect physical contact. Impurity is removed by immersion in a body of water—a natural spring or a *mikveh*—after a prescribed period of time. Of particular note in this section is the law of *niddah*, under which husbands and wives are forbidden from engaging in sexual intercourse for the seven days following the onset of the woman's menstrual period.

Acharei Mot

אַחֲרֵי מוֹת

DL: Acharei Mot translates to "After the Death," referring to the death of two of Aaron's sons, which we discussed two parshas ago in Shemini. God killed Aaron's sons when they offered a fire pan without being instructed to do so.

AP: Their sin is still hard for me to fathom.

DL: This parsha picks up after that event. God tells Aaron what special rites he must perform and the sacrifices he must offer if he wants to enter into the Holy of Holies, the innermost sanctum of the Temple.

AP: Which very few people ever saw.

DL: Correct. Only the High Priest was permitted there.

AP: In addition to everything that Aaron has to do inside the Temple, there is also a list of rituals he must complete outside to cleanse us of our sins, which includes conscripting an animal to schlep our sins off into the sunset.

DL: Is "schlep" in the King James Version?

AP: Funny. But there is an animal that must bear this burden and shoulder our sins.

DL: Correct, and which poor animal is chosen for this task?

AP & DL together: The GOAT!

AP: We are talking about the famous—or infamous—goat. Not the most poetic animal on which to offload our missteps, but yes, this explains the origin of the word "scapegoat." I find that a fascinating tidbit. So, what is this goat supposed to do for us, Dov?

DL: Well, in biblical times, sin was thought of as a concrete, metaphysical reality—not just a state of mind but something that existed in the world. It wasn't an object you could hold, but it was still there; it was a burden on your back, and it would weigh you down. In fact, when the Torah describes God's method of forgiving sins, it says God is *nosei avon*, which means "carries the sin." God lifts the sin off our backs.

AP: That's relevant here because the goat is doing the carrying.

DL: Right.

AP: Let's look at the verses. We're going to read Leviticus starting at 16:8:

> And Aaron shall cast lots upon the two goats. One lot for the Lord, and the other lot for Azazel. While the goat designated by lot for Azazel shall be left standing alive before the Lord to make expiation with it and to send it off to the wilderness for Azazel.

So, there are two goats, one of which will be killed and the other will be sent off. Tell us, Dov, what's Azazel?

DL: It will come as no surprise that the explanation is a matter of debate. Some understand Azazel to be some demon or demonic force. Others translate it as "wasteland" or "desert."

AP: Or a kind of hell?

DL: Yes, or a kind of hell. But let's get back to the goat. Keep reading.

AP: Jumping ahead to verse 16:21:

> And Aaron shall lay both his hands upon the head of the live goat and confess over him all the iniquities of the children of Israel and all their transgressions and all their sins, putting them upon the head of the goat; and shall send him away by the hand of a fit man into the wilderness. And the goat shall bear upon him all their iniquities unto a land not inhabited, and he shall let go the goat in the wilderness.

Basically, we're talking about a goat getting heaped with all our sins and then being sent off a cliff to its death.

DL: In the Bible, this actually makes sense because, as we've been saying, sin was an almost tangible reality; it could crush us with its weight. Here, rather than God lifting sin off our backs, which God will sometimes do, the High Priest—the *Kohen Gadol*—takes the sins off of us and places them on the goat. And now the goat is carrying those sins out into the wilderness, far away from us. And it's through this ritual that we cast our sins away and achieve atonement.

AP: Which is like *tashlich*, when on Rosh Hashanah afternoon, we go to a river or another body of moving water and throw bread pieces into it as a way of ridding ourselves of our sins.

DL: Right. Which is why I don't do *tashlich*. It feels like cheating: we do some ritual and that's how we achieve forgiveness. But I say, "No way!" It's too easy; it's unearned.

AP: Wait a minute, you don't do *tashlich*? An Orthodox rabbi skips *tashlich*?

DL: I'm one of those *tashlich*-averse Orthodox rabbis. Maybe you've heard of us. This breadcrumb-tossing thing is really a later custom; it's post-Talmudic; it's a custom and not truly required by *halacha*. I feel that it distracts us from the real work that we need to do on Rosh Hashanah.

AP: And when you say "real work . . . ."

DL: *Teshuvah*—repentance—excavating your character, thinking about those you've hurt in the past year and from whom you must seek forgiveness, feeling remorse, trying to do better in the future . . . .

AP: I agree that the real work of atonement is internal. It's private, and it should be more painful, in a way. We should be suffering. It shouldn't be easy.

DL: I don't feel it needs to be painful, but it definitely needs to be hard, internal work. And it's not always necessarily private either. If it's a sin between you and another person—as opposed to a sin that is just between you and God—then you need to ask forgiveness directly from the person that you hurt.

AP: Just to get back to *tashlich*, I like the "physicalization" of atonement. I realize that breadcrumbs can be used to replace penitence and the elbow grease of really doing that work of repentance. But our tradition gives us something to *do* for change, not just something to ruminate about. Obviously, I've never tried saddling a goat with my sins—it's kind of attractive to me—but I do look forward to, once a year, tossing my mistakes in the water. I will admit that. That ritual, which I did with my children each year, so it's meaningful and pretty concrete to them, requires me to focus on each crumb as I throw it.

I do ask myself, what am I ashamed of? What am I promising to do better?

DL: Wow, Abby, that is inspiring. I've never heard somebody be that intentional about *tashlich*. And I have to tell you that—

AP: Are you rethinking it? Am I persuading you?

DL: You know, you are. As with many things, it's not just about the ritual but what you bring to it. And actually, I have recently been considering taking this ritual up again. Maybe I've been mellowing and deciding I'm not going to be such a purist.

AP: I don't think you're mellowing, Dov.

DL: Okay, well, in my own mind. I do think that, though the focus of *teshuvah* really needs to be internal, rituals are really powerful. And as Jews, of course, that's our emphasis on *mitzvot*. We believe in the power of our actions.

AP: *Mitzvot* meaning "commandments."

DL: Yes. And these are not only objectively good things, but they shape us, our character, our beliefs, and our inner spiritual life. If we are really doing the internal work that we need to do on Rosh Hashanah and Yom Kippur, I can definitely get behind a ritual expression like *tashlich*.

AP: I'm so glad that I persuaded you even slightly. You made an interesting point when we were studying this parsha together before today. It lays out only the ritual; our to-do list is very clear in the text. But it doesn't say what we're supposed to *strive* for, how we're supposed to repent. That's not in the text at all.

DL: That's correct. We have to separate those two ideas. "Atonement" is the end result; when our sins are forgiven, they're wiped clean, and we get a fresh start. We're not being held accountable for what we did in the past. "Repentance" is a process of remorse and taking responsibility and trying to fix what was done, while making sure it won't happen again. We always assume that you need the *teshuvah*—the repentance and the remorse—in order to achieve the atonement. But in the Torah, atonement is much more about sacrifices and these ritual acts than it is about the internal work.

AP: That bears repeating: in the Torah, atonement is more about offering animal sacrifices or sending goats off into the sunset, and there's very little about how to look honestly at ourselves. That's kind of incredible.

DL: It is, and the Rabbis really were the ones to change our focus to repentance. But even when it comes to a communal sacrifice like the scapegoat, the Torah is telling us that our sins do, in fact, weigh us down, and our guilt over past actions prevents us from achieving our fullest potential. So, one day a year on Yom Kippur, it's like amnesty day. The Torah is saying, "Just show up, and you get a fresh start." Because sometimes the best way to become a better person is to leave our past mistakes behind rather than spending all of our time and efforts obsessing over them.

AP: Ah, but then what will become of Jewish guilt?

DL: I don't think we're at risk of running out of that anytime soon.

Acharei Mot to Kedoshim

In an extended rebuke against the risk of idolatry, God repeatedly reminds the Israelites that they may not simply slaughter animals for sacrifice wherever they please, but rather must do so before God in the sanctuary, and later, the Temple. Moreover, they are forbidden from eating the blood of the animals they are otherwise permitted to consume, because blood is the source of an animal's life-force. The people are similarly told that when they slaughter birds or wild animals for consumption, they must make sure to cover the blood with dirt.

God then pronounces a series of decrees regarding sexual practices, which include prohibitions against incest, bestiality, and adultery. It is here that the Torah also prohibits a man from sleeping with another man "as he would with a woman." The overarching purpose of these restrictions is to distinguish the Israelites' way of life from that of the Canaanite nations, who failed to abide by God's sexual ethics.

Kedoshim

קְדֹשִׁים

DL: Our next parsha is Kedoshim, which means, "holy" or, in context, "You shall be holy."

AP: Let's give people a sense of where we are in the story.

DL: Exodus ended with the building of the sanctuary—the *mishkan*. Leviticus started with all the laws of the sacrifices, then it got into the laws of purity and impurity, and laws about forbidden sexual relationships. Now we have reached a new set of laws, which opens up with this mandate about being holy.

AP: Let's start in Leviticus 19:2. It says, "Speak to the whole Israelite community and say to them: You shall be holy, for I, the Lord, your God, am holy." I want to talk about that line first because it was not self-evident to me exactly what it means when God is saying, "You"—that's us—"*shall be holy, for I, the Lord, your God, am holy.*" Does that mean we are automatically divine because God created us and because God says so? What makes us holy? What does that line tell us about why we are suddenly holy?

DL: It's a mandate, a call to action. It's not saying, "You are holy because I am," it's saying, "You *shall* be holy." It's about *becoming* holy, not about *being* holy. But what does holiness mean? It's not explained here. It has something to do with God, so we know we should try to become more Godlike, more like God. But it's up to us to figure out what holiness is.

AP: I do want to push back on the "for" in that sentence: "You shall be holy *for* I, the Lord, your God, am holy." The "for" is a "because," right?

DL: Yes.

AP: So does that mean, "Because I have attained this, you should try"?

DL: Well, let's say the verse said, "You shall be compassionate—you shall care for the orphan and the widow because I, the Lord, your God, am compassionate and care for the orphan and widow." Would you understand that?

AP: Yes, I would understand that better.

DL: Why is this harder to understand?

AP: Because holy feels like a state of being, not an action.

DL: Would you ever describe somebody as *being* holy, or is that not part of our lexicon these days?

AP: No, not so much. Would you?

DL: Very few people. But somebody who is pious and always thinking about God and about others, I could imagine myself saying, "He is a really holy person."

AP: Let's look at what the laundry list of holiness amounts to in this parsha. These are just a few of the examples. In 19:11: "You shall not steal; you shall not deal deceitfully or falsely with one another"; 19:12: "You shall not swear falsely by My name, profaning the name of your God"; and in 19:13: "You shall not defraud your fellow. You shall not commit robbery. The wages of a laborer shall not remain with you until morning." It goes on, "You shall not insult the deaf or place a stumbling block before the blind . . . You shall not render an unfair decision; do not favor the poor or show deference to the rich; judge your kinsmen fairly . . . You shall not take vengeance or bear a grudge against your countrymen. Love your fellow as yourself." We know that famous line.

DL: It's why we consider this parsha the core of Jewish ethics.

AP: Yes, that's a pretty comprehensive list, and it's an inspiring one. It's clearer than most things in the Torah, wouldn't you say?

DL: Absolutely. Reading those verses makes it clear that holiness has a lot to do with living an ethical, moral life. It describes a person who cares about others. When we think about holiness or religiosity, we tend to think about ritual things that make us different from everyone else—the way we dress, keeping kosher, keeping Shabbat. And when we think about people who lead moral, ethical lives and care about other human beings, we just say, "Oh, that's morality; that's not religious." But here we are being told what a holy life is really about.

AP: Do you think holiness requires doing *all* of it? Is everything in this litany required to be holy, or does one act of decency suffice?

DL: The Torah expects us to do it all. But as I've said, our lives are about *becoming*, not of being. Becoming holy is a helpful way of thinking about what we're always striving toward. I noticed you did a little cherry-picking in the verses you chose. You focused on the ones about morality—and there are plenty.

AP: Is that a criticism of the examples I chose?

DL: It was a friendly jab. Because, in addition to the verses you cited, there are also a lot that are about more ritual, religious types of activity. It starts with Leviticus 19:3: "You shall each revere your mother and your father." Okay, that's fine, basic to the way we treat our parents. But then it says, ". . . and keep My sabbaths: I am the Lord, your God. Do not turn to idols or make molten gods for yourselves: I am the Lord, your God." And then the verses explain how to bring a sacrifice and how you should eat it. So right at the beginning, it gives us all these ritualistic actions, and then it transitions to the moral and the ethical. What are your thoughts about that?

AP: They are very integrated. The blueprint is both; you have to live morally, but that's a more universal road map. You don't necessarily need to be a Jew to do those things; we all should be doing them. The God piece makes it particularistic: this is what *Judaism* requires.

DL: You are saying that they are related because you have the universal part of Judaism and the particularistic part of Judaism.

AP: Right, the fact that you are raising all these moments where it says, essentially, "You have to do this, I am the Lord your God. You shall fear God." Even in 19:14, "You shall not insult the deaf, or place a stumbling block before the blind. You shall fear your God, I am the Lord." You could say that's a non sequitur, but it's linked. They are integrated; you don't put a stumbling block before the blind, and you should fear your God.

DL: I would also add one verse. Many people know the Talmudic teaching that "Love thy neighbor as yourself" is a core Jewish tenet. But verse 19:18 says, "You shall love your neighbor as yourself: I am God." It sounds to me that you are reading this as two things going on that complement each other—there's the religious and there's the ethical.

I would say not that they complement one another, but that the ethical is being framed in the context of the religious. What the Torah is saying—and not everyone would agree with this—is, "Don't act morally just because it's the right thing to do; act morally because I am God, and I am telling you this, and it is part of your relationship with Me.

AP: I like that. To me, it's part of what it means to be in a covenant; that's the contract we've signed.

DL: Yes! And maybe that's what "being holy" is about. We started with 19:2: "You shall be holy," and maybe being holy means if you live a moral life, that's part of your relationship with God, and if you live a ritual life, which highlights your relationship with God, then all those things combined is what a holy life is about. Some people in the more observant community, when thinking about *mitzvah* observance, focus just on the more ritualistic, particularistic aspects, and they don't pay as much attention to the interpersonal and ethical. For some people in the less ritually observant community, it's the reverse. The Torah is saying here that these intertwine, and they are all part of a life in relationship with God. It can't be about just taking care of the poor; it also has to be about fasting on Yom Kippur.

AP: We agree for a change.

DL: Yes, we are just coming at it from different angles.

AP: I wish holiness for you. I'm going to be measuring you against everything on this list.

DL: And I wish for you a life of *becoming* rather than a life of *being*.

AP: I appreciate that wish for me. It's something to strive for.

DL: Shabbat shalom, Abby.

Kedoshim to Emor

God continues to set forth a wide range of laws and regulations for the Israelites to follow. Each of them, in its own way, is meant to help the people pursue the directive to "be holy"—to orient themselves toward God and God's ways, which includes both ritual and ethical *mitzvot*. These *mitzvot* include, in rough order: respecting one's parents and rising before one's elders; observing Shabbat; injunctions against idolatry, sorcery, and witchcraft; agricultural gifts to the poor; prohibitions against stealing, cheating, withholding wages, and swearing falsely; prohibitions against putting a stumbling block before the blind, miscarriage of justice, being a tale-bearer, and standing idly by when someone's life is at risk; not to hate another person or take revenge; not to cross-breed animals or plants; prohibitions against tattooing; the *mitzvah* to have just (fair) weights and measures; and the *mitzvah* to love the stranger. This extensive list of *mitzvot* concludes with a repetition of many of the laws of sexuality.

From here, the Torah turns its attention to the *kohanim* and lays out an elevated code of ritual purity for them—they may not come in contact with a dead body, nor can they marry a woman who has been divorced. We are told that a *kohen* with a physical blemish may not serve in the Temple, and animals that are blemished may not be offered as sacrifices. The Torah then discusses all the holidays, starting with Shabbat, and the special rituals associated with each of them: eating *matzah* on Passover, blowing the *shofar* on Rosh Hashanah, fasting on Yom Kippur, and sitting in a *sukkah* and taking the *lulav* and *etrog* on Sukkot.

Emor

אֱמֹר

DL: We're discussing Emor, which means "speak" or "say." God is telling Moses to speak to the *kohanim*, the priests, and to command them in the priestly laws. The parsha then goes on to enumerate other commandments relating to sacrifices and the Temple, as well as reviewing the holidays of the annual cycle. In the middle of all of that comes a verse which talks about gifts that are given to the poor.

AP: Let's look at the verse. We're reading Leviticus 23:22, which says, "And when you reap the harvest of your land, you shall not reap all the way to the edges of your field or gather the gleanings of your harvest. You shall leave them for the poor and the stranger." Essentially, "Don't take everything you're entitled to—leave some for the person you've never met and the person who has no land or harvest at all, who might need a little bit to survive."

DL: Correct. It's really important to try to imagine the scene. We're in an agricultural society, and everybody's out there harvesting—the owners of the farms, their families, their workers. Then, here you are, a poor person who comes after the workers are done, and you finish the work. You pick up the gleanings—what they let drop—and you're cutting the grain that's left in the far corners of the field. A person in need is not just receiving a handout; they are *working* for what they're taking. When you're harvesting and gathering like everyone else, you feel more like an equal member of society.

AP: Which is more humane than just giving them the food.

DL: Right, exactly.

AP: It also strikes me that this kind of charity is essentially anonymous. You're not likely to see who takes your vegetables or strawberries from the corners of your field.

DL: Yes. The value of this anonymity is reflected in Maimonides's hierarchy of *tzedakah*, usually translated as "charity." Giving anonymously is seen as being a better way to give, because it saves the recipient from possible embarrassment. Then there's the quite different phenomenon, which is when a big donor puts his or her name on a building or scholarship. Of course, for those of us who run institutions, we are more than happy to accept those types of donations as well. I do also believe that giving publicly has real power because it inspires others to give too.

AP: Is that a shameless plug for Chovevei Torah's annual campaign, Dov?

DL: Well, we recently finished this year's campaign, but we can definitely get an early start on next year's!

AP: I absolutely agree; giving is contagious. I don't think you or I value anonymous giving *more* than any other kind, but it's incredibly admirable. But I'm still not entirely clear how Emor is a blueprint for giving back. Most of us don't have farms.

DL: Yes, that's true. And that's why in the Talmud, which was written when we shifted from an agricultural society to a more commercial one, and when we weren't living in the Land of Israel, the concept of *tzedakah* expanded to include the idea of straight monetary gifts. Later, the practice developed to giving 10 percent on a regular basis.

AP: 10 percent of your earnings or worth?

DL: Of your income. This practice was based on agricultural tithes in the time of the Torah, and then later, when we were no longer an agricultural society, it morphed into a monetary tithe.

AP: Is that pre-tax, that 10 percent?

DL: Ha! It's a debate. There are different *halachic* opinions, depending on whom you ask.

AP: How would you respond to someone who says, "Charity is well and good, but why should I have to give up something that I worked hard to make? Whether that's crops or money. Why should I give it away for nothing to someone who didn't work for it?"

DL: This gets us back to the translation of the word *tzedakah* as "charity," which is a translation that I hate.

AP: It's a lazy translation?

DL: Yes.

AP: Lazy to those of us who use it? You can be judgmental; just put it all out there.

DL: All right, I will. "Charity" comes from a Latin word that means "benevolence," "mercy," or "compassion." Those are very Christian ideas about charity. The Christian answer to the question, "Why do we give charity?" is that "Benevolence to the weak is Christian love in its highest manifestation." But that is not the Torah's idea of what this is about, because it reinforces the power imbalance that we've been talking about. The Hebrew word *tzedakah*, on the other hand, comes from the word *tzedek*, which means "justice." Justice is very different from benevolence or compassion. Maimonides explains it this way, he says: "Today you may be rich and somebody else is poor; tomorrow it might be the reverse. We have all received from others and, therefore, we contribute back to the world."

AP: That just underscores that I shouldn't keep everything I've earned. Just like I shouldn't keep my whole strawberry field—some strawberries should go to someone else. That's where we started with this parsha.

DL: That's right, and guess what? Nowhere in the Torah does it say you should give *money* to the poor. The model is always to leave these agricultural gifts.

AP: Wait, that's going to shock a lot of Jews I know, so we have to say it again: nowhere in the Torah does it tell us to give money to the poor. People think that idea is found all over the Torah.

DL: Yet another myth we're busting: it isn't! You'll see that idea all over the *Talmud* but not the Torah. The Talmud is where the Rabbis expound and expand on the *mitzvot* and the commandments—

AP: Just to remind our audience at home that the Talmud is the Rabbinical commentary on the Torah.

DL: Right. It also says in the Torah that you have to *care* for the poor.

AP: You don't give money to the poor; you care for poor people.

DL: Yes. In this parsha, we have all the agricultural gifts—*pe'ah*—which is what we've been discussing—

AP: *Pe'ah*?

DL: Yes, the corners of the field, which were left unharvested so that the poor could come and harvest it for themselves. And again, that's through their agency and participation. Then there were some others:

leket and *shikhhah*, which were sheaves or stalks of grain that had been dropped during the harvest—

AP: Which people could pick up and keep.

DL: Exactly.

AP: But it isn't money.

DL: Not money. I'm talking about the general ethos of caring for the poor. We have the famous verse in Isaiah 58:7 where Isaiah says, "Share your bread with the hungry," and, to paraphrase, "If you see the poor, downtrodden person, bring them into your home. If you see a naked person, cover him." But in terms of money, the Torah speaks only of *lending* it, not giving it as a gift.

AP: You can give a loan, but you can't give a gift. Isn't a loan worse?

DL: I didn't say you *can't* give a gift. There just isn't an explicit *mitzvah,* a commandment, in the Torah to give a gift.

AP: But that's what the Torah talks about—lending, and not just giving a gift outright. Isn't that just the same thing or worse in some way, because now the poor person has to pay the loan back.

DL: True, but foremost, it allows the person to preserve his or her dignity. A loan is an exchange between equals in a way that a gift or charity is not. Then the Torah says, "You can't charge interest." So the borrower won't lose anything in the exchange. Then it goes further and says, if the borrower can't pay the loan back, the debt is wiped clean after seven years. It's annulled. This lets a person borrow money with dignity, even if the loan is never repaid.

AP: But if they don't pay it back, then a loan becomes a handout. So, it's still charity.

DL: Yes, but it's a charity retroactively; it isn't charity at the time of the exchange. It's like the corners of the field. It allows us to recognize a person as an equal member of society.

AP: Which is my takeaway from this parsha. It also has great relevance today. Ultimately, if you're going to help someone, you must try to do so in a way that doesn't diminish them.

DL: Absolutely. That's core to what *tzedakah* is all about.

AP: I'll take a loan.

DL: I'll take a gift.

Emor to Behar

Following the descriptions of the festivals, God explains the procedures for lighting the menorah and setting up the twelve loaves of show-bread known as *challot* in the Tabernacle. The *challot* are to be set out before each Shabbat as an offering to God and eaten by the *kohanim*.

Next, we hear the story of a man with an Israelite mother and a non-Israelite father, who, in the heat of a dispute with an Israelite, blasphemes the name of God. The blasphemer is sentenced to death, and the Torah lays out the rules of like-for-like punishment, with the principle of "an eye for an eye, a tooth for a tooth."

Behar

בְּהַר

AP: Dov, why don't you place us in the story. We are at the foot of Mount Sinai, where we've been for a while. We got out of Egypt, and then we were in the desert. Why have we been sitting at Mount Sinai for all these verses?

DL: We've been receiving all the *mitzvahs*, building the Tabernacle, receiving all the laws of the sacrifices, which, I'm sure, have been a very gripping part of the book of Leviticus for our audience. And now, a book-and-a-half later, we're still at the foot of Mount Sinai.

AP: This is Leviticus 25:4–7:

> But in the seventh year, the land shall have a sabbath of complete rest, a sabbath of the Lord: you shall not sow your field or prune your vineyard. You shall not reap the aftergrowth of your harvest or gather the grapes of your untrimmed vines; it shall be a year of complete rest for the land.

Basically, this is an enforced work-stop. We are not to harvest, till the soil, or touch the land in any way. We are letting it breathe.

DL: Exactly.

AP: How are people supposed to eat?

DL: Presumably, they have stored food in preparation or will find things that grow wild, but it's a real problem. The Torah refers to this period as "Shabbat," a sabbath. The same way you rest one day of the week, you rest the land one year out of the seven. But here's where it gets interesting: elsewhere in the Torah, this seventh year is referred to as *shmita*—a relinquishing. It speaks about letting the poor eat from the produce. The concern is for the poor, not for the land.

These two ideas don't necessarily work well together. When you don't work the land, what good does it do to let the poor eat from the produce? How much produce will grow on its own? At least the rich can eat from food that they've stored up, but for the poor, it's not at all clear how they will be taken care of.

AP: As I was reading about this parsha, there is an acknowledgment that it is an economic hardship. There was value in letting the land rest, but there was risk in it as well.

DL: Absolutely. The Talmud says, quite shockingly, that when they reentered the land to build the Second Temple, they didn't sanctify the entire land of Israel precisely so there would be land where these laws did not have to be practiced and so the poor would have sustenance during these years.

AP: It does seem to inevitably echo this moment we're in right now during the coronavirus—the fact that everything has basically ground to a halt. It's not something we chose; it has been foisted upon us, and there is tremendous economic pain. But in some ways, there is value too. You see those before-and-after pictures of smog in China; you see how the desecration of the land has had to pause. I was reading Rav Kook, who wrote about this parsha in a book called *The Sabbath of the Land*—I'm sure you're familiar with it, Dov—but I loved this quote:

> Life can only be perfected through the affording of a breathing space from the bustle of everyday life. The individual shakes himself free from ordinary weekday life at short and regular intervals every Sabbath. What the Sabbath achieves regarding the individual, the *shmita* achieves regarding the nation as a whole. A year of solemn rest is essential for both the nation and the land; a year of peace and quiet, of equality and rest.

We are certainly in an enforced rest now.

DL: That's really a beautiful vision and ideal. I was just thinking about what it means to slow down now that I only go grocery shopping once a week instead of every day. But I'm concerned in two ways: first, I wonder whether we are really getting any benefit as a society from this pandemic experience; and second, how much is it going to last beyond this moment? In the Torah, the *shmita* occurred every seven years, and it was built into the fabric of society. People did it because they were commanded to, but with an understanding that it was to achieve a certain goal. Here, in the year 2020, it is for a very different reason. I really wonder if the same kind of gains can be achieved.

AP: You're saying that this forced reset doesn't necessarily mean we'll go back with our eyes open about the damage we were doing?

DL: I hope we will, but I'm skeptical. You have experiences while you are living through them where you think, "I'm really going to learn from this, and I'm going to be different," and then two weeks later, you're back to your old habits. That's what I'm concerned about. Do you have any thoughts about how we could really own and integrate this pause to last beyond just this moment?

AP: Part of the *shmita* year was to remind people, "God gave you this. This is God's land; these are God's crops. This is not yours." Not only is there humility in that but it's also a reminder of a certain democracy of ownership, as well as a relinquishment. One of the things the pandemic has done is make us step back from the things that we own and do—whether it's materialism or violating the environment—the things that are the downside of our great productivity, ingenuity, and innovations.

DL: That's a beautiful point. Whether or not we're able to integrate these lessons beyond the pandemic, it is so necessary to ask what it is telling us about how we're taking care of the planet and one another.

I want to go back to the idea you raised earlier about the hardship that came from the *shmita*, because, to me, that's one of the major parts of what is going on today. People in poorer communities without access to healthcare are unable to get COVID tests; people who don't have paid sick leave *have* to work to put food on the table and are the most endangered in the current reality; some kids go without lunch because they're not going to school; some people don't have access to the internet. A lot of the inequities and hardships of society come to the fore. The coronavirus hits everybody, but suffering is greater in certain segments of society, and certainly in the way it is disrupting the economy. I wonder what your perspective is about the trade-offs here.

AP: I think the jury is still out. When we look back on this time in history, there is ultimately going to be a verdict as to whether the trade-off was worth it, whether the sacrifices we've made were an overcorrection or the only thing that kept this from being a greater disaster.

DL: I think if there is a lesson we can take from *shmita*, it's that if we want to live according to certain values, we have to find a way to incorporate those values into the fabric of our society. Maybe we need to step back and reflect on what we've learned during this horrifically difficult period and think about how we can bring those lessons into our lives and into our societal structures.

AP: Let's end with the words of Rav Kook and the idea of "a breathing space." I wish you a breathing space, Dov. In a way, the pandemic has become a breathing space where many of us have gotten back to basics—our families, reading books, and enjoying this downtime—yet, at the same time, we are feeling so weighed down by so much daily loss.

DL: Amen, amen.

Behar to Bechukotai

In addition to the sabbatical year, which is practiced every seven years, the Torah also mandates a jubilee year, to take place every fiftieth year, at the culmination of seven sabbatical years. During the Jubilee, all slaves are to be freed: "You shall proclaim liberty throughout the land to all its inhabitants thereof" (Lev. 25:10), and all lands are to return to their original owners, even if they have been sold and resold during the last fifty years. The Torah then directs us to create a society of greater equity and freedom, commanding us to redeem a relative who has sold himself into slavery, to treat our slaves as hired workers, not to give them back-breaking labor, and to not charge interest when we lend money to one another.

Bechukotai

בְּחֻקֹּתַי

AP: The parsha of Bechukotai—"by my decrees"—lists all the terrible tragedies that will befall the Jewish people if they violate God's commandments. It's a pretty terrifying list.

DL: And it goes on and on and on.

AP: For me, the main question that came up in reading this parsha was, should God—or should we—threaten people to get them to do the right thing? If you're asking me, that's a really bad motivator.

DL: Yes, I agree it's not ideal, but I do think that often it's necessary—in life and even in religion. I'm okay with that. I think this tension plays out a lot in parenting.

AP: Parenting? You mean, all of us perfect parents who never threaten our children?

DL: Right, listen, it's not standard parenting procedure. But I think sometimes when our kids aren't listening to us or they're misbehaving, we often do have to threaten punishment.

AP: Maybe *your* kids aren't listening to you, Dov.

DL: Sure, it's just me, Abby! Look, I'm ambivalent about it. We're human. We're driven by what we might get in return, what motivates us—a salary, a reward, a nice trophy—or by punishments or negative consequences if we do something wrong. Sometimes people are going to do their best work because they are being held accountable.

AP: Let's read the text we're discussing. It's Leviticus 26:15:

> If you reject My laws and spurn My rules, so that you do not observe all My commandments and you break My covenant, I in turn will do this to you: I will wreak misery upon you—consumption and fever, which cause the eyes to pine and the body to languish . . . I

> will go on smiting you sevenfold for your sins. I will let loose wild beasts against you, and they shall bereave you of your children and wipe out your cattle.

Not sixfold, mind you, sevenfold—*many* folds.

DL: Just to point out, you're skipping a couple of verses.

AP: You're right, there's more that's much bloodier—starting at 26:25:

> And if you withdraw into your cities, I will send pestilence among you, and you shall be delivered into enemy hands . . . You shall eat the flesh of your sons and the flesh of your daughters. I will lay your cities in ruin and make your sanctuaries desolate, and I will not savor your pleasing odors.

God is saying we'll cannibalize our kids! Goodness!

DL: Well, that does echo our previous discussion about child sacrifices.

AP: These are fighting words—"I will send pestilence among you . . . you shall be delivered into enemy hands." They are actually God's words. It's kind of heart-stopping.

DL: Yes, but let's remember that it started with a list of all the blessings you will receive if you keep the *mitzvot*.

AP: God started with the good, right?

DL: Yes, there you go. And this is a core religious principle of reward and punishment. We say it every day in the *Shema* blessing—the affirmation of faith—that if we do the *mitzvot*, we'll have rains in the right season; if we transgress, we'll be driven from the land. It goes back to the Garden of Eden. God says in Genesis 2:17, essentially, "Don't eat from the Tree of Good and Evil, because on the day you eat from it, you will surely die." Our actions have consequences.

AP: I can relate to that as an abstract principle, but I'm stuck on the idea that God needs to threaten us with this shocking litany of if/then promises or threats to get a desired result. That seems antithetical to faith. I can't accept that God really wants our obedience or our kind acts to happen because we are terrified.

DL: I agree. But there's a reason why religions have been talking about hellfire and damnation for millennia—because often, people aren't doing things for the right reason; they are doing it because of a fear of consequences.

AP: Hellfire works.

DL: Hellfire does work. Maybe it's not always necessary, but it works for a lot of people.

AP: I think we get better results as parents—as you mentioned—or as employers, if people are motivated by purer things.

DL: Like what?

AP: Wanting to do a good job because you take pride in excellence. Wanting to help someone because it's gratifying to see what kindness can do for another person. There are a million examples. It makes me think that love of God or of Judaism isn't sufficient for us to abide by those commandments, those *mitzvot*, and that somehow God—or the men who wrote God's words—knew it.

DL: I fully agree with that. But can we acknowledge that it also isn't always sufficient? The Rabbis have a saying that if it's not possible to do a *mitzvah* for the right reason, do it for the wrong reason. Because if you do something for what is *not* the right reason, you'll eventually come to do it for the right reason. What does it mean for you to do the *mitzvot* for their own sake?

AP: I do it because it's meaningful, ethical, and the right thing to do.

DL: I do it primarily because God commanded me to do it.

AP: But it's still not the same as when you find meaning in it on your own, no? When I was writing about every Jewish holiday for my book, *My Jewish Year*, I struggled with the six fasts. I'd never done all six before, and it's not just that I was hungry. It was hard to connect to the destruction of the Temple. Four out of the six fasts are related to that destruction, which feels like a very remote symbol—the idea that one building is the center of observance. It felt especially hard to connect to the fast of *Tzom Gedalia*, when we fast for this obscure Jewish general who was assassinated by his fellow Jerusalemites. I did stick with it, because I was committed to doing everything that was required. But since my year-long immersion ended, I haven't continued to fast for Gedalia's sins, and I'm not proud of that. I would say, one food abstention a year on Yom Kippur is enough for me. But you, Dov, fast all six times every year, even for the minor fasts. Aren't you annoyed somewhat by the remoteness of their meaning? Aren't you thinking, *I'm really hungry, I'm uncomfortable, and the reasons for this fast are antiquated and obsolete. Why am I still doing this?*

DL: Absolutely, Abby, and you are certainly not the only person who has a problem with *Tzom Gedalia.* When I'm fasting, sometimes I'm thinking exactly that—*I'm hungry, I'm uncomfortable, and this isn't religiously meaningful.* And for the most part, when it's not Yom Kippur, I find fasting counterproductive. It's hard for me to focus and be religiously in touch with the day, or to be productive in any way for that matter, when I'm fasting. But at the end of the day, I'm committed to *halacha*, and there's no question that I'm going to fast, and that's where I find meaning. I'd like to find the meaning you talk about, and I often do, but if, in the end, the only meaning is because of my observance and commitment to *halacha*, that's sufficient.

AP: But what would you say is your *internal* driver or obligation that keeps you from grabbing that English muffin?

DL: That God commanded me; that's my obligation.

AP: I guess I can get there. We do it simply because it's what we do. But I will never be thrilled by the idea that God needs to intimidate us to get results.

DL: We don't have to love it or be moved by it, but we have to do it. Ideally for the right reason, but if it takes a little external motivation, so be it.

AP: So be it.

Bechukotai to Bamidbar

THE FINAL SET of divine commandments in Leviticus concerns the practice in which a person sanctifies an animal or his house or his land to God. The one who sanctifies these things may either transfer the property itself to the Temple or redeem it by paying its value plus an additional 20 percent and donating that money to the Temple.

NUMBERS

בְּמִדְבַּר

Bamidbar

בְּמִדְבַּר

AP: This parsha puts me in a little bit of a bad mood. Virtually every other parsha has spoken to me in some way, but this one I scroll through verse upon verse, and it's just a tedious list.

DL: There's a reason it's called Numbers.

AP: Yeah, because it's *numb*ing. How about that?

DL: Exactly, exactly.

AP: We are in Bamidbar in Numbers, and basically, we are counting. Tell the folks at home what we are counting, Dov.

DL: We are counting the members of each tribe. The Israelites have still not left the foot of Mount Sinai. They are about to move forward, along with the whole camp, and the Torah is basically saying, "Here are the numbers for each tribe, here is where each tribe has to be situated in the processional, the Tabernacle must be in the middle, and this is how you are to move forward when it's time to head off to the Holy Land."

AP: There is something powerful about keeping track of everyone—that's my takeaway—the granular specificity of every tribe, every name. What's the traditional explanation for why this list was so detailed?

DL: It's exactly that: thoroughness. Rashi, the eleventh-century classic French commentator, says:

> Because the people were so dear before God, God counted them at every moment. When they left Egypt, God counted them; when they fell as a result of the sin of the Calf, God counted them; when they came to have the Tabernacle in their midst, God counted them; when they came to move from Mount Sinai, God counted them.

The Torah's message is, "Every single one of you matters, and I am constantly checking who is here."

AP: In the context of Jewish history, this text could not have anticipated the future persecution and, ultimately, the extermination, of so many lost over so many generations, and there was almost a desperation during those horrors to keep track of people. In April, we were marking Holocaust Remembrance Day—*Yom HaShoah*—and naming the names of the perished, which is one of the rituals. When you read a list of family members, the names can sometimes go on for hours. It's like the *yahrzeit* [anniversary of the death of a loved one] list in synagogue; we take the time.

DL: Absolutely. You've heard about the project called "Names, Not Numbers"? The big numbers are abstractions, and here in this parsha, the Torah says that they were counted according to their families. There were so many members of *this* family, so many members of *that* family, and every individual counts. I am feeling that same kind of urgency with the current pandemic; you hear of those who are sick and dying from the coronavirus, and it obviously pains you when you hear these large numbers, but it really strikes home when it's people you know. Many have passed away who were just one degree removed from me—a father of a friend, a mother of a friend—and all of a sudden, these abstractions become real, and every number is a human life.

AP: Also, there were entire clans who perished from this virus. You look at Italy, where experts explain that one of the fatal errors—even though it's completely understandable—was that families sheltered in place together when even one person was sick, and ultimately entire families were infected and sometimes many members died. There is a sense of that kind of enumeration in this list we're discussing: this is a family clan that is marching through the desert and maybe dying together.

I also wanted to talk about the standards mentioned in this parsha—the flags. The instructions were to make the march almost like a parade: "You're going to stand over here with this flag; you're going to stand over here with this shield." There's a formality—a pomp—almost like a military formation.

DL: That's true. The Torah uses a lot of that military language. There is a term here that is sometimes translated as "hosts," but it also means "armies"—and in contemporary life, the Chabad Hasidim calls themselves "God's Army." They are out there to fulfill their mission, to do what God wants of them like troops following God's command. The Torah never really connects the dots as to why it uses this type of military terminology. It could be because they are going to go into the Promised Land to conquer it, but it doesn't really seem to be about that. Do you have any thoughts, Abby?

AP: In this society they are building, there's going to be structure, and after slavery, we are no longer just a mass; we are very specific and organized, there are demarcations, and there are names and hierarchy. Freedom is found partly in the ability to assign roles and titles; there's an organization to it. And now we are doing that for ourselves. No one is doing it for us; no one is bossing us around and telling us who we are.

DL: Yes. We were structuring a society. When you mentioned the flags, it made me think of the Israel Day Parade—remember those days before the pandemic when we used to have parades? Various groups would march with their banners, each showing their support for Israel. It's a message of representation—of different backgrounds, denominations, schools, or affiliations—and one of, "We are all here, coming together." It's like the question of whether America is a melting pot or salad bowl. We are enriched by our diversity, but there also has to be a way in which we are all in this together. Here in Numbers, we are all surrounding the Tabernacle; we are all one nation despite our differences.

AP: That's a perfect note to end on because it's also a snapshot of this podcast—we are two very different Jews sitting together regularly and talking about this same text. We disagree a lot, we were educated differently, and our sensibilities are different, yet that's part of what makes it a fruitful dialogue. And it's built into the DNA of our tradition: this parsha, as boring as I said it was at the start, possesses both contrast and collaboration at the same time.

DL: I'd like to think that the Torah can function now in the same way the Tabernacle did in the past. Just as the Tabernacle was the focal point for the different tribes, pulling them all together, it's my hope that the Torah can be at the center of our lives and will serve to bring us all together in all our varieties and differences.

Bamidbar to Naso

IN PREPARATION FOR the Israelites' impending journey through the desert, the Torah lays out the way the Israelites, divided into twelve tribes, are to encamp and move. This begins with a census of all the men twenty years and older, so as to determine the number of battle-ready men in each tribe. The tribes are then situated around the Tabernacle, three on each side. At the center of the encampment are the Levites, who will be responsible for transporting the Tabernacle and all its contents. The Levites are subdivided into three families, with each assigned a specific task. The *Kohathites*—the family to which Moses and Aaron belong—must transport the sacred items such as the Ark and the menorah. The Gershonites are to transport the screens and coverings, and the Merarites, the Tabernacle's heavy beams.

Naso

נָשֹׂא

DL: Today we're talking about Naso, meaning "to lift up." In the Torah, to count someone is to "lift up" their head. God is telling Moses to count the members of the different families of the Levites and assign them to their various functions of the Tabernacle. The parsha then goes on to present a number of laws and introduces a particularly challenging ritual—the *sotah*.

AP: And we're asking a pretty fundamental macro question: How do we deal with parts of the Torah that make us squirm?

DL: Yes. What do we do with a text that's both sacred and, at the same time, in conflict with our contemporary values, seemingly going against some of our most basic ethical principles?

AP: There's some tough Torah on the table today. *Sotah* is a ritual in which any woman who is suspected of infidelity is forced to undergo a barbaric test to prove her guilt or innocence.

DL: I'm not sure I'd say it's barbaric, but I agree that it's pretty demeaning and degrading.

AP: Which *is* barbaric, in my estimation.

DL: We can debate that.

AP: Okay, here we go. We're in Numbers 5:12.

> If any man's wife has gone astray, and broken faith with him, in that a man has had carnal relations with her unbeknown to her husband, and she keeps secret the fact that she has defiled herself without being forced, and there is no witness against her, but a fit of jealousy comes over him [the husband] and he is wrought up about the wife who has defiled herself, the man shall bring his wife to the priest.

Let's pause and summarize the bizarro ritual she has to do, Dov, just for the sake of time.

DL: The woman is brought to the Temple before the priests, and a priest takes off her head covering and dishevels her hair, which is a form of debasing her. It's like stripping her naked because the hair of married women was covered at that time. Then there's a declaration of curses that will befall her if she actually did commit adultery—but it's pretty much assumed that she has.

AP: Then the priest scrapes off the words of the curses from the scroll they were written on.

DL: Right.

AP: How do you scrape off words?

DL: You write them with ink on parchment and then, when the ink dries on the surface, you scrape them off with a knife into water, which is mixed with dirt from the Temple floor. Next, the woman is made to drink this mixture, and if she's guilty, the verse says her belly will expand, her thighs will collapse, and it leaves to the imagination what will happen next. But if she's innocent, no harm will befall her, and she will be fertile and conceive a child.

AP: The text reads—Num. 5:19:

> If no man has lain with you, if you have not gone astray in defilement while married to your husband, be immune to harm from this water of bitterness that induces the spell. But if you have gone astray while married to your husband and have defiled yourself, if a man other than your husband has had carnal relations with you . . . may the Lord make you a curse . . . may this water that induces the spell enter your body, causing the belly to distend and the thigh to sag.

DL: I'm going to go out on a limb and say that you have a lot of trouble with this.

AP: That's an understatement. As far as I can tell, there's no redeeming lesson or moral in this chilling ritual. It honestly reminds me of the Salem witch trials. I should mention that I played a brilliant (if I do say so myself) Abigail in *The Crucible* in fifth grade. A woman is humiliated here; she is hauled before a kangaroo court of some kind, because I guess it's a priest's business whether or not she had an affair. While, I'll point out, no man is called to account for the same exact crime of adultery. Then the woman is made to drink dirt, which presumably is going to sicken her, and she's lucky if her belly doesn't blow up.

DL: I also have real problems with this. For me, the difficulties begin even before the ritual. The fact that the husband can bring his wife to the Temple just because he's jealous or suspicious, with absolutely no evidence whatsoever—that gives him unilateral and unchecked power over his wife. It's almost like she's his property, which was sort of the reality in patriarchal societies—the woman has no rights. And it doesn't work in the reverse, as you said. If the wife suspects her husband of adultery, sorry, she can't do anything about that; she has no power over him. She is considered defiled through an adulterous act, but not he.

AP: It's been a long time since anyone would say this feels like a justifiable way to handle a situation like this in a marriage. So, how do you deal with these affronts to our moral sensibilities today?

DL: The first way is to put it in historical context.

AP: You're already worming your way out of it by saying, "This is of the time."

DL: Yes, and honestly, this is an *improvement* over the way things had been done. In past societies—and in some places even today—a husband who suspected his wife of adultery could just take the law into his own hands and have her killed. This *sotah* ritual represented progress for those times. Because, instead of the husband being able to act capriciously and unilaterally, he had to bring her to the Temple for the priests to adjudicate the situation.

AP: Let me get this straight: you're okay with a biblical passage that runs entirely counter to our ethical sensibilities because it was better than the bad thing that was the norm of the time? If this is truly from God, shouldn't it be good in the absolute sense and not just relative to the time period?

DL: Yes, but the Torah was also given to human beings. Maimonides writes that sometimes society isn't ready for radical change, and the Torah has to take a step in the right direction. Not everything in the Torah is the absolute moral ideal. It is moving society to a better place, and the *sotah* ritual was a step in the right direction.

AP: Even if it was a watered-down trial of a woman—

DL: "Watered down," ha ha!

AP: Very funny. I didn't even intend that double entendre. The woman is still debased, and she can still be found guilty.

DL: Right, but let's face it, it's not likely that any woman has ever blown up from drinking dirty water. It won't happen unless God intervenes miraculously to make it happen, which God—I think it's fair to say—did not tend to do. So, at the end of the day, she gets debased, which allows her husband to feel she was punished. Then she's found innocent because God doesn't intervene miraculously to prove her guilty. Subsequently, they both go home and live happily ever after.

AP: You're saying this test was essentially designed so every woman would pass it, and therefore, it's not so offensive? She's going to drink a potion that's *not* going to make her belly distend, so who cares if she has a little bit of nausea—no harm done? Then they go home and everything's fine? You're good with that?

DL: His jealousy is put to rest, and they're able to get on with their lives.

AP: I'm so glad he feels better.

DL: It's bad by our standards, but it's better than the alternative.

AP: I can see that, but I don't agree.

DL: We're going to have to agree to disagree here. But I do continue to struggle with this text because of how it's been used to justify harmful attitudes and behaviors toward women. And also because it's had lasting implications in Jewish Law.

AP: In what way?

DL: For one, the Rabbis say that because the Torah refers to the wife as having been "defiled," this teaches us that any woman who commits adultery is subsequently off-limits to her husband—that she and her husband are forbidden to have sex.

AP: You're saying that even if they've reconciled, they can't have make-up sex?

DL: Forget make-up sex. They can't continue to live together as husband and wife. But there are workarounds.

AP: *Workarounds!*

DL: Yes. First of all, we make it very hard to prove adultery has ever really happened. Even if the woman herself admits to it, we take her testimony as inadmissible.

AP: It seems sometimes like a lot of commentary is a workaround.

DL: Anyway, that's how I deal with this parsha. What I'm really wondering, Abby, is how do you, as a Reform Jew, deal with this? Does this challenge your notion of the Torah as sacred?

AP: I don't love the question being framed with "as a Reform Jew . . . ." I'll answer as a Jew. I have a problem with this text. I reject this ritual. I still think the Torah is a sacred document. I can hold both thoughts, because the Torah is sacred in the sense that it is enduring, inherited, magical, extraordinary, challenging, and resonant. But it isn't a blueprint for living; it's not a handbook. It's not meant to be followed to the letter in that sense. I know it hasn't been followed to the letter by Orthodox Jews either.

DL: What do you mean by that?

AP: You're not stoning someone who doesn't correctly observe the Sabbath. There are plenty of times that your community has chosen—*selected*—what you feel is comfortable in terms of *halacha*. It's not like all 613 *mitzvot* are being met every moment. I once interviewed an Orthodox rabbi on Tisha B'Av who wasn't fasting.

DL: I'm not going to ask who, but okay.

AP: My point is that Orthodox Jews may accept the text as divine, but it is not an instruction manual.

DL: I didn't say that. We *do* accept it as divine, and we deal with difficulties through interpretation. But I want to know how *you* deal with difficult passages.

AP: I identify them as just that: difficult. I'm interested in unpacking them and discussing them, but I am not wrestling with whether to live by them. It feels like you are pretzeling yourself to accept a text as holy that is offensive to you.

DL: I start with the principle that it is holy and divine, and I have to square that with a belief that God is good. That's what the Rabbinic enterprise of commentary and interpretation is all about.

AP: I can engage with the *sotah* ritual, but it is not our religion to me. Part of grappling with our religion includes rejecting parts of it. That's sometimes hard. But in this case, it's not hard for me. It's in the tradition; it's in the text, but I'm not struggling to find meaning in it.

DL: Well, I will continue to struggle.

Naso to Beha'alotcha

Following the law regarding the woman suspected of adultery, the Torah introduces the concept of the Nazirite—a man or woman who wishes to achieve a certain degree of holiness by separating from society in certain defined ways. If a person takes a vow to be a Nazirite, he or she must abstain from drinking wine or eating grapes or any grape product, must let his or her hair grow wild, and must not come in contact with the dead. At the end of the period of the vow, the Nazirite brings a sacrifice to terminate their special status and resume normal life.

The Torah next introduces the Priestly Blessing, often given by parents to their children prior to the Shabbat meal on Friday night: "May God bless you and keep you. May God make His countenance shine upon you and be gracious to you. May God lift up His countenance upon you and give you peace" (Num. 6:24–26).

The text then returns us to the consecration of the Tabernacle and describes the valuable gifts that the heads of each of the twelve tribes offered in its honor. Collectively, they donated six covered wagons and twelve oxen for its conveyance as well as individual offerings of silver and gold vessels and sacrifices of flour, oil, incense, and livestock. As a final step in preparing the Tabernacle to become fully operational, God gives detailed instructions as to how the Levites must be purified and consecrated in order to perform their ritual Temple duties.

Beha'alotcha

בְּהַעֲלֹתְךָ

DL: Beha'alotcha means, "When you cause the flame to rise up." It's about Aaron lighting the menorah in the Tabernacle. A year has passed since the tribes left Egypt, and they've been standing at the foot of Mount Sinai after crossing the sea. They are getting ready to travel to the Holy Land, which is why there is all this discussion earlier in Numbers about setting up the camp. Now, it's time to bring the Paschal sacrifice once again because this was intended to be a yearly sacrifice. Just like our annual seder, the Paschal sacrifice was an opportunity to reconnect every year to the foundational story of what makes us a people and the events of the Exodus.

AP: I'm going to read from Numbers 9:13 "But if a man who is clean and not on a journey refrains from offering the Passover sacrifice, that person shall be cut off from his kin, for he did not present the Lord's offering at its set time; that man shall bear his guilt." First of all, what's the crime here?

DL: His failure to bring the Paschal sacrifice, which is a sin of omission as opposed to commission.

AP: Okay, please explain this part for us: "A man who is clean and not on a journey . . . ."

DL: There could be practical reasons why you were not able to bring the sacrifice. You might have been impure because you'd come in contact with a corpse, which happened to some people in the story told a few verses earlier. Or, you could have been on a journey and weren't able to get to the Temple in time to bring the sacrifice. The Torah gives you dispensation in those cases; it says you can bring the sacrifice the following month. But if you were *able* to bring it and *didn't*—if you willfully kept yourself out of this communal experience—then you are deserving of *kareth*, being cut off.

AP: Let's talk about *kareth*, because when I had a *bat mitzvah* at age forty—not to make this about me—I read from the parsha of Emor, which also mentioned this idea of *kareth* or being "cut off."

DL: Correct.

AP: There's a question about what that means and what you are cut off from. It says you are cut off from your kin—does that mean your fellow Jews, the Jewish people generally, or God? What is the traditional understanding?

DL: The Rabbis explain it in two ways. One is metaphysical: that if a person dies without repenting this sin, their soul does not get into the World-to-Come. I should note that the idea of the World-to-Come—a place where the soul lives on after the person has died—is not found anywhere explicitly in the Torah, but the Rabbis understood it to be central to the Torah's theology. So, for them, *kareth* meant they would be cut off from this afterlife. The Rabbis also said that *kareth* can mean that person will die young, in his fifties.

AP: I heard about a rabbi who turned sixty and had a party. He said, "I got past the *kareth* mark; I survived it!"

DL: True story.

AP: It's interesting that *kareth* appears something like thirty-six times in the Torah.

DL: Yes.

AP: It should be noted that we are instructed to love the stranger thirty-six times in the Torah also. And because I know numbers matter in the Torah, that's an interesting parallel. I think about how, in our tradition and in our culture as Jews, there are times when we symbolically cut each other off, or we worry about being cut off. Speaking for myself, there are times when I am not acting ethically or perhaps as God might want me to, and I have the sense that there is the threat of some kind of excommunication or a metaphorical exile. Maybe that's my own therapized neurosis of fearing that I've disappointed God.

DL: I really appreciate that perspective. Sometimes a sin can be so grievous that you feel you deserve punishment, that you are cut off from God, or that you've violated your own integrity—that you've cut off part of yourself. Then there are sins in which you distance yourself from your connection to the Jewish people. For example, the Torah assigns *kareth* to someone who does not bring the Paschal Lamb sacrifice or to a man who does not have himself circumcised—these are fundamental signs of being part of the nation.

AP: As you see Orthodoxy evolve these days to a more egalitarian and progressive model—and you have been part of this evolution, Dov—do you worry that one step too far on those changes could risk *kareth*?

DL: Chovevei Torah, the rabbinical school I head, has received, in its twenty-plus-year history, some nasty attacks from the more Haredi right-wing Orthodox community. It's over things that, from a *halachic* perspective, are trivial. For instance, a greater role for women in the synagogue—there are almost no *halachic* issues when it comes to some of these roles, but there are people who feel that women in a leadership role makes you not really Orthodox. There have, sadly, been those who have tried to cut our seminary off from the Orthodox community. The reality is that we are deeply anchored in *halacha* and Orthodoxy, and I find particularly deplorable the whole enterprise of self-appointed gatekeepers seeking to delegitimize others in their community with whom they disagree. But it's fascinating how, for some people, it has become the cultural issues—such as women's roles—and not the halachic ones that define who's in and who's out. I'd much rather invest my energy worrying about how to keep people *in* and engaged in our faith than who I think deserves to be kicked *out*.

How about you, Abby? I'm really interested in your perspective. What makes you worry about *kareth*?

AP: There are times when I think about the fact that I'm not keeping kosher or not fasting during all six fasts, and I ask myself why. Ultimately, it's not something I'm ready to take on as a regular practice. It's not necessarily that I'm worried God is going to punish me for neglecting to fast or keep kosher; it's more a question of why I'm resistant to doing a difficult thing that would be meaningful and would connect me to my tradition and to my people.

DL: For the examples you gave, is it just a question of how much you are fully connecting to the tradition, or is it also because so many of those practices are about social grouping and being part of the community? Observance of holidays is a fundamental way in which we celebrate as a community; keeping kosher is about the foods we eat—these are very social experiences. Is that a piece of it?

AP: That may be. Our tradition and our Jewish family is constantly throwing us back together, and that's where *kareth* is such a threat or so ominous—the idea of being cut out of the family. I'll be honest, I dated someone who was not Jewish in my twenties, and my mom, despite all of her liberal politics, became very reactionary. The idea that I would be cut off was kind of her message—not necessarily from her, although I do think something would have been severed between us—but she was essentially saying, "You're turning your back on your people and your story." That was unsettling to me. I do think there's some kind of modern-day specter of losing your family.

DL: Let me get this straight: you're saying that you feel it's wrong to intermarry and that doing so cuts somebody off from the people, or *should* cut someone off from the people?

AP: No, that's too simplistic. I think interfaith partnerships create a more challenging road for a number of reasons—in terms of melding two backgrounds and building a life and family with very different religious perspectives, traditions, and practices. But I feel very strongly—and I think you suggested it—that to turn your back on an interfaith couple is often to lose the Jew in that union, and that is to our people's peril. There has to be a way to open the tent and have that conversation in a way that's more honest and allows for more definitions of what it means to build a family with two religions. I will say, personally, that you and I are part of a larger Jewish family that is too often judgmental, which makes it harder if one chooses to marry "out." That is something I was aware of because it was painful for my mother, who comes from a generation where the mentality is still: "We survived this long, and now you're going to break the chain?" If that perspective has been ingrained in your DNA, it's hard to shirk a certain sense of responsibility.

DL: I don't want to end this discussion without commenting on how things have become less absolute or less final nowadays in the community I inhabit. For example, there are a lot of rabbis in synagogues today who have interfaith couples in their synagogues, and there is a very clear understanding that you do not cut people off. You can make it clear you don't approve and state what your lines are, but there is still a Jewish soul in front of you, and, from our perspective, if the mother is Jewish, then the kids are also Jewish. So, how do we keep them connected to the tradition even though they have married out? I think there is a real emphasis today to not make *kareth* an absolute line and to know we can't afford to lose people.

AP: We can't.

Beha'alotcha to Shlach

The Israelites are finally ready to proceed toward the Promised Land, and they take their marching orders from the movement of the divine cloud, which covers the Tabernacle by day (along with the pillar of fire by night). When the divine cloud rises up and moves forward, the people move in the direction of the cloud and encamp where it comes to a rest.

At last, the Israelites continue toward the Promised Land, almost exactly a year after arriving at Sinai. It is at this moment that Moses entreats his father-in-law, Hovav (elsewhere called Yitro), to travel with them to the land that God has promised, but Yitro refuses, saying he will return to his own land.

The people start to traverse the desert, but before long, dissatisfied with the manna and missing the delicacies of Egypt, they begin to grumble. God instructs Moses to assemble seventy elders to help him bear the burden of leadership. God also sends a massive flock of quail to assuage the Israelites' appetite for meat, but subsequently strikes down many people in a plague when they respond with gluttony.

As the nation journeys on, Moses's own family faces a crisis when—as punishment for speaking derisively about Moses's wife Tzipporah—Moses's sister Miriam is struck with *tzara'ath*. Though Moses pleads to God on Miriam's behalf, she is nonetheless forced to wait outside the camp for seven days until she can regain ritual purity. The people wait for her to recover, after which they resume their journey through the desert.

God commands Moses to send twelve men—a leader from each tribe—to scout the land of Canaan in preparation for their war of conquest. The spies, who include Caleb and Joshua, are told to survey the land, identify whether the people are strong or weak, find out if their cities are open or fortified, and to bring back samples of the fruit growing in the land when they return. After scouting the land for forty days, the spies return, carrying with them huge clusters of grapes, figs, and pomegranates, and with a report of the ominous giants they have seen.

Shlach

שְׁלַח

AP: We're in Shlach, which means "send." Who is sending what?

DL: Moses is sending a chieftain from each tribe to go scout out the Land of Canaan.

AP: Okay. What's our theme today?

DL: A major theme of this parsha is courage—who has it and who doesn't.

AP: We would assume that the Torah is pro-courage, but I was surprised to learn it's really not that simple. When you focus on courage in the Hebrew Bible, other than Moses and King David, there aren't a million iconic stories where bravery is held up as the way to be in the world.

DL: I'm not even sure Moses would be described as courageous. If you think about it, he had to be cajoled into his role. Are there other people who demonstrated courage in the Torah? I guess Judah comes to mind; he stands up against his brothers when he tries to save Joseph.

AP: You mean when they're going to throw Joseph in the pit?

DL: Yes. And Joseph represents a different type of courage. He's willing to stand up to Potiphar's wife when she tries to seduce him. That's a type of moral resolve; he's willing to expose himself to whatever consequences there might be. But you're right, there aren't many other obvious examples of bravery.

AP: Maybe we should back up and see what the verses say. Just to situate us, we're in the desert, it's post-Egypt, and we're finally reaching the Land of Israel. This parsha describes the twelve spies, each representing one of the Tribes, whom Moses sent out to do reconnaissance. They were told to scout out the Promised Land so the Israelites would know what to expect when they arrived there.

This is Numbers 13:27:

> This is what they [the spies] told him. "We came to the land you sent us to; it does indeed flow with milk and honey, and this is its fruit. However, the people who inhabit the country are powerful, and the cities are fortified and very large; moreover, the people are mightily strong" . . . Caleb hushed the people before Moses and said, "Let us by all means go up, and we shall gain possession of it, for we shall surely overcome it." But the men who had gone up with him said, "We cannot attack that people, for they are stronger than we."

DL: So, ten of the spies are saying there's no way we can win the war. And Caleb is saying, "Yes, we can." One way to look at it is as a strategic debate between generals.

AP: But then the spies start whipping up fear among the people saying, "The land through which we have gone to search, it is a land that eats up the inhabitants thereof." Basically, "They're going to devour us."

DL: Yes. "Destroy us."

AP: "And all the people that we saw are men of a great stature" (Num. 13:32). They're huge and scary.

DL: Right.

AP: "And there we saw giants . . . We were in our own sight as grasshoppers, and so we were in their sight." In other words, we were as puny as insects to them because they're so formidable.

DL: Exactly. A key point is how we perceived *ourselves*: "We have no chance." What comes next is totally predictable. The people are so filled with fear that they say, essentially, "Oh, if only we never left Egypt! We might as well die in the wilderness. Why did we come here?"

AP: The majority of Moses's spies freak out and doubt God, just as the people did at the Red Sea.

DL: Had they been thinking straight, I think the spies would have believed in God's ability to help them conquer the Land. But they were gripped by fear, and fear can paralyze us. It can take away our ability to think rationally and spreads like a contagion, so that soon, everybody is terrified.

AP: To me, it seems pretty rational to be afraid of a stronger opponent in a foreign land that you'll be entering blindly.

DL: Yes, but hear me out. Given what the people have experienced so far—God taking them out of Egypt, performing all these miracles, and saving the day time and again—the rational thing is for them to believe God will save them once again and that they will conquer the enemy, no matter how crazy the odds are.

AP: You're saying that because miracles saved them before, they should believe in one now?

DL: Yes, and I think the comparison you made to standing at the Red Sea was a good one. They were at the edge of the sea, and the Egyptian army was in hot pursuit after God had just unleashed ten plagues upon the Egyptians. The rational thing would be for them to say, "God has done these miracles. God will save us." Instead, they all froze!

AP: I see your point, but I still think it's entirely rational to doubt a miracle.

DL: Yes, I hear that. The question we should ask now is, "Why were Caleb and Joshua undeterred?" They have faith, and they're unafraid. Why is that?

AP: Maybe they're the *irrational* ones. Maybe it takes some irrationality to be courageous. I'm struck by Caleb's certainty here. He says in Num. 13:30 about the land of Canaan, "We shall gain possession of it, for we shall surely overcome it." He is sure, based on nothing except God's promise and the sense that, if God believes in us, we should believe in ourselves. We should not view ourselves as grasshoppers but as giants. Without being too melodramatic, that's a message for our time now.

DL: How is this a message for our time? God isn't making us direct promises these days, last I could tell.

AP: I like the idea that faith gives you strength—not just to believe in the next miracle—but to believe in your own fortitude, your capacity to face things. Faith shouldn't make us stupid or rash, but it can give us a kind of armor we didn't know we had. Maybe sometimes we need to believe that if we do our part, we will be taken care of; if we leap into the next proverbial land, we're going to be safe there and it's going to work out.

DL: I really like that, Abby, and it goes back to the grasshopper point. If you see yourself as a grasshopper, that's how the enemy will see you. Caleb and Joshua didn't see themselves as insects—they saw themselves as giants. And in the verse, God describes Caleb as, "Imbued with a different spirit."

AP: I love that quote.

DL: I do too. And I think the "different spirit" here is something to strive for. It's a spirit of jumping without a visible net. Even without these past miracles and promises, it's finding a mettle we didn't know we had that allows us to really affect things.

AP: To bring it to a contemporary moment, that reminds me of the student in Charlotte, Riley Howell, who recently charged a gunman in his school, taking bullets that would otherwise have hit other people. He was imbued with a different spirit.

DL: Yes, and same with Lori Gilbert Kaye, who, during the 2019 synagogue attack in Poway, San Diego, held her ground between the shooter and the rabbi. That was incredible.

AP: The rabbi of that synagogue, Rabbi Goldstein, also stood firm and didn't run. I think of the insane courage it took to stand firm when the shooter was aiming directly at him. His first thought was for the children standing off to the side, watching, frozen and terrified. His instinct was to protect them right away. If I'm honest, I worry that my instinct would just be to duck.

DL: I have the same thoughts. They had that different spirit. Do we? Part of the lesson here is that having courage is not always about religious faith. I'm thinking of the extraordinary courage of first responders during the pandemic, which we are now in the middle of. They literally run into a fire. They have a different spirit, with or without this faith in God or miracles.

AP: They also have training, which the first Jews didn't.

DL: That is true, and that does kick in. Sometimes the different spirit is about God, sometimes it's about training and preparation, and sometimes it's about having strong moral convictions without believing in God at all.

AP: I'm sure many would identify with that take.

DL: I think what we're missing is that there are times when doing what Caleb did wouldn't be considered courageous at all—it would just be plain stupid. It could have turned out that way in the Caleb story.

AP: I'm not following you.

DL: Caleb's courage wasn't the kind we're talking about in Charlotte or San Diego. He wasn't putting himself at risk to protect others; he was insisting that the entire people go into the land of Canaan against a stronger enemy. He was putting everyone at risk.

AP: If he was wrong, everyone could have perished.

DL: Exactly. Is it courage if a general whips his troops into fighting a battle where the odds are totally against them and they get slaughtered?

AP: No, that's irresponsible. So, returning to what we were talking about earlier, you're saying what makes it courage here—as opposed to stupidity—is God's promise. This is what's *supposed* to happen, and it will end well because God ordains it. Caleb trusted what God guaranteed.

DL: Right, and therefore it wasn't a stupid risk. So, whether we call it "rational" or not, it made sense for them to believe in God. God was in Caleb's corner, God was in the Israelites' corner, and God was going to back the army. Do you think that Caleb and Joshua's courage—the "different spirit" we've been talking about—is rare in the Torah?

AP: There aren't a lot of brave patriarchs who come to mind. Nachshon does pop into my head, from the *midrash* on Exodus. He wasn't a patriarch, and he's not as famous, but he's an unsung hero. He waded into the Red Sea when no one else would, before the waters had even parted. He said, "I believe God won't let us drown." He kept moving forward into those seas, even when the waves were lapping at his nose.

DL: Yes, that story is powerful. I also think about Abraham—he was willing to leave everything to follow God. I think there *are* such stories in the Torah. My question for you—for both of us—is, do we strive for that kind of courage?

AP: I'd definitely like to find a little more Nachshon in my *kishkes*, yes.

DL: Obviously, so would I. I'd like to have the courage that comes from an unshakable belief in God, like Abraham, Nachshon, and Caleb. I'd also like to have the fearlessness to do the right thing, even if it means putting my life at risk to save and protect others.

AP: Here's to the courage of a different spirit.

Shlach to Korach

Despondent at the spies' ominous report, the Israelites cry out in protest. They insist they would have been better off had they never left Egypt and even talk about appointing a new leader and returning there. When Joshua and Caleb call on the people to have faith in God, the crowd nearly stones them to death. Furious, God appears and is prepared to wipe the nation out entirely and start again with just Moses. Moses intercedes on the people's behalf, arguing to God that damage would be done to God's reputation, as well as to God's mercy, if God were to destroy an entire people. God relents.

God takes an oath, however, that the entire generation will spend the next forty years wandering the desert—one year for each day the spies scouted the land—until the dying-out of the entire generation that left Egypt. The only Israelites who will enter the Promised Land—from that generation that left Egypt— will be Joshua and Caleb. The people now recognize their sin of doubting God, and some of them try to enter into the Land against God's command, only to be beaten back by the opposing armies.

The Torah instructs the people about the *mitzvot* that will apply in the Land of Israel, including the *mitzvah* of *challah*—the separating of a bit of dough every time they bake bread—to be given as a gift to the *kohen*. They are also given additional laws relating to sacrifices for unintentional sins.

Sometime later, an Israelite man is found gathering wood on the Sabbath—a violation of the holiday's laws. He is sentenced to death and duly stoned. God subsequently instructs the people to attach fringes called *tzitzit* to the corners of their garments as a reminder to follow the Torah's commandments.

KORACH

קֹ֫רַח

DL: Korach is a person's name, and he was from the tribe of Levi.

AP: A rebel.

DL: Yes. He gathered together 250 people and challenged the authority of Moses and Aaron by saying, "Why should you guys be the leaders? Other people deserve to be the leaders."

AP: They're on their way to the Promised Land, and there is an insurrection.

DL: Exactly. The end of last week's parsha, Shlach, was about the sin of the spies; it was decreed on all the people that they wander in the desert for forty years. Their whole lives had been directed toward going into the Promised Land, and now they are told they're all going to die out and only their children will see it.

AP: This was punishment for those ten out of twelve spies who came back from scoping out the Land and were entirely doomsday about their survival against the enemy.

DL: Correct. They said, "There's no way we can conquer this place; it's filled with giants." This wasn't just the people complaining—they were *rejecting the land God had promised them.* So, God's response was to decree that they would never make it into the Land.

AP: In a way, they are being penalized for their pessimism and the fact that they have given up on God.

DL: Yes, they were punished for their lack of faith.

AP: The reason we are revisiting that parsha is because it's important context for Korach. There's this backdrop of, "Just when you are on the verge of getting more agency post-slavery and making your own society, we're slapping you down."

DL: Yes, there's a tremendous sense of despondency and loss for everything they had devoted their lives to and had been hoping for. One can imagine that this also led to a crisis of faith in the leadership. That's where Korach steps in.

AP: That's good background for Numbers 16:1:

> Now Korach . . . gathers a group, to rise up against Moses, together with two hundred and fifty Israelites, chieftains of the community, chosen in the assembly, men of repute. They combined against Moses and Aaron and said to them, "You have gone too far! For all the community are holy, all of them, and the Lord is in their midst. Why then do you raise yourselves above the Lord's congregation?" When Moses heard this, he fell on his face.

Let's take it from there. This rebellious group, led by Korach, is essentially saying to Moses, "Who died and made you king?"

DL: Exactly, and he also strikes an egalitarian note: "Everybody is equally holy, so why should you or anybody be the head of us?" It was a populist message but with a very non-populist goal: Korach wanted to be king. He wanted to be the ruler, but he pitched it through this message that would appeal to everybody.

AP: What particularly strikes me is when Moses falls on his face. First of all, it's dramatic; and second of all, it seems out of character. It feels like defeat, enervation, like, "I have done everything I've been asked to do, and it hasn't been easy. It's been a long journey, I didn't ask for this leadership role in the first place, and now I have a mutiny on my hands?"

DL: I'm totally with you. To me, that's such a striking scene. Rather than Moses responding, "Let me ask God," or challenging Korach by saying, "How dare you?"—which he *does* say a little bit later—he just becomes totally paralyzed. It's almost like he was reeling from a gut punch. I have certainly experienced this in my professional life: you give 110 percent, you're sacrificing for others, all you're doing is for the people you're serving, and they're either ungrateful or asking, "Who died and made you king?"

AP: I'm playing the world's tiniest violin for you right now, Dov.

DL: Oh, I'm sure!

AP: You've had such a hard road.

DL: It's okay, I survived! But I've probably had some of those Moshe moments—

AP: It's thankless, right?

DL: Thankless, yes. And it leaves you stunned, speechless, and questioning your position altogether.

AP: All right. Back to the parsha. Ultimately, the Korach rebels are severely chastised. There's not a lot of tolerance for this kind of mutiny.

DL: No, there's not.

AP: The earth opens up . . . .

DL: Yes, there are two very dramatic events: one is that the rebels bring incense—and we know from an earlier story that when Aaron's sons brought incense improperly, a fire came down from heaven and killed them both—so this is almost a setup, a trap set by Moses. Moses says, "Hey, if you want to be the priests, bring incense to the Temple," and a fire comes down and consumes them. And then another faction, which is probably the one challenging Moses's political leadership, gets obliterated. The Torah says, "The earth opens her mouth and swallowed them up . . . and they went down alive into the pit" (Num. 16:32–33). Some type of earthquake sucks them into the very bowels of the earth.

AP: The takeaway for me is that you do not dare challenge either God's plan or God's messenger. It's pretty clear here—there's nothing admirable about Korach and his minions.

DL: That is a really good issue to discuss. I wonder if the punishment they received was about the challenge they were presenting or how they approached it. If somebody had come and respectfully questioned certain aspects of Moses's leadership, I don't think it would have gotten this response. We know people came to Moses in the past and questioned his rulings. Just two parshas ago, we read that people who couldn't bring the Paschal sacrifice asked Moses why they should be excluded just because they were deemed impure? Moses asks God, and he resolves their problem. So, I don't think challenging Moses is the issue; it's the way they were attacking him. That's how I read it.

AP: What resonates for me is that Moses is disappointed in his own people. He was disappointed they'd built the golden calf before he came down from Mount Sinai—like, "Seriously? You couldn't wait for me? I told you I was coming back." Then his people are *kvetching* in the desert constantly. I have a sense that they are not learning from their own deliverance, or they are not absorbing the gift of it. They just keep focusing on its deficits—the glass is constantly half-empty.

DL: I agree with that, and it makes me wonder if Moses isn't learning either. How much has he still not fully internalized that he is on a different level than the people? He is right up there with God—he sees everything in absolutes, and he cannot tolerate human fallibility, so everything is met with a certain harshness. I think there is definitely some learning that Moses needs to do as well.

AP: As parents, it is certainly true that we have to not just honor but be patient with our kids' defiance and questioning of our authority—it can't be scorched-earth when they disappoint or challenge us.

DL: Absolutely, and I'm also thinking about it from my perspective as a teacher. I used to be a pretty harsh instructor—very exacting—but I have mellowed with the years. I think that it was this same issue: I needed to understand where my students were coming from and to not hold them to impossible standards. There is a beautiful scene at the end of the parsha where Aaron's staff and the staves of all the tribes are brought into the Tabernacle, and Aaron's staff blossoms forth with flowers. To me, that is a metaphor that leadership can't be through the staff—it can't be through harshness; it has to be with something that cultivates a sense of growth and beauty, and that's really the leadership we need.

AP: Let's close with the flowers. I like that ending much more than the swallowing of people into the earth.

DL: Or burning them alive! Yes, we need the kind of leadership that blooms.

AP: We choose flowers.

Korach to Chukat

THOUGH KORACH'S REBELLION has been crushed, the rest of the Israelites are enraged at the deadly punishment the rebels received. As they gather around Moses and Aaron, God appears and brings a plague that strikes down nearly fifteen thousand more Israelites, until Aaron, offering up incense, causes the plague to cease.

God then instructs the chieftain of each tribe to inscribe his name on a staff and place it in the Tent of Meeting. Aaron's staff—placed on behalf of the tribe of Levi—blossoms into flowers. The staff is then placed inside the Holy of Holies together with the Ark to serve as a reminder of the chosenness of the *kohanim* and Levites for divine service.

With the *kohanim* and Levites' status comes responsibility: they must serve in the Temple and guard and protect it from impurity. As they are to be fully dedicated to serving God, they are not to become farmers and work the land, and thus—as a tribe—they will not be given a portion in the Land of Israel. Rather, the *kohanim* will receive various priestly gifts, including certain parts of the sacrifices, the firstborn of the flock and cattle, and *terumah*, a first offering of the grain. The Levites will be given a tithe from the grain and agricultural produce of all the other tribes.

The Torah next delivers instructions for purifying a person who has come into contact with a corpse or grave. They center on the ashes of an unblemished red heifer, which must be mixed with water and other substances to perform the purification process.

The people then proceed through the desert, thirsting for water. They gather around Moses and Aaron, setting the scene for Moses's famous—or infamous—smiting of the rock.

Chukat

חֻקַּת

AP: Chukat means "statute," Dov. What statute is relevant in this parsha?

DL: The parsha opens with the statutes, or laws, of purification from coming in contact with a corpse. From there it moves on to some very interesting narratives.

AP: The most famous being the story of Moses hitting the rock and being told that *he* can't enter the Land of Israel.

DL: Yes and we've decided to focus on the question, "Did Moses get a fair deal?"

AP: My answer is "No."

DL: Why could I have guessed you'd say that?

AP: Where is the justice when great visionaries don't get to see their visions realized in their own lives? Here's the verse—Numbers 20:7: "The Lord spoke unto Moses, saying, 'Take the rod and gather thou the assembly together, thou and Aaron, thy brother, and speak ye unto the rock before their eyes and it shall give forth His water.'" So, just to be clear, when God says, "Speak ye unto the rock," that's an instruction for Moses to literally coax water *verbally* from the stone.

DL: Right, or, if not to coax it from the stone, to command it. And then, through a miracle, God will make the water come out.

AP: Okay, to continue:

> And Moses and Aaron gathered the congregation together before the rock . . . And he said unto them, "Hear now, ye rebels, shall we fetch you water out of this rock?" And Moses lifted up his hand and with his rod he smote the rock twice and the water came out abundantly and the congregation drank, and their beasts also.

DL: Let's pause for a moment and point out that Moses did not *speak* to the rock as he was commanded. He hit it; he smote it twice.

AP: God's not pleased at all with the smiting, as we see in these final verses from Numbers 20:12: "But God said to Moses and Aaron, 'Because you did not trust Me enough to affirm My sanctity in the sight of the Israelite people, therefore you shall not lead this congregation into the land that I have given them.'" That's that. Moses didn't follow God's instructions, so he can't enter the Promised Land.

DL: Right, game over. After forty years of selfless service, it all went down the drain in an instant. "Sorry Moses, you blew it one time. Now you're not going into the Land."

AP: Aaron couldn't go in either. It sounds like Aaron is punished for Moses's mistake, or maybe he's being slapped retroactively for the golden calf sin, which happened a long time before. It just doesn't make any sense to me, honestly. What exactly was Moses's fatal error here? The Torah does not lay it out.

DL: That's another really curious part of this story. The assumption that the Rabbis tend to make is that the sin was hitting the rock as opposed to speaking to it. But even if that's true, what's so terrible about that? It's not exactly what God instructed, but at the end of the day, why is that a reason to be kept from the Land?

AP: I researched this parsha, and I found that the commentators give many explanations of Moses's sin that kept him from the Promised Land. I thought it might be interesting to share some of them.

DL: Go for it.

AP: I'm sure you know them all by heart, Dov. The first is that Moses called the people "rebels," and he displayed his anger, which was out of control.

DL: That's Maimonides.

AP: See? You do know all the commentators by heart. Impressive.

DL: Thank you. Go on.

AP: The hypothesis from Nachmanides, the thirteenth-century Spanish commentator, is that Moses screwed up by implying it was *he*, not God, who was making the water come out of the rock.

DL: Oh, interesting.

AP: Others believe it was because Moses and Aaron ran away from their people when the rebellious congregation initially confronted them.

DL: Which goes back to our previous episode on courage.

AP: Right, they didn't have it. Regardless of what Moses's sin was, let's talk about where the justice is in this. It's such a severe punishment, all kidding aside. If you consider everything that Moses did, the degree of self-sacrifice, all of which was leading to bringing the people into the Land, and then it's just, "Sorry." He did all the work and gets no reward.

DL: Okay, so here's a theory: maybe Moses wasn't being punished at all. Maybe there was a deeper issue about his leadership, something that made it clear he could not be the one to bring the people into the Land.

AP: You're saying Moses failed the leadership test in a way we can't necessarily see? Like, maybe his poor anger management—which was Maimonides's explanation—was too problematic a trait to have in the leader who's going to take you into the future. That it was a dealbreaker.

DL: Right, but I would move beyond just the anger issue. I think it was more specific. Moses struck the rock rather than speaking to it, and I think that shows, symbolically, that Moses is stuck in his old ways. Because forty years earlier, when they came out of Egypt and were thirsty, God told him to hit the rock, which he did, and that was just fine. Now God is saying, "Let's see if you can do something different this time—*speak* to the rock." And Moses just falls back into his old patterns. That's a problem. As a leader, you are going to face new realities in the Land of Canaan. Are you going to be able to adapt? Are you going to be able to change, or are you stuck in your old ways? This is a new generation. They're more mature, and they're not whiny and immature people like the slaves who came out of Egypt. They deserve a leader who can talk to them like adults, not one who is going to try to hit them over the head as if they're children.

AP: Nice metaphor. But I'm not satisfied. We still haven't answered the basic question—which I'm not just harping on for its own sake, but because, it seems to me, it's the essence of the turn that's taken here—between slavery and freedom, the old life and the new. Where is the justice in the fact that this leader, Moses, whom we have held up as an icon of our tradition and our faith, is getting short-changed here? He's out. If we look back at the fact that he didn't want the job in the first place, his hesitancy was a virtue. When God said, "You have to lead the people out of Egypt," he said, "I'm not the man for the job." God pushed him to do it, and Moses did it beautifully, heroically. And now one rock-smite, and he's sidelined. To me, humility is a sign of real leadership.

DL: I agree with all of what you said, but that's a separate conversation. Moses was a great, humble leader, but that doesn't mean he should be the one to take them into Canaan. Even with his initial hesitancy to lead, we have to acknowledge that he got the job by fiat. God decreed it; he was not chosen by the people. His leadership was a top-down appointment, and he governed in a top-down manner. That wasn't the right model for an independent, empowered people, who were about to enter the Land of Canaan. It all goes back to a leadership style that's about hitting the rock, not speaking to it. Maybe the Torah is also instructing us to pursue solutions through words instead of violence.

AP: Then let's discuss this next question: Did Moses get recognition in his own time? The Torah text suggests that he was not praised until his death, so he is dying as *persona non grata* after being this hero.

DL: I feel for Moses, but—

AP: It doesn't sound like you do.

DL: Well, maybe I have to work on that. But it's not like he didn't get his day in the sun. The entire Torah is named after him. It's called *Torat Moshe*, "Moses's Torah," for God's sake. (That's not a pun!) In the tradition, he's known as Moshe Rabbeinu—"Moses, our Teacher." He is the number one figure in our religion. He might not have taken the people into Israel, but he gets credit for the whole shebang.

AP: After he's dead.

DL: Okay, I get that. You're right—in his life, he gets very little in the way, of kudos. But it's like that for a lot of leaders. There's a lot of aggravation and ingratitude, absolutely. But I think there are still some significant markers of Moses's status. First of all, the text says that after he came down from Mount Sinai, they saw that his face glowed, and they were afraid to draw close to him. That's not exactly recognition or gratitude, but it's a type of awe. There's clear realization of who he was.

AP: But that's not enough. He worked all his life to get to this point, and he deserved to enter the Land. He got a raw deal.

DL: Do you think Moses should have gone in even if he wasn't the right leader?

AP: I think he should have at least been able to see it.

DL: He did see it. God took him up to the mountaintop and showed him.

AP: Taste it, feel it.

DL: What if that would have compromised Joshua's ability to be the right leader, living in the shadow of Moses?

AP: This is what it was all for, and he should have the peak moment. A chance to take it all in and feel the earth beneath his feet and taste the milk and honey. He earned that. It's not just recompense, it's also right for the people that he go with them. That bothers me as well.

DL: But you agree that, if it weren't right for the people, it might make sense for him to be denied?

AP: But who decides that? Who's determining that?

DL: Well, in the Torah, it's God.

AP: We know God is not always fair. We know God's not always right.

DL: What happens when an individual suffers, and it isn't fair, but ultimately, it's for the greater good?

AP: Why does it hurt the people for Moses to go?

DL: Because any future leader will always live in Moses's shadow. He is a larger-than-life figure, and if he enters into the Land with them, their narrative about building a new society is going to start with Moses.

AP: Or maybe what you're getting at is that as long as Moses is with them, their story in the Promised Land will always start with slavery. We need to think like free people now; we have to remake ourselves as liberated people, and he reminds us too much of our oppression.

DL: Exactly, and if you buy into that—which I'm not saying you do—you find a way to live with the fact that he might have to suffer some unfairness.

AP: I'll have to think about that.

Chukat to Balak

Despite the decree that he will not enter the Promised Land, Moses continues to lead the people there through the desert. He sends messengers to the King of Edom to ask for passage through their territory, only to be refused. The people arrive at Mount Hor, and God tells Moses that Aaron will die here. Following God's instructions, Moses brings Aaron to the top of the mountain and transfers Aaron's priestly clothes and authority to his son, Eleazar. Aaron dies and the people mourn him for thirty days.

Following Aaron's death, the Israelites—with God's help—fend off an attack by the King of Arad, conquering his cities. They then ask for passage through the lands of Sihon, King of the Amorites, only to again be refused, and they find themselves facing Sihon's armies in battle. In a complete turnaround, the Israelites decimate Sihon and his troops and take possession of major territory east of the Jordan River. This feat is then repeated with Og, King of Bashan, who similarly initiates war against the Israelites only to be soundly defeated and whose territory is taken over by this new nation.

The people now move to the plains of Moab, immediately to the east of the Jordan River, preparing to enter into the Land of Canaan. Seeing these Israelites, and fearful that his nation will be the next to fall, Balak, King of Moab, sends a prophet named Balaam to curse the Israelites, with the intent of enabling the Moabite army to drive them out. God warns Balaam against the mission, but under continued pressure from Balak, the prophet eventually sets out toward the Israelite camp. Ignoring signs from God—delivered via Balaam's donkey—to turn back, Balaam reaches the Israelites and tries three times to curse them. Each time, words of praise come out of his mouth, one of which is the famous blessing from Numbers 24:5: "*Mah tovu ohalekha, Yaakov!*" ("How goodly are your tents, Jacob!") This enrages Balak, but Balaam reminds him that he, Balaam, is beholden to God's will. Before returning to his land, Balaam gives a prophecy about the future of many nations of the region, including a vision where Israel rules over Moab. Balaam then returns to his homeland.

Balak

בָּלָק

AP: We are in Numbers, about to talk about Pinchas. This is another one of those hard stories where it feels like the Rabbis twist themselves into knots to put a good spin on some questionable behavior. Tell us where we are in the Torah narrative, Dov.

DL: We are continuing to follow the Israelites' travails traveling through the wilderness for forty years. Most of this parsha devotes itself to a fascinating story about a talking donkey and Balaam, a Gentile prophet who was hired to curse the Israelite people and failed.

AP: I know we're not planning to get into Balaam in this conversation, but what do you mean he was "hired" to curse the Israelites?

DL: A king of Moab named Balak offered Balaam money to harm the Israelites because he feared they would defeat him, as they had other kings in the area.

AP: Okay, what happens next?

DL: Balaam tells King Balak that he can't curse the Israelites if God hasn't directed him to do so, but he suggests, in the meantime, that Balak lure the Israelites to sin by tempting them with non-Jewish women, in the hope that this will bring God's punishment upon them. Indeed, Midianite and Moabite women—women from the tribes that were trying to curse the Israelites—seduced the Israelite men to have sex with them and to worship their gods.

AP: It's always the women's fault.

DL: It's truly unjust. And it was this, the illicit sex and idolatry and not Balaam's curses, which succeeded in bringing harm to the Israelites. God responded as God tends to respond—by sending a plague and calling on the people to punish the sinners.

AP: When in doubt, send another plague.

DL: Exactly.

AP: Does it say what kind of plague he sent?

DL: No. It says, "God's anger was kindled against the people" (Num. 25:3). God then said, essentially, "The only way you are going to stop this plague is if you take the responsibility into your own hands. Gird your loins, take your swords, and kill all the people who are sinning."

AP: I am going to read Numbers 25, starting with verse 6:

> Just then, one of the Israelites came and brought a Midianite woman over to his companions, in the sight of Moses and of the whole Israelite community who were weeping at the entrance of the Tent of Meeting.

To clarify—an Israelite named Zimri flagrantly brings a *non*-Jewish woman right in front of Moses and the whole Israelite community—

DL: Correct; it's a *shanda* [disgrace].

AP: Continuing the text, Pinchas is pissed:

> When Pinchas, son of Eleazar, son of Aaron the priest, saw this, he left the assembly and, taking a spear in his hand, he followed the Israelite into the chamber and stabbed both of them, the Israelite and the woman, through the belly. Then the plague against the Israelites was checked. Those who died of the plague numbered twenty-four thousand.

So, this is vigilante justice.

DL: Or close to it. God basically said, "If you want this plague to end, you have to take responsibility and do something about it," but everybody is paralyzed to act except Aaron's grandson, Pinchas, who metes out justice on his own without doing so as part of a judicial system.

AP: Even so, Pinchas is rewarded; he gets the priesthood for this. I am just reading on here, though this section comes at the beginning of next week's parsha (Num. 25:11):

> God tells Moses, "Pinchas . . . has turned back My wrath from the Israelites by displaying among them his passion for Me, so that I

> did not wipe out the Israelite people in My passion. Say, therefore, 'I grant him my pact of friendship. It shall be for him and his descendants after him a pact of priesthood for all time.'"

So the reward is pretty clear, which surprises me.

DL: You mean why is such a violent act being rewarded? Let's remember that God was often quite violent in his punishment, so maybe it fits that theme. It's worth pointing out that the key word in Hebrew is "*kana*," which you read as "passion," but it's actually a word more related to anger and zealotry. It really is describing Pinchas as a zealot: "He was a zealot for My sake" (Num. 25:13).

AP: The Sefaria translation is: "He took impassioned action for his God."

DL: The word has both meanings. In the end, this story raises serious questions about whether zealotry is something to be praised. The modern Hebrew word *kanai* is defined as a crazy extremist who lashes out against people he thinks are not acting the way they should from a religious point of view.

AP: I am extremely uncomfortable with it. We've seen where zealotry gets us, and the idea that this is any kind of model for behavior does not feel Godlike at all. It's one thing for God to issue punishment, but for human beings to do it when we are supposed to be—as I understand it—God's agents on Earth, feels very dangerous.

DL: I totally agree with you. So much of the Torah is a shifting away from this tribal vigilantism and toward creating a whole judicial system with due process. This situation seems to say, "If the judicial system isn't doing its job, you have to step up and do it." But for us, that can be very destructive to the fabric of society, and it's hard to understand why it is being praised.

AP: When I was reading up on this, I saw that our ancient Rabbis also wrestled with it. They talk about a moral ambivalence here. I am going to quote from *Sanhedrin* 82a in the Talmud, because it really struck me. The sages are saying what Pinchas did was wrong:

> Although his act was lawful, the sages nonetheless said that, had Zimri turned around and killed Pinchas instead, he would be deemed innocent since he acted in self-defense. And had Pinchas

> asked a court of law whether he was permitted to do what he was about to do, the answer would have been no.

My goodness, the Rabbis do not approve of Pinchas's actions, but God *does*?

DL: That is a perfect passage because the Rabbis are trying to reconcile zealotry with a new judicial system woven into the fabric of society. What they are saying is, "After the fact, we might look back and say that was praiseworthy, but we would never allow it in the moment."

AP: Where do you come out on Pinchas? In your gut?

DL: I am troubled by his actions. The Rabbis did a lot to blunt the edge of that event, and I think maybe the Torah did too. After Pinchas's act, God says—and this is in next week's parsha—"I am giving him my covenant of peace" (Num. 25:12). I would like to interpret that as God saying, "What you did was violent, but that's not the way you are supposed to act." We are supposed to find peaceful solutions, even if that was a moment when violence was necessary. We read about Pinchas's later life in the Book of Joshua, and Pinchas became a peace-seeking diplomat. So, I think the Rabbis—and even the Torah itself—are trying to say that, as a rule, this is not acceptable behavior. But I ask myself, if there have ever been cases when somebody acted outside the rules of society, where afterward, we said it was a good thing because we'd be in a much worse place if they hadn't taken action? How about you? Does that resonate at all?

AP: No.

DL: It doesn't?

AP: It really sets a bad precedent. I understand that you can believe something is wrong and act on that belief, but there's a reason why we have judicial systems.

DL: Sometimes judicial systems are created or corrupted by flawed human beings who misuse it.

AP: True. But as a rule, it seems that unless lives are being threatened, as soon as you think you can take justice into your own hands, *anybody* can begin to justify an act because they are outraged by some behavior they consider to be crossing the line.

DL: Your point about how it hurts the fabric of society is correct. That's why we can never condone it *in the moment.* But I do wonder whether we can allow for exceptions. I am thinking about how, in movies, for example, somebody finds a child molester or a serial murderer, and if they don't stop this person, he's going to keep on doing what he's been doing. The character kills the bad guy in the movie without any judicial due process. I think most of us are like, "Yeah, good for you! That's exactly what you should have done."

AP: It's interesting that you're saying this now. We are talking a few days after the horrific George Floyd video came out—the Minneapolis incident where a police officer put his knee on George Floyd's neck to the point of killing him. There were a lot of bystanders. There were other law enforcement officials standing around doing nothing, and some were even helping. If that was a Pinchas moment, I would change my mind and say that someone should have thrown their body on that cop or done something besides just film it. I'm glad there's video documentation, but there were a lot of people who did not act physically to stop it. That kind of action might have saved his life.

DL: I think both of us are grappling with the same things the Rabbis did. We want to say that you are never allowed to be a vigilante, and you must always follow the rule of law. But after the fact, sometimes we're happy that certain people did what they did even though it violated certain strictures.

AP: What exactly was Pinchas avenging? What did he see happening? What was the sin?

DL: They were having sex in the context of the worshipping of idols.

AP: It's sinful because the Midianite woman is not a Jew?

DL: Well, yes, but it seems the Torah is much more concerned with the fact that this was connected to idol worship, taking the people away from God.

AP: Am I wrong in thinking that Zipporah, Moses's wife, was a Midianite woman?

DL: Yes, she was. The Rabbis pick up on this and say Zimri went to Moses with this Midianite woman and said, "Moses, am I allowed to have sex with a Midianite woman?" And Moses said, "No." So Zimri said,

"Well, what about you and your wife?" Moses didn't have an answer, so Zimri went and acted as he did—to demonstrate that it should be permissible. The Rabbis never reconciled the problem, though.

AP: So the lesson in this parsha is to resist seduction, resist idols.

DL: I think we should end on this note: Pinchas was given God's blessing of peace, which is what we should always be striving for.

Balak to Pinchas

WITH THE PLAGUE against the Israelites now over, God directs both Moses and Aaron's son Eleazar—who is now in charge of the *kohanim*—to conduct a census of the remaining people. For military purposes, the census only counts able-bodied males over the age of twenty. The results of the census are announced tribe by tribe, and they add up to approximately 600,000 men overall. They are told that the land will be allotted to the tribes (with the exception of the Levites) proportionally, with larger areas going to more populous tribes. By the time this count takes place, the only people remaining from those who originally left Egypt are Moses, Caleb, and Joshua.

PINCHAS

פִּינְחָס

AP: Before we get started, I have to ask why this parsha is called Pinchas when we've left his story behind in the previous parsha.

DL: Good question. It can be confusing, but a parsha is always named for one of its first words, and Pinchas is mentioned at the top of this parsha—almost like a coda from the last, before moving ahead.

AP: Got it. So where are we in our story?

DL: We are on the cusp of entering into the Land of Canaan, and the Torah has just gone through listing all the major families of each tribe by name and counting all the people.

AP: That's why it's called "Numbers," because we're counting. Taking a census.

DL: Exactly, and it's saying that these are the tribes among whom the Land is going to be divided.

AP: We should at least note that we're talking about women, for a change. There aren't a lot of female characters in the Torah, so that, at least, is striking. Although, the fact that this parsha is more obscure underscores how rare it is that people talk about women in the Torah. But enough preamble, here we go. We're in Numbers 27:1, and I am reading the end of that first verse: "These are the names of his daughters—" Whose daughters are these?

DL: A person named Zelophehad.

AP: That's literally a name you would make up for a comedy sketch. One more time?

DL: Zelophehad.

AP: All right, "These are the names of his daughters: Mahlah, Noah, Hoglah, Milcah, and Tirzah."

DL: As you said, it is very unusual in the Torah to have women named.

AP: "And they stood before Moses, and before Eleazar the priest, and before the princes"—the heads of the tribes—"and all the congregation at the door of the Tent of Meeting saying, "Our father died in the wilderness, and he was not among the company of them that gathered themselves together against the Lord in the company of Korach."

DL: You'll recall from a previous parsha that Korach, a cousin of Moses, was a rebel who tried to undermine Moses's leadership—

AP: And there was a battle—

DL: Yes. Korach got a group of Israelites to back him.

AP: Right, and these daughters of Zelophehad are saying essentially, "Our dad was not part of that Korach-led rebellion; our family was not guilty of mutiny against Moses."

DL: Yes.

AP: The daughters continue: "Why should the name of our father be done away from among his family because he had no son? Give unto us a possession among the brethren of our father." They're saying, "Why should our surname—the name of our father—be lost because he didn't have a boy to carry on the name?"

DL: More like: Why should the memory of our father's line be lost because his property transfers only to his brothers and their children? Let *us* inherit the property, and by keeping the property with his direct descendants, his name, his lineage, and his memory will be kept alive.

AP: What possessions are we talking about here?

DL: They mean a portion of the Land of Israel. By the Bible's laws of inheritance, before this event, property would only pass on to the males. If there were no sons, it would pass on to the father's brother or to the father's nephews, but it would never go to any daughters. These daughters are saying, "If we follow those conventions, then the land will pass away from our father's line."

AP: By the way, that wasn't just in just biblical times. That practice continued for a long time.

DL: Absolutely.

AP: Numbers 27:5 says,

> And Moses brought their cause before the Lord, and the Lord spoke unto Moses, saying, "The daughters of Zelophehad, thou

> shalt surely give them a possession of an inheritance among their father's brethren, and thou shalt cause the inheritance of their father to pass unto them. If a man dies and has no son, then ye shall cause his inheritance to pass unto his daughter."

This is one moment of real justice.

DL: Major move for a proto-feminist God.

AP: The progressive God is saying, "Yes, daughters; you can have the land."

DL: We should acknowledge that it's a half-measure. It's still huge but—

AP: It's a portion, as opposed to nothing.

DL: Right, but women only receive the land when there are *no* sons. If there are both sons and daughters, the sons still get everything. Even if there's one son and ten daughters, the one son gets it all. But, as a second tier, the daughters come before any other men like brothers or nephews.

AP: My first reaction is that it's one of the rare times when someone argues for something and gets it. There are so many times when someone asks for something in the Hebrew Bible, and they are denied. They pine or long for it, but this time the daughters made a good argument and won.

DL: Yes. This goes back to the fairness point, which has come up in previous episodes. In fact, the first word that God says in response to Moses—this is in Numbers 27:7—is the Hebrew word *kein*, which translates to: "properly they (the daughters) have spoken"; "rightly they have spoken"; "their claim is a just one." One word: *kein*. "Yes" in modern Hebrew. That's a strong statement. They are right. They will get justice. It may not be total equality—let's acknowledge the realities of the time—but it's a big step forward.

AP: It signals that it's worth arguing for your piece of the pie.

DL: Absolutely.

AP: That's something that isn't necessarily a regular takeaway from the Torah, particularly for women: You are entitled to something. You should inherit this.

DL: It's also interesting to note that, in pursuit of their claim, these women are showing they know how to navigate the patriarchy. They come to Moses and to all the leaders of the tribes. There's no question about male authority here; they're not challenging that. They don't say, "Give it to us because it wouldn't be fair otherwise. We're our father's children as well." What they say is, "What will this do to our *father's name*?" which is a legitimate concern within the patriarchy.

AP: Do you think they really care about that, or are they just making the best argument to get what they want?

DL: There's no way of knowing, but I think it's a recurring theme when women get what they're asking for in the Bible. It's often because they know how to navigate the realities of the society in which they live, which, as we know, was patriarchal. That *is* the best argument they could have made. It's the one that resonates most deeply with the males in charge. Which raises interesting questions for today: How much do you challenge the whole system, and how much do you try to work within it?

AP: Also, this parsha makes me think about the power of continuing a name—what a legacy of family means. Your wife, for example, did not take your name—if I may be so personal.

DL: That's correct.

AP: Did that bother you?

DL: It didn't bother me, but it did bother one of my parents, I'll say that.

AP: Who shall not be named . . . .

DL: Who shall not be named. When we lived for a few years in Boca Raton, Florida—

AP: Are there Jews in Boca?

DL: Isn't Florida God's waiting room? Anyway, when I went to pick up our dry cleaning once, I said, "Linzer," and they said they didn't have anything under that name. I asked them to look under my wife's last name, and they asked, "Why does your wife have a different last name than you?" There's still a very patriarchal mentality around taking the husband's name.

AP: But it's not clear in this parsha *why* God sees it the daughters' way. That confuses me. What's persuasive?

DL: Right; is God saying, "This is how we do justice by Zelophehad—to make sure his name continues"? Or is God saying the daughters deserve the land on their own merits, and it has nothing to do with preserving their father's name? There's no mention of their father

Zelophehad in God's response, which is an excellent point I've never thought of. It's all about the women and the rightness of their claim. It's about *kein*.

AP: Do these daughters ever come back in the Torah?

DL: Yes, right at the end of the book of Numbers, they reappear. It's an interesting story, because the other members of their tribe come to Moses and say, "What if they marry men from another tribe? That portion of our tribal land will transfer to that tribe." And Moses acknowledges that they're right.

AP: So they reverse the—

DL: No. The women are told they must marry men from their tribe. So, it limits their freedom to some degree.

AP: Of course it does.

DL: It's balancing the realities of the patriarchy—or of the division of the land according to tribes, which is *connected* to the patriarchy—but the amazing thing is that the Rabbis come to the rescue here because they say this rule stood for only that one generation. For all future generations, when women inherited the land of their fathers, they could marry whomever they wanted.

AP: As we finish up, what's your takeaway from this parsha?

DL: It would be really nice to live in a time when you can go to a rabbi or leader like Moses and say, "This isn't fair," and they could say, "Let me check with God," and God would resolve the conflict. I would love to be able to say, "Let me take that to God," and have God come back and say, "*Kein!*"—they're right. Their cause is just.

AP: Maybe you can.

DL: For Modern Orthodox Jews, for myself, the challenge is to partner with God, because that's what it means to interpret and apply *halacha*. We try to figure out if we can find a path. We can't *revise*, but can we find a way that's both true to *halacha* and acknowledges the truth of the claim and of the human reality?

AP: You know where I come out on that: I hope you can always find that path to a fair result.

DL: Me too.

Pinchas to Matot–Masei

Knowing he will not enter the Holy Land, Moses asks God to choose the next leader of the people. God instructs Moses to take Joshua and, in the presence of Eleazar, the High Priest, and all the people, to lay his hands upon him and to charge him, thereby endowing Joshua with his glory and status, ensuring his acceptance by the people.

Moses and the Israelites next receive instructions from God regarding the procedures for daily, weekly, and monthly sacrifices, as well as for those required during the various festivals. These offerings include animals, grain, and wine, and are to be offered in the Tabernacle by the *kohanim*.

The Torah next addresses the laws of oaths. Vows that impose an obligation on oneself are binding and may not be violated. However, reflecting the patriarchal society of the time, under certain circumstances, a father can annul the vows made by his daughter, and a husband can annul those made by his wife.

At God's command, the Israelites wage a war of vengeance against the Midianites, killing all the men and capturing the women, children, and livestock. Moses is furious that the women—who had seduced Israelite men into idolatry—had been spared, so he issues the death penalty for all women who have had sexual intercourse. Per God's instructions, the remaining spoils of war are distributed among the *kohanim*, the Levites, and the rest of the nation.

MATOT-MASEI

מַטּוֹת-מַסְעֵי

AP: We're looking at a double parsha today.

DL: Yes, we'll be discussing Matot and Masei. Matot, which means "tribes," is the first, and Masei, the second, means "journeys." It's common to combine these two parshas.

AP: We're still in Numbers, and we'll be zeroing in on something I find very powerful yet difficult. It's a reiteration of something we saw in an earlier parsha that we did not discuss in detail: the Israelites are not going to make it to the Promised Land. This is stark, because the entire basis of our history and story is that we escaped 400 years of slavery in Egypt only to be prevented from—

DL: Realizing our dream.

AP: Precisely. This is Numbers 32:10:

> Thereupon the Lord was incensed and swore, "None of the men from twenty years up who came out of Egypt shall see the land that I promised on oath to Abraham, Isaac, and Jacob, for they did not remain loyal to Me—none except Caleb son of Jephunneh the Kenizzite and Joshua son of Nun, for they remained loyal to the Lord."

Those were the two spies of the twelve who weren't wholly pessimistic about what lay in wait for them in the Promised Land.

DL: Right.

AP: "The Lord was incensed at Israel"—Israel being the people—and he made them wander in the desert for *forty* years until the whole generation that had provoked the Lord's displeasure was gone. In other words, if you were under the age of twenty, you'd make it in, but if you were over twenty, too bad; you die in the wilderness after escaping Egypt, crossing the Red Sea, and getting to Mount Sinai.

DL: I will share with you a graphic image in the Talmud, which horrifies me every time I think about it. The Talmud says that, after they were told they were all going to die out in the wilderness, they would dig a grave every night and sleep in it, so if they died that night, they would already be partly buried.

AP: That's chilling.

DL: Truly. So, did the people accept their fate? When Moses first tells them of God's decree—that they will die out in the wilderness—they reject it; they are in denial. Some say, "No, no, no! We are going to go into the Land," and they send troops to fight their way in, but they all get wiped out. Eventually, they become resigned to their fate.

AP: But God promised this. It's even in the language: "None of the men from twenty years up who came out of Egypt shall see the land that I promised on oath . . . ."

DL: True, but God didn't promise to give it specifically to this generation who came from Egypt. I can tell that this bothers you, Abby. What are you thinking?

AP: When we sit at the Passover seder and talk about the Exodus, rejoice in it, and talk about redemption and deliverance, the average child at the seder table thinks that it's a happy ending—that our ancestors escaped and got to the Promised Land. It's a bit of a betrayal to learn they did not. I'm not saying it would have been better for them to have stayed in Egypt, but so much of this journey was the promise of milk and honey, of a better day, a better land, a home, and to never see it feels like an extremely tragic conclusion.

DL: Yes, and it's important to realize that in this week's parsha, Moses is afraid that the people are once again going to lose faith and refuse to continue on to the Promised Land. The tribes of Reuven and Gad approach Moses and say, "It's so beautiful here on the east side of the Jordan"—these were lands they had just conquered in a battle they weren't expecting—"and we want to stay here and not go into the Land." Moses thinks this is history repeating itself, so he lectures them about the mistakes of the past and how giving up on the Land of Israel forty years earlier led to an entire generation dying out in the wilderness.

AP: You're saying Moses is predicting they will make the same mistake again—doubting God—and that more generations will lose out on the Promised Land?

DL: Yes. Moses is afraid they are being seduced by wealth and the ease of living outside of the Land, and they are rejecting God's promise. I'm left wondering how much these choices resemble the ones we make today. I often feel guilty about not living in Israel. Am I living outside of Israel because I have a nice, comfortable life here in America? I don't believe that's true, but it's a central question I ask myself. Does that resonate for you?

AP: Before I answer, why aren't you living in Israel?

DL: The honest answer is that I would love to live there, but there are family reasons and other factors that don't make it possible.

AP: I love Israel, and I love it when I'm there, but it's never been in the lexicon of my upbringing to live there permanently. I recently read Francine Klagsbrun's book about Golda Meir—*Lioness: Golda Meir and the Nation of Israel*—which is an amazing tome, and it made me think about what an extraordinary thing it was to have been part of it, to put down roots there. But in reading the biography, I felt that it's too late for me. Everything we study about the post-Temple evolution of Judaism tells me there's been a shift from the Temple focus and the Israel focus to a diaspora Judaism, where you are Jewish and connected wherever you are. That's the Jewish DNA I grew up with: less focused on place and more focused on being Jewish and finding meaning where you are—building the story where you live.

DL: Framing it in terms of that evolution is very helpful. Yes. In Biblical times, you had a Jewish nation in Israel. We had self-governance, and that was where you needed to be. Otherwise, you were outside of your homeland, and you were in diaspora. But, together with the destruction of the Temple and the decentralization of Jewish society, it might be that the biblical centrality of the land doesn't have to remain part of our Jewish self-understanding. But for me, the Biblical vision of us as a Jewish people living as a nation in the Land of Israel, as well as the religious significance of the land itself, has always loomed quite large. So not making Aliyah leads to some guilty feelings.

AP: Moving to Israel was a core message of your childhood?

DL: Yes. It's very hard to let go of the deep things that were said to us and the way we were taught to look at the world when we were children. So even though I greatly appreciate and understand your perspective, it's deeply ingrained in me that we all should be living in Israel, and if we're not, there'd better be a good excuse. Or, if you don't have a good excuse, at least admit that you're selling out a little bit. It's sort of like what Moshe was afraid of in this parsha—that his fellow Israelites were selling out. Until the modern State of Israel, Jews had been in exile for the last 2,000 years—in Babylonia, in Western and Eastern Europe, wherever, and they couldn't do anything about it. All they could do was dream of being in Israel. And every day, they would pray in the direction of Jerusalem, pray for a time when Jerusalem would be rebuilt and the Jews would once again live in the land. Now you have the opportunity, so stop saying, "Next year in Jerusalem!" unless you mean it and do something about it. I carry that guilt/aspiration/religious feeling with me about going into the Land. So, when I read the verses where Moses critiques the tribes who want to stay outside of the Land where the living is good, I take that in and start asking myself some hard questions.

AP: I understand now. Shabbat shalom.

DL: Shabbat shalom, Abby.

Matot–Masei to Devarim

THE TEXT RECOUNTS the Israelites' journey from Egypt, enumerating every one of their stops through the desert all the way to their current location at the plains of Moab. God gives Moses orders to pass on to the Israelites: when they cross the Jordan River and enter the Promised Land, they are to destroy all the idols and places of pagan worship. God specifies the borders of the area they are to conquer and assigns a chieftain to ensure the proper distribution of each tribe's portion. Because the tribe of Levi will not receive a portion of its own, they will be granted cities with surrounding pastures, within the other tribes' sectors. These will also serve as cities of refuge where a person who unintentionally commits murder can take shelter from the victim's relative who would want to avenge the blood of his kinsman.

The leaders of the tribe of Manasseh approach Moses with a concern: the daughters of Zelophehad—who are now landowners within the tribe—might marry men who are not from the tribe of Manasseh. This would result in sections within their tribal land being owned by members of other tribes. In response, God declares that the daughters must marry within their own tribe, and the Book of Numbers ends by telling us that, following this directive, the daughters of Zelophehad married their cousins, keeping the tribal land complete.

DEUTERONOMY

דְּבָרִים

Devarim

דְּבָרִים

AP: Let's talk about the very start of the final book—Deuteronomy 1:11. What's interesting here is that Moses is essentially retelling the entire Torah.

DL: Exactly—the whole story from Exodus to the end. You have an entire book of the Torah that is, more or less, Moses's valedictory speech—given over the course of a month—in which he recounts all that came before. "Deuteronomy" means "second law," because it's a retelling of the laws and the *mitzvot*, but also of the narratives, the stories.

AP: Yes, but it's a selective retelling.

DL: That's an excellent point. It begs the question: why is Moses doing this, and what happens when you recount past events? Retelling a story allows you to try to organize and make sense of the past while doing so through the lens of the present.

AP: And maybe it's an opportunity to try to improve it the second time.

DL: That's another good point.

AP: Let's hit the verses. Deuteronomy 1:11. "May the Lord, the God of your fathers—"

DL: This is Moses talking to the people.

AP: Right. "May the Lord, the God of your fathers, make you a thousand times as many as you are"—

DL: In other words, multiply your families and your population—

AP: ". . . and bless you as He hath promised you. How can I myself alone bear your cumbrance and your burden and your strife?"

DL: Moses is saying I can't be responsible for all of you.

AP: He says that explicitly in Deuteronomy 1:10: "I cannot bear the burden of you by myself."

DL: Right. This is Moses as the reluctant, often weary, leader.

AP: We continue with Moses's instructions to his people: "Get you from each one of your tribes wise men, and understanding, and full of knowledge, and I will make them heads over you . . . ." Moses is telling them to designate wise leaders, and he will give them authority. "And you answered me and said, 'The thing which thou hast spoken is good for us to do.'"

DL: In other words, "You"—my fellow Israelites—answered me and agreed it was the right course. And Moses, in the next verses, says these new leaders should adjudicate disputes fairly, without fear or favor.

AP: Yes. And Moses tells them if they get stuck and can't decide the right verdict, to bring the conundrum to him and he will assist: "For the judgment is God's, and the cause that is too hard for you, you shall bring unto me and I will hear it" (Deut. 1:17). So Moses is telling his people: "I couldn't adjudicate disputes alone, I couldn't lead by myself, and neither can you. You need to deputize, delegate, and feel free to ask for my help if necessary." We've heard this admonition before.

DL: Yes, we did—straight from God and from Moses's father-in-law, Yitro. This parsha gives us an opportunity to explore what happens when a story gets retold.

AP: Let's talk about when it was *first* told in Exodus.

DL: It is from parsha Yitro, which is the parsha of the Ten Commandments. The Israelites are at the foot of Mount Sinai, and before they receive the Ten Commandments, Yitro travels from his homeland to where the Israelites are encamped. The Torah tells us that Yitro is a Midianite priest, a religious man who has heard about the miraculous exodus from Egypt and is drawn to connect to the God who has performed these miracles. After he arrives, he sees that Moses is spending the entire day adjudicating the people. Moses has a line a mile long; he has to hear all their complaints, and Yitro says essentially, "You're going to burn out."

AP: "You can't do all of this yourself."

DL: Let's look back at Exodus 18:17:

> And Moses's father-in-law said unto him, "The thing thou dost is not good; that will surely wear away both thou and the people

with thee. For this thing is too heavy for thee; thou are not able to perform it thyself alone. Harken now unto my voice. I will give thee council and God shall be with thee. Be thou for the people towards God, that thou may bring their causes before God. Moreover, thou shalt provide out of all the people able men such as fear God, men of truth, hating covetousness. And place such over them: be rulers of thousands, rulers of hundreds, rulers of fifties, rulers of tens, and let them judge the people at all seasons."

Yitro tells Moses that trying to take on too much isn't just bad for him, it's also bad for the people.

AP: We see the parallels between this Exodus parsha and the start of Deuteronomy. In both, the lesson is: don't go it alone. No one person can judge, lead, or advise *everyone else*. No man is an island.

DL: Yitro continues:

"And it shall be that every great matter they bring unto thee, but every small matter they shall judge. So shall it be easier for yourself, and they shall bear the burden with thee. If you do this thing and God commands you, you shall be able to endure, and all of the people shall go to their place in peace." And Moses harkened unto the voice of his father-in-law and did all that he had said.

There is a real power to this story. Here, this non-Jew, Yitro, who was not part of the Exodus, is the one who lays out how to set up their legal system and leadership. And Moses follows Yitro's suggestions.

AP: What is your response to this?

DL: I'm shocked and impressed at the same time. What does it mean that, right in the middle of this narrative about God giving the Torah to the Israelites, we hear that the Torah is open to all voices, even those of a non-Jew, like Yitro? I'm struck by the fact that the way in which the Torah is going to be implemented in practice—the leadership structure, the judicial structure—is based on the advice of this foreigner. And then you get to our parsha in Deuteronomy, and Moses is saying—

AP: He's appropriating Yitro's advice as his own!

DL: Yes! Moses is essentially saying, "I realized I couldn't handle the burden of adjudicating the people by myself, so here's this idea I came up with: I'll appoint other judges and delegate some of this responsibility." Moses is stealing the credit.

AP: Plagiarism!

DL: I'm not sure he's *intending* to steal the credit, but for whatever reason, he leaves Yitro out of the retelling. And that means, in this version, we've lost the power of that story: that we can learn from outsiders—from a Yitro—even when it comes to what it means to live by God's Torah.

AP: I'm bothered by that. It's extremely symbolic that Moses doesn't just learn from an outsider but that he is directed by him and listens. Moses should have acknowledged that his teacher was Yitro.

DL: I agree. Absolutely. Maybe the *point* is that we have both stories. The other story with Yitro still exists; both are still in the Torah, so we haven't lost the first story.

AP: That brings us back to the question of, "Why retrace our steps? Why go through this all again?" I think people who come to the Torah anew don't understand why things need to be repeated. As if it didn't sink in the first time.

DL: That might be the case, because the first story was experienced forty years earlier, chronologically; many of the people hadn't even been born at the time these retold events took place. I think maybe you answered your question—now that we're about to enter the Land, maybe the Israelites need past events recapped in a certain way so they will internalize the lessons that Moses believes they need to learn.

AP: So I shouldn't focus on the fact that the story is redundant, because it's being retold through a different lens and to different people.

DL: Right. The *mitzvah* of the Passover seder is not to tell the story, it's to *retell* the story. We don't read the verses in the Bible at the seder table even though it's a great Exodus story. Why *not* just read it? Because by *retelling* it rather than repeating it, we shape it and frame it, emphasizing the parts that we think are most important, the lessons we have to learn. That's what's going on here. Every time we read this retelling, we should ask ourselves, "What is the *new* lesson? Why is Moses presenting it this way to the people, and how is that supposed to guide them in a different way than the previous version?"

AP: Let's also touch on what the content actually says. It's very striking to me that this is the foundation of our judicial system and that it is very explicitly talking about balance, fairness, and impartiality. "Hear out your fellow Israelites and decide justly between one party and the other—be it a fellow Israelite or a stranger" (Deut. 1:16).

The Hebrew for "You shall not be partial to any person"—as I understand it—is "do not recognize, or be partial to, the face of any man," which means any race or creed.

DL: It means if you're adjudicating a dispute that involves someone you know, you can't allow that relationship—that recognition—into the courtroom.

AP: I'm struck by the directive in 1:17—"You shall hear the small and the great alike." That's an admirable judicial system.

DL: Again, in theory. It's not always realized, but yes.

AP: It's the way the system is built, but not necessarily the way it's carried out.

DL: That's true. There are admirable structures in place. But to hold up a model—and tell me if this is too political, but if you ask a politician—

AP: You can get a little political.

DL: If you were to ask politicians what their primary objective is once they get into office, and if they were fully honest about it, they would almost always say, "To get reelected." I'd like to hear the politician who says, "To do what's right, to act justly toward the people, and to fight for their well-being." It's important to hold that up as an ideal, even if we don't always achieve it.

AP: Going back to verse 1:16—here's a slightly different translation: "Hear the causes between your brethren, and judge righteously between a man and his brother and the stranger that is with him." If there are more apt words for our time, I don't know them. I believe the stranger that is with us—the person who feels foreign or alien—is often stigmatized, not necessarily honored or heard.

DL: Yes, and to tie it to our opening discussion, the takeaway for me is the stories we tell ourselves about who we are as a people—whether as a Jewish people or an American people. What are our values? What are we striving for? Values shape society. That has a huge impact on how these systems play out in reality.

AP: To your point about the fact that the first story—with Yitro—was a long time ago, it's true that every time we hear something, we absorb it differently, depending on where we are in our lives. So, maybe we do have to keep retelling it again and again.

DL: You're right, Abby. There can be wisdom in repetition.

Devarim to Va'etchanan

Moses continues his public recounting of the Israelites' journey. There is a retelling of how the spies brought back a grim report about the dangers in the Land, resulting in God's punishing decree that the Israelites spend the next forty years wandering through the desert. This retelling differs from the first in that the people—not God—are the ones who ask that the spies be sent to scout out the Land.

The story continues: God instructs the Israelites to pass through Seir—the land of Esau's descendants—and through Moab without doing anything that might provoke either area's inhabitants. The Israelites comply, but when they reach the land of Heshbon, its king, Sihon, refuses to let them pass. The Israelites go to war against him, destroying his army and seizing the spoils of war. The same occurs with Og, the king of Bashan. God assigns the lands formerly under Sihon and Og's control to the tribes of Reuban, Gad, and the half-tribe of Manasseh, on the condition that they cross over the Jordan River with the people and fight alongside them in conquering the land of Canaan.

VA'ETCHANAN

וָאֶתְחַנַּן

AP: Va'etchanan means, "And I supplicated." Who is supplicating, Dov?

DL: Moses is supplicating—humbly begging—God. We are retelling the whole story of the Exodus leading up to the edge of the land of Israel, and Moses is telling the people that when he was told he could not go into the Land, he supplicated God to let him enter.

AP: This is the only time that he says, "Please let me in."

DL: Correct. Earlier, when God tells Moses he can't go into the Land, the narrative just continues, without recording any response. Here, when Moses is retelling the story to the people, he is letting them know that he prayed and begged God to let him in.

AP: This is Deuteronomy 3:23:

> I pleaded with the Lord at that time, saying, "Oh Lord, God, You who let Your servant see the first works of Your greatness and Your mighty hand, You whose powerful deeds no god in heaven or on earth can equal! Let me, I pray, cross over and see the good land on the other side of the Jordan, that good hill country, and the Lebanon." But the Lord was wrathful with me on your account and would not listen to me. The Lord said to me, "Enough! Never speak to Me of this matter again!"

It feels a little unfair that God stops Moses from even appealing to him; Moses has earned the chance to be heard this one time.

DL: You're right. What does it mean that Moses's appeals have been "too much"? How relentlessly has he been going on about this? We only have a few verses recording his prayers. One interesting way of reading this is that the words in 3:26 for "Enough!" are *rav lach*—meaning "it's enough *for you*," and God is saying, "Moses, you have done enough. You have achieved enough. Step back and let somebody else take the mantle."

AP: I like that interpretation a lot.

DL: There's also another way of reading 3:26, where Moses tells the people, "God got angry against me for your sake," or "on account of you." We would normally read that word as, "*You* are to blame. It is all because of how you have acted that I can't go into the Promised Land." But perhaps "for your sake" actually means: "I can't go in because you need a different type of leader, somebody without all this baggage and this relationship to God, who is not larger than life. You don't need me with you in order to bring some miraculous deliverance. That is why God has told me not to enter."

AP: This is going to sound mundane, but in our lives, there are times where we have lobbied for ourselves—say, for a promotion or some kind of recognition—and someone has said, "Enough! Stop asking." It's not necessarily about humility but about taking a step back because it's not the best plan.

DL: That's a great parallel. You know, in the earlier verse, Moses does not even say, "Let me *lead* the people to the Land." He says, "Let me, I pray, cross over and *see* the good land" (Deut. 3:25). It's as if he is saying, "I don't need to lead them, but all my life has been building up to entering the Land; let me at least get a taste of that." But God won't allow that. It's, "You really need to step back and let somebody else step forward."

AP: Let's jump ahead a bit. Moses accepts the fact that he's not going, and then he tells his people essentially, "You need to understand how remarkable this thing is that you're inheriting." It's almost like he is selling it to them and, at the same time, admonishing them to be good citizens and be observant of God's laws. I'm in Deuteronomy 4:9:

> But take utmost care and watch yourselves scrupulously, so that you do not forget the things that you saw with your own eyes and so that they do not fade from your mind as long as you live. And make them known to your children and to your children's children.

And then later, in 4:32:

> You have but to inquire about bygone ages that came before you, ever since God created man on earth, from one end of heaven to the other: has anything as grand as this ever happened, or has its like ever been known?

And then finally, 5:23:

> For what mortal ever heard the voice of the living God speak out of the fire, as we did, and lived?

DL: He is finding different ways to persuade them that they have to live life according to what God has said. One of his approaches is, "Look how amazing your relationship with God is! Remember what you experienced. You saw that God has done all these incredible things. If you internalize that, then hopefully you will be motivated to live by what God has told you." A lot of the Book of Deuteronomy is Moses seeing the people as rebellious and disobedient and perhaps even thinking, *They now have to go into the Land and follow God's* mitzvot *and commandments while building a society, but this is going to be a real struggle for them; what is going to keep them on the right path?* That's the way I see it.

AP: Even now, when we are living through such discord, debate, and strain on our social fabric after the killing of George Floyd, it's extraordinary to see the world we have been given, to watch the people working through it. And even more so during the virus, because we're not out of the pandemic as we talk today. We have seen snapshots of humanity, of people lifting each other up, of a world that is both extraordinarily difficult and selfless all at once. Maybe I'm getting mushy, but when we feel lucky to be alive, things come into focus. Do you relate to that at all?

DL: The verses are speaking about when you have experienced something supernatural that is unequaled ever in history. God spoke to all of us at Mount Sinai—

AP: And there was God's miraculous parting of the Red Sea.

DL: Yes, but what you are speaking about is a gratitude that we don't acknowledge. That's a little different.

AP: I guess I am talking about daily miracles, and you are saying they're not miracles.

DL: Oh, I definitely agree that we can and should look at them as miracles, and it seems you're doing a better job at that than I am. That's a great way to translate these messages into our world, our reality, and it is such a needed message. I see the verse, however, as pointing us to something beyond the everyday. If I had to connect what's going on in our nation right now to this verse calling on us to remember the giving of the Torah at Mount Sinai, I would go back to the founding principles of the country—the Constitution and the ideals that this country was founded upon. In the last few years, I fear we may have lost our bedrock belief in those principles, what it means to be living by and inspired by those values, that vision for a "more perfect union." That's how I would bring this parsha into this present moment.

AP: A lot of these lines repeat the sentiment, "Do you understand how lucky you are?" when the text says, "For what mortal ever heard the voice of the living God speak out of the fire, as we did, and lived?"

DL: It's pushing the people, saying to them, "And therefore you have to live your life according to the commandments." Another important point is that the verse also states, "You shall pass this on to your children." This is talking about the obligation of transmission. It's an interesting question to stop and ask ourselves what we are transmitting. Normally, we think we are transmitting ideas: we believe in an ethical God. Or we are transmitting *halachot* laws, such as *Shabbat* observance, *kashrus* [kosher laws], and so on. But the Torah is telling us more—that we should *transmit the experience of Mount Sinai*. Part of a lived religion is connecting to those powerful experiences. What do you think, Abby? How do we reconnect to the giving of the Torah at Mount Sinai? What ritual should we have?

AP: We should stand in the wind and the thunder and the rain.

DL: Maybe! Some people say that the reading of the Torah in the synagogue is a way to recreate that moment at Sinai, but it doesn't have the same power.

AP: I understand the resonance of Mount Sinai intellectually and symbolically more than I do some kind of physical experience. Whenever I have observed the holiday of Shavuot, which marks the receiving of the Torah and involves the ritual of studying all night, I mostly just get tired; I'm stimulated by the learning, but I'm not feeling the earth shake.

DL: In my community, the Modern Orthodox community—and I won't speak for all of us, but at least based on what I've experienced—we do really well at educating the mind. Like, "Here are all the laws. Here is what the Torah says. Here is what the commentators and the Talmud say." But I don't think we do well at all in terms of transmitting the experience of feeling connected to God, of what it means to really feel like you are reaching out to God in prayer, what it meant in the past to stand at Mount Sinai. The experiential aspect is a significant part of what I think is missing from our religious lives. I don't mean totally, but that issue of transmission is one we need to improve upon.

AP: Maybe we end with the hope that we have a little more thunder, fire, and lighting in our lives.

DL: Amen to that.

Va'etchanan to Eikev

Moses elaborates to the Israelites on the importance of them remembering the events of Mount Sinai, the direct experience of God's commanding voice, entering into a covenant with God, and receiving the Ten Commandments. Moses warns them against the seductions of idolatry and the desire to create a physical representation of God. They are told that after many years in the Land they will succumb to the temptations of idolatry, and will experience the punishment of exile, but they will eventually return to the worship of God.

Moses emphasizes to them their unique relationship with God and the critical importance of loving and obeying God, and it is here he articulates the *Shema*: "Hear O Israel, the Lord is our God, the Lord is one" (Deut. 6:4). This is Judaism's primary declaration of faith. The people are told to do "what is right and good in the eyes of God" (Deut. 6:18) and to tell their children the story of how God took them out from Egypt and how their relationship with God is the key to all their future success.

Moses then urges the Israelites to remember that it is thanks purely to God's love that they will get to enter the Promised Land. They are told that God freed the Israelites from Egypt so they could become a holy nation, and to this end, they have a responsibility to conquer the land and destroy all its idols and must not intermarry with the other nations who inhabit the land. They are to know that God will ultimately reward and bring kindness to those who keep God's covenant.

EIKEV

עֵקֶב

DL: Our parsha today is Eikev.

AP: Which means?

DL: "On account of" or "Due to."

AP: "Due to." That's a scintillating title.

DL: The verse is saying, "*Due to* your keeping of the commandments, God will bless you in all ways." From there it goes on to say what might lead you away from observing God's commandments.

AP: Okay. I'm starting at verse 8:11.

DL: Here, Moses is retelling the story of the Torah, preparing people to enter the Land and anticipating what it's going to be like.

AP: To set this up, he's giving them a warning:

> Take care, lest you forget the Lord, your God, and fail to keep His commandments, His rules, and His laws, which I enjoin upon you today. When you have eaten your fill and have built fine houses to live in, and your herds and flocks have multiplied, and your silver and gold have increased, and everything you own has prospered, beware lest your heart grow haughty and you forget the Lord, your God—who freed you from the land of Egypt, the house of bondage . . . And you say to yourselves, "My own power and the might of my own hand have won this wealth for me." Remember that it is the Lord, your God who allows you the power to get wealth, in fulfillment of the covenant that he made on oath with your fathers, as is still the case.

DL: In other words, "You have accomplished nothing. It's all because of Me." How does that work for you, Abby?

AP: What I love about this is that God is basically saying, "You can't take credit for the bounty and success you have in your life; it is a gift bestowed." Yes, God is speaking, but I feel like it's less about God wanting credit and more about the word "haughty" or the Hebrew word for it.

DL: The word is *ram*—"lifted up" or "high."

AP: Yes, in other words, "Don't think so much of yourself." It's about humility in the face of incredible blessings you did not earn. To me, it's very relevant for the current generations of, "Me, me, me. I did this. I made this. I deserve this."

DL: You're saying that even if we take God out of the equation, it's about appreciating the privileges you were born into—living in America, the society, protections, rights, and systems that have *enabled* you to succeed.

AP: Yes, but also look at what I wake up to: I have the breakfast that I choose. I live in this incredible land and city. What's around us that we take for granted? In some sense, we stop seeing those things because we lose sight of the fact that we're not entitled to any of it. It's all from the grace of—whether it's God or some other force in the universe—that we were given these blessings. Without being all mushy about it, I think it completely changes your perspective to just feel *lucky*.

DL: It's cultivating a sense of gratitude or, as Abraham Joshua Heschel would say, a sense of awe.

AP: Right. "Radical amazement." Wonder.

DL: A chapter earlier, the Torah talked about reciting a blessing after you've eaten a meal, to appreciate that everything is from God. It's mainly for this reason that the Rabbis told us to recite blessings throughout the day—before you eat, when you wake up in the morning and hear the rooster crowing, before bed.

AP: I don't wake up to many roosters in Manhattan.

DL: You get the idea. We are supposed to feel blessed from the moment we open our eyes each day.

AP: And even when you go to the bathroom.

DL: Yes, we're grateful to God that the internal plumbing is in working order. As an Orthodox Jew, I think the challenge is connecting to the power of those statements of gratitude and what they're supposed to cultivate within us rather than just, "Check, check, check. I said all the blessings; I did what I had to do."

AP: I say *Modah Ani*, "I give thanks to you," every morning before I put my feet on the floor.

DL: I didn't know that.

AP: It's something I have been doing for years. It's just a way of taking a moment and saying, "Oh my God, I get another day. Thank you."

DL: A wonderful thought.

AP: Gratitude reorients you. Instead of waking up with all that is wrong or annoying in my mind, or the things that I messed up or forgot, I think instead, *Look how lucky I am; I get another chance*, or, *I get to breathe again and have my morning coffee and see my family and friends and do interesting things* . . . . It's kind of amazing that this Torah text exists, because I think it's so applicable to the modern moment, where we often say, "It's my own power and the might of my own hand that have won this wealth for me." Remember when President Obama got in a lot of trouble when he said, "You didn't build that," and people were saying, "Yes, I did! Why are you taking that away from me?" I think what the president was saying was, "We have to watch the solipsism of our success. There's so much we obtain simply by way of good fortune, because we happened to be born somewhere, because we live next door to someone, because we had that opportunity, that privilege." It doesn't mean you can't take pride in what you accomplish; it's not about demeaning your own accomplishments.

DL: That's interesting because the verse warns, "You're going to say, 'My strength and my power did this for me.' It's not you. It's God." I think you and I would like to add, "It's not *just* your strength. You contributed, but God is also a part of that." It occurs to me that maybe that's what the Torah means. The verse says, "For God is the one who gives you the strength to create wealth." It's true, what you achieved was through your effort, your dedication, and your talents. But who gave you those talents? Where did your strength come from?

AP: When you look at that line I quoted in Deuteronomy 8:12: "When you have eaten your fill and built fine houses to live in . . ." that's again what you were saying about forgetting to give thanks after you eat. There are so many riches—although not everyone has access to them, and there's so much grave poverty and struggle—but God is essentially saying, "For those who are sated, pay attention, be careful." There is a caution in that, and to me, these are the verses that every Jewish person should be thinking about: What is at our core? Humility or hubris?

DL: Right, and I want to translate that into the practical. What's a concrete consequence of that? What does it mean when we realize that it all comes from God or when we fully appreciate all the gifts that we're given from society? I think it would translate to, "It's not all ours," and to asking the question, "What (or who) do we owe for our success?" Which would lead to giving back—through charity and philanthropy. Why are people philanthropists? Because they realize they've been blessed, and they want to give back.

AP: It can also be guilt.

DL: Maybe. Depends. But from a religious perspective, if this is all from God, then I should use my material blessings in a godly way. We can't deny that the Torah's emphasis is not just about gratitude, it's about God. The Torah wants God to be central to our lives and for us to see God in everything.

AP: What makes you think I'm leaving God out of that? I'm talking about being grateful to God—not about being grateful *generally*. The Divine *is* operating for me, but it may not be for other people. What I'm saying is: at least get to gratitude, one way or another. Maybe some people don't talk about who bestowed all of this upon them because they don't believe in a deity, but I do, so I'm conscious of that. To me, it's a reorientation. Instead of, "I did all this," it's "I've been given a heck of a lot."

DL: Absolutely, I just didn't want to lose sight of the centrality of God.

AP: You never want to lose sight of the centrality of God, and I appreciate that. But to push you on what you mean by it: and therefore what?

DL: Therefore, "What do I do with this bounty? How do I use it? Do I give it to the poor?"

AP: Are you saying you have to imitate God—or try?

DL: Yes, you *should* imitate God. And, you must realize that our blessings coming from God is meaningful in a purely religious, experiential way. I want to live in a world of meaning and God's presence, not a world devoid of God.

AP: Maybe we should end by rereading verse 8:18, because it's at the core of all of this—the word "covenant." Here it is: "Remember that it is the Lord, your God who gives you the power to get wealth, in fulfillment of the covenant made on oath with your fathers, as is still the case." What I love is that part of the contract is to remember how you got here and how you've obtained what you have; that's part of the covenant we've signed on for.

DL: You're spot-on. And what I'm going to take away from this parsha is to aim for more intent when I say those morning blessings.

AP: You could call me on the phone after you pray, and I'll say, "Did you mean it, Dov? Did you really mean it? Say it like you mean it."

DL: I will!

Eikev to Re'eh

The Israelites are told by Moses that God will bring them into the Promised Land, described as a place of "wheat, barley, grape, fig, and pomegranate; a land of olive oil and date-honey" (Deut. 8:9). When the people eat and are satisfied, they must give a blessing to God "for the good land that God has given you" (Deut. 8:11). This later becomes the practice of *birkat ha'mazon*, Grace After Meals.

Moses charges them to follow the path of God, who brings justice to "the orphan, widow and loves the stranger to give him bread and clothing," and that they likewise "should love the stranger, for you were strangers in the land of Egypt" (Deut. 10:18–19).

It is here that the second paragraph of the *Shema* appears: Moses tells them that if they do the *mitzvot*, God will bring the "rain in its time," and if they abandon the *mitzvot*, they will suffer exile. They are to bind *tefillin*—phylacteries—as a sign of God's Torah on "your hearts and between your eyes," and to put the words of the Torah on the *mezuzot* [doorposts] of their homes—the *mitzvah* of *mezuzah*. Finally, they are commanded to teach Torah to their children and to study it constantly, ". . . when you sit in your home and walk on the street, when you lie down and when you wake up" (Deut. 11:19).

The Torah now shifts to focus on how the people must protect themselves against the threats of idolatry when they enter the Land. They are to destroy all the idols and idolatrous places of worship. Unlike the pagans who offer their sacrifices "under every leafy tree," the Israelites will have only one single place to worship God, a place that God will choose—later to be identified as Jerusalem.

The kashrut laws are reiterated, as are *mitzvot* relating to the giving of tithes and the *mitzvah* to free Hebrew slaves after six years of servitude.

The people are told to observe the Sabbatical year when all debts are to be annulled. When approached by someone in need, they must respond generously: "Open up your hand to him . . . sufficient for what he is lacking" (Deut. 15:8). These verses serve as the basis for the *mitzvah* of *tzedakah*.

Re'eh

רְאֵה

DL: The name of this parsha—Re'eh—means "see." Moses is saying to the people: "You are about to enter the Land. *See* that I have placed before you two paths. Will you choose good, or will you choose evil? It is in your hands. How will you build that new society? How will you live your life? Which path will you walk?

AP: And the good path means following God's commandments.

DL: Right. We are done with the narrative thread in Deuteronomy—there's no more storyline. Moses has been retelling the whole story of the Exodus leading up to when his people are about to enter the land of Israel. But now he is also reiterating many of the laws that have been given in the past. "Deuteronomy" means "the second law," so we are in a heavy section of laws.

AP: Often, we hear Jewish parents say, "I want to pass on Jewish values to my kids," but I would defy most of those same parents to actually say where they are located in the Torah. That's not me being judgmental—that's just the reality; I include myself.

DL: I hear that.

AP: Here's where most of them are located, in an extremely definitive way, which I find moving. This is Deuteronomy 14:29:

> Then the Levite, who has no hereditary portion as you have, and the stranger, the fatherless, and the widow in your settlements shall come and eat their fill, so that the Lord, your God, may bless you in all the enterprises you undertake.

And then, in 15:7:

> If, however, there is a needy person among you, one of your kinsmen in any of your settlements in the land that the Lord, your God, is giving you, do not harden your heart and shut your hand against your needy kinsmen. Rather, you must open your hand and lend whatever is sufficient to meet the need.

And then the final one from 15:10, which I think is among the strongest about helping someone in need:

> Give to him readily and have no regrets when you do so, for in return the Lord, your God, will bless you in all your efforts and in all your undertakings.

Obviously, on its face, the upshot of this is that you have to be compassionate. It's a directive, an instruction to be kind.

DL: I see this not as a mandate to be kind. I think the *mitzvah* of *tzedakah* is not to be nice to people, it's that you have a *responsibility* to people; that's what I read in this verse. Compassion is like extra credit and not a fundamental moral obligation. In other words, if I have a responsibility to someone and am not living up to it, I have wronged them.

AP: So, it's about what you do, as opposed to what you feel. You're saying, "I don't really care what your internal motivation is; this is simply what you need to *do*."

DL: Right.

AP: That's very Jewish. You can *feel* all the compassion you want, but what are you doing about the problem?

DL: Exactly. You should always act out of kindness because part of the *mitzvah* of giving *tzedakah* is not just the money; it's making the person feel loved, cared for, and recognized. That's obviously a core part, but I think that the driver is the responsibility. "Charity" comes from the Latin word—not that I know much Latin—*carus*, which means "love" or "dear," and it's rooted in a Christian concept that acts of charity are acts of love toward one's fellows. It comes across as, "Because I love you, I'm kind to you." An act of charity is an act of kindness. In stark contrast to this is the Jewish word *tzedakah*, which comes from the word *tzedek*, which means "justice." We recognize, as a fundamental function of society, that we must take care of everyone; we have an interconnected responsibility to everyone.

AP: The name of the parsha is "See," and that feels like so much of what all of us are reckoning with right now when it comes to who is still struggling or being shortchanged in this country. "You need to open your eyes. You need to open your eyes to what you have not seen or refused to see or neglected to see." I recognize that charge in this parsha—that each of us personally has an obligation to open our eyes and then to do something about what we see. Many of us have said, "I thought I *was* seeing," then realized how much we still weren't.

DL: That's a great point. In terms of how it plays out for the poor in this parsha, how many times are people in our community invisible to us? Do we know what's happening with our neighbors two blocks down? Sometimes, we may pass someone on the street who is sitting on the sidewalk asking for money, but we really don't even see them.

I think that the next verse speaks to the structural, societal issue that I was referring to earlier. Verse 15:11 of this section says, "For the poor will never cease from the land; therefore, I am commanding you to open up your hand to your brother, to your poor, to the destitute in your land." Why say, "The poor will never cease"? Is it to remind us there is an ongoing obligation? I think the Torah is saying, "This is the nature of society. There are always going to be people who are rich and those who are poor. Don't look down on the poor; understand that this is something systemic."

AP: And this isn't charity, it's dignity. That's something we talked about in a previous parsha. People are surprised that Judaism teaches you to not just give a handout, but to give a hand-up. There needs to be a way in which you are restoring someone's sense of self by not making them feel infantilized or diminished by some kind of financial rescue. You have to make sure they have an education, a job, equal pay. Economic justice goes beyond the temporary Band-Aid of some money or groceries.

DL: Absolutely. The verse constantly repeats, "Your brother in your land," like, "Look at this person as an equal. Nobody should think they are somehow lesser than you because you are more well-off." It's about affording fundamental dignity to everyone. Maimonides has a classic list of the hierarchy of *tzedakah*, and at the top of the list is giving someone a job. It's not giving them a big check, it's allowing them to maintain their dignity—to be a productive, equal member of society. If you read the parsha closely, it doesn't talk about giving a gift of money; it talks about *lending* money. Lending money recognizes somebody as your peer, someone you trust to pay you back, not somebody who is simply accepting your largess.

AP: As I listen to you, I feel like you're speaking even more to this moment where a lot of Black Americans are saying, "Enough with your compassion; we want action." All these organizations, whether they're law firms, publishers, or fashion designers, are being forced to look—to *see*—inside their own house. "Look at your colleagues; who is working there? Is it a diverse group? Is everyone paid fairly for their work?" These are the questions that are being asked right now; it's not about whether you are *feeling* their pain. It goes right to the parsha's directive: "Do people have dignity? Is equality made manifest factually, as opposed to just emotionally?"

DL: Let's all think about what we can do to live up to, not just kindness, but also to the mandate of justice and equality.

AP: I'll end with the line that you repeated from 15:11. "For there will never cease to be needy ones in your land, which is why I command you: open your hand." Open your hand.

Re'eh to Shoftim

Moses reiterates the laws of the festival of Passover, which commemorates the Exodus. The holiday's most fundamental requirements are the sacrifice and communal consumption of a lamb and a seven-day abstention from eating or possessing leavened bread. Following Passover, the Israelites must count off a seven-week period that culminates in the festival of Shavuot. In the fall, once the harvest has concluded, they will observe the seven-day festival of Sukkot—a joyous celebration of God's bounty. Each of these three holidays will include a pilgrimage to a holy place of God's choosing, thus they are known as *regalim*, or "pilgrimage festivals."

Moses further reminds the Israelites that they must establish a genuinely fair court system in order to ensure a just society. They are told that if there is a matter of law that is too difficult for them, they are to bring it to the "*kohanim* and the judge" who reside in the place that God chooses—later Jerusalem—and they will determine the meaning of the law. The people are then admonished to strictly follow the teaching of those authorities. These verses serve, in the Talmudic period, as the basis for the Rabbinic authority to interpret the laws of the Torah.

Shoftim

שֹׁפְטִים

AP: Shoftim is the plural for "judge"—because Moses is explaining God's command to appoint judges in the new judicial system. But we'll be zeroing in on the idea of a king, because Moses is telling the people, "You are going into this Land without me, and you're going to want to make a king." Dov, why don't you summarize before we read the verse?

DL: Moses predicts the people will say, "We want a king like all the nations around us." So Moses lays out some very particular parameters about what that king will have to do and keep to, in order to be a proper king for the Israelites.

AP: At that time, if you had a society, you had a king. But Moses is saying, "You can't have a king without strictures, without guardrails." We're in Deuteronomy 17:14:

> If, after you have entered the land that your God has assigned to you, and taken possession of it and settled in it, you decide, "I will set a king over me, as do all the nations about me," you shall be free to set a king over yourself, one chosen by the Lord, your God. Be sure to set as king over yourself one of your own people; you must not set a foreigner over you, one who is not your kinsman.

We can liken that to America today—the president must be an American citizen. The verse continues at 17:16:

> Moreover, he shall not keep many horses, or send people back to Egypt to add to his horses, since the Lord has warned you, "You must not go back that way again." And he shall not have many

> wives, lest his heart go astray; nor shall he amass silver and gold to excess.

What do you make of that? Is Moses basically saying, "Anyone who is to become king must remember who they are and where they've come from"? So they can't just suddenly become some fancy guy on a throne.

DL: Yes, it's exactly that. We might be concerned that a king not abuse his power for self-gain and self-aggrandizement, but the Torah is more focused on serving both the people and God. It's not about status, wealth, ego, and pride. The whole concern about the horses is that the king will lead the people back to Egypt, and the Torah wants us to stay out of Egypt.

AP: Moses continues about this new hypothetical king: "When he is seated on his royal throne, he shall have a copy of this Teaching written for him on a scroll by the Levitical priests." Basically, "Keep the Torah at your side. Don't lose sight of the official road map."

DL: Exactly. The Hebrew word for "teaching" is, in fact, *Torah*. The monarchy that is envisioned here is one that is bound by the laws of the Torah—something like a constitutional monarchy—and this verse is saying, "You're not above the law; you are bound by the law." And also, "You're under God."

AP: Here is the last verse of this section, 17:19: "Let it remain with him and let him read it in all his life, so that he may learn to revere the Lord, his God, to observe faithfully every word of this Teaching as well as these laws." It's pretty powerful to say to any future king, "Don't let the education stop. Don't get complacent. Don't get lazy. You're not just a leader, you're a learner, and you are going to keep studying."

DL: That's actually very beautiful, I don't think I've ever noticed that. I always read it more as, "You are ultimately under God, or under the Torah. You must live up to the Torah and represent it to the people." But I really like your point about humility and always being open to learning and growing—I hadn't thought about it that way.

AP: Isn't the point of humility knowing you really don't know it all?

DL: Yes. Part of being a leader is recognizing that you don't have all the answers, and you should constantly be learning. It's a really beautiful insight.

AP: I know we're supposed to avoid politics, but I do think about reports that President Trump doesn't read a lot. Or at least, doesn't study up—whether before a meeting, a summit, or in general. This idea in the parsha—"Let him read in it all his life" is compelling: that any king—and by analogy—any president, prime minister, or leader—has to have humility about knowledge, learning. We're missing that in our current "king," in my opinion.

DL: If you ask someone what books are on their nightstand and the answer is, "None," that's a problem.

AP: The idea of study being connected to leadership is a big takeaway for this parsha.

DL: Yes, definitely. What do you make of the fact that it also says in the immediately preceding verse, "And it shall be, when he sits upon his royal throne, that he shall write him a copy of this Torah . . ." Would there be meaning in the act of putting the words directly onto paper, or rather parchment?

AP: My translation from Sefaria reads: "When he is seated on his royal throne, he shall have a copy of this Teaching written for him."

DL: That's a possible translation, but it's not the only one. A more literal translation is that he must write it himself. If we go with that read, what would be the point of the king writing the Torah himself?

AP: There is more personalization—and frankly more retention—if the king has to copy the words of the Torah himself without scribes to do it for him.

DL: I agree. You've written books, Abby. I'm in the middle of working on one, too, and I think there's a profound sense of connection when you are the one putting the words to the paper. Even if it's just copying the words of the Torah, as it is in the case of the king, I can see it creating a close sense of identification and ownership. Remember the verse that says, "It should be with him all of his days." For the Rabbis, that meant it was something the king physically carried with him everywhere he went.

AP: It's a discipline, in a sense; you're incomplete without it.

DL: I wonder what draws you to the idea of being a lifelong learner. Why does it speak to you so much?

AP: Because it's more than just an idea or slogan to me. Continual learning is something to strive for. I guess it's how I've tried to approach my own Jewish path. When I wrote *My Jewish Year* and was researching and observing every holiday in the Jewish calendar for the first time—which I know you have done since you were in utero!—I was very careful to confess that, "I am a sojourner here. I am trying not to parachute in and say that what I am learning means that I know more or have mastered anything." It's just the opposite. I was asking rabbis and scholars to bring me along, to help me fill in the blanks. And to a rabbi, to a scholar, no one turned me down when I asked for guidance, for education. Everyone said, "Yes, let's talk about Tu B'Shevat for two hours!" To me, that was the richness of the journey more than anything: having a kind of accessible laboratory—so many people from so many directions in terms of Jewish life and observance saying, "I'd love to talk to you about that. I'd love to help you there." That generosity from teachers is hopefully not just making me a better writer and a better journalist. It's making me a better Jew.

DL: And a better person.

AP: Hopefully. I'm still shamefully flawed, and my therapist can tell you all the ways why. But when I think about a king, I think about exactly that same kind of humility—a sense of how small you are in the universe.

DL: Do you think that learning engenders humility? Or do you think you came in with that? Because when some people learn, it feeds arrogance and a sense of superiority.

AP: I feel like the more I learn, the more inexpert I become. Because the landscape is overwhelming as much as it is awe-inspiring. It stops a lot of would-be learners from even starting, because it feels like, "I'll never know all this; it's too late to begin." But for someone like you, who has mastered such a sizable amount—and I say this not just to praise you, but because you're living this learning and teaching it on a daily basis—how does this tension play out between mastery and humility?

DL: When I took the position of president of our seminary, I came into the job knowing I did not have all the answers. I've been a lifelong teacher, a scholar—not the head of an institution. I knew I had a lot of learning to do and that I'd need a lot of people to collaborate with me. It's made me a better leader, and people have, I think, responded to that. I still have a lot to learn, but when I see leaders make mistakes, I feel it's often because they are too self-confident and not open to learning. There's a sense that they always have to project that they know the answers. When something doesn't go the way we hoped at the *yeshiva*, my mantra to the staff is: What can we learn from it? How can we be better going forward?

How about you? You were president of Central Synagogue. What was it like for you in that role?

AP: Genuinely humbling. I think when you're representing the congregation from a layperson's perspective, you have to pay closest attention to other people's stories, concerns, and experiences. I saw my role not as a leader-in-chief but as a listener-in-chief. That doesn't mean I never made decisions or weighed in on hard calls. But I hope that I never did it without a lot of listening first, which is essentially what this parsha is asking us to do. You cannot be a leader without listening, which is, to me, analogous to learning.

DL: May we both always be learning and always be growing.

AP: Amen to that.

Shoftim to Ki Tetze

Moses cautions the Israelites against requesting or listening to the counsel of any type of sorcerer, as to do so runs counter to faith in the one God. While God will provide prophets for the Israelites in future generations, the people must also remain vigilant against being seduced and misled by false prophets.

Moses then highlights certain elements of the justice system, such as the laws of witnesses and cities of refuge designated for a person who kills someone unintentionally and needs to be protected from the victim's kin who is seeking vengeance.

Warfare, too, is subject to God's laws. A specially designated *kohen* is to play a role in preparing the people for battle. He is to go out with the troops and proclaim that God will be with them and will ensure their success in battle. The *kohen* then announces that those who have unfinished business—those who have betrothed a woman but not consummated the marriage or built a house but have not begun to reside in it—are exempt from serving. That is also true, somewhat surprisingly, of anyone who is overly fearful of the upcoming battle, lest his fear spread throughout the troops.

The people are then commanded that when they prepare to besiege a city, the city must first be offered terms of peace before any attack. They are warned against destroying fruit trees for the sake of using their wood to build implements of siege—*lo tashchit* ["you shall not destroy the trees"]—which later becomes the *mitzvah* against wasteful destruction of property or of anything on God's planet.

KI TETZEI

כִּי־תֵצֵא

DL: Ki Tetzei means, "When you go out . . . ." In this case, "When you go out to war" or "When you take the field against your enemies."

AP: Who's going out?

DL: "You" refers to the people of Israel who are waging war against the enemy.

AP: Things kind of get ugly in this parsha. It's one of the challenging moments in the Torah that we might want to obscure, forget, or excise, because it's tough stuff. But I'm going to read it because it's there, and we do not dodge our own texts. This is Moses speaking in Deuteronomy 21:10:

> When you take the field against your enemies and the Lord, your God, delivers them into your power and you take some of them captive, and you see among the captives a beautiful woman and you desire her and would take her to wife, you shall bring her into your house, she shall trim her hair, pare her nails, and discard her captive's garb.

Let's pause here. Why is she cutting her fingernails?

DL: I think the best explanation is that this is a ritual of mourning, and we are giving her an opportunity to mourn for her parents.

AP: That's kind of a gross detail, but you're going to come back to it.

DL: I am.

AP: I can't wait. To continue 21:13:

> She shall spend a month's time in your house lamenting her father and mother; after that you may come to her and possess her, and

> she shall be your wife. Then, should you no longer want her, you must release her outright. You must not sell her for money: since you had your will of her, you must not enslave her.

Oh, that's so nice. "You raped her, but you can't enslave her." That's her redemption, her deliverance—that you didn't make her a slave. Even though you obviously already enslaved her.

DL: The word that was translated as "possess her" is more accurately, "have sex with her."

AP: I wonder why they soft-pedal that. They're essentially saying, "If you're at war, and you see a woman you desire on the enemy's side, take her if you want her."

DL: Let's talk about why this is so troubling to us.

AP: It's not that complicated.

DL: But I think it will help to spell it out. We're talking about taking people captive and having sex with a woman against her will. But what was the historical reality at that time? Until very recently, people would go to war, take captives, enslave them, and the female slaves were used as sexual property. So, this is taking place within a particular context.

AP: Ah, context.

DL: That said, we would have hoped the Torah would have done more to repudiate this reality. The Rabbis don't so much mitigate the laws of the story, but they do acknowledge the problem. They say the Torah is speaking against man's evil inclination, meaning that this is a law that ideally should not be on the books, and the only reason it is, is because men—particularly men at war, outside of civilized society—will act in unrestrained ways and rape women on the battlefield. The Torah is saying, "Let's try to get control of this situation." It's not ideal, but at least—

AP: So the justification is that this kind of thing happens in war—women are taken and raped, brutalized, and traumatized. And it's almost like the Rabbis are assuming that default behavior and saying, "Okay, knowing that bad things are going to happen in times of war, at least you cannot take a woman and make her your slave."

DL: That's after you've returned from war and taken her into your house. You then have a choice—either marry her or set her free. But the

Torah places limits on the soldier's behavior even before that, while he is still on the battlefield by saying, "Don't act at that moment when you see her. Don't rape her on the battlefield. If you take her captive, she can become your wife, but you have to go through this procedure."

AP: What "procedure" are you referring to?

DL: That the woman must first spend a month in your house grieving her lost parents. This allows you time to calm down and decide if you just want her sexually—in which case, you may not have sex with her and must set her free—or if you are prepared to marry her. You're back in society as opposed to being on the battlefield, so hopefully society's constraints will exert some influence. That's how the Rabbis read it: that by requiring this delay, it would hopefully lead to a change of heart instead of them acting on their worst impulses.

AP: I want to give another example in this parsha where the Rabbis try to soften thorny things. The part I want to talk about is how we deal with the wayward son—the son who is drunk and disobedient. This is a few verses later in 21:18 of Deuteronomy:

> If a man has a wayward and defiant son, who does not heed his father or mother and does not obey them even after they discipline him, his father and mother shall take hold of him and bring him out to the elders of his town at the public place of his community. They shall say to the elders of his town, "This son of ours is disloyal and defiant; he does not heed us. He is a glutton and a drunkard." Thereupon, the men of his town shall stone him to death. Thus, you will sweep out evil from your midst: all Israel will hear and be afraid.

You are publicly stoning your son to death because he drank too much.

DL: Exactly. Here the Rabbis don't just contextualize it, they significantly limit its scope in practice, almost to the point of non-existence. They say this never actually occurred—no parent ever stoned their son for being rebellious or for being a glutton and a drunkard. They interpret the verse as demanding impossible-to-be-satisfied criteria before this stoning can take place. The Rabbis do this type of thing in other cases as well. For example, the Torah often talks about imposing the death penalty for various sins, but the Rabbis say it would have been practically impossible for a court to gather testimony sufficient to execute anyone.

AP: Then why are these laws in the Torah?

DL: The Rabbis have an answer for that, too. They say, "So we can learn from it." They never tell us exactly *what* we're supposed to learn from it, and that's the essence of the question we're asking—what is the constructive lesson we can learn from this thing that will never happen?

AP: Is the Fifth Commandment at play here—that you're supposed to honor your mother and father—and this stoning threat is the extreme of what could happen if you don't?

DL: Absolutely. But are we really supposed to believe that it would go that far? That someone would be stoned to death for getting drunk? Do you have any thoughts, Abby?

AP: You answer first. You posed the question.

DL: The verse ends by saying, "All Israel will hear and be afraid." I think there might be a fear that rebelliousness against one's parents will undermine the institution of parental authority. It's not just, "My son disrespected me, and therefore he deserves to die," but if people can flagrantly and publicly defy their parents without consequence—and maybe it's more about the defiance than it is about the drinking—what will this do to the institution of parenthood? And while this is extreme, it's a recurring complaint that people have, which is like, "Ugh. Kids these days! It used to be that they were seen and not heard. Whatever happened to respecting your parents?" I believe that's a piece of this.

AP: There's also a reluctance for parents to share their disappointment in their kid's failures. We all fear that our communities will find out our child tripped up in some way, particularly when there is drug or alcohol abuse involved, or if a child drops out of school. The humiliation of feeling like you've failed as a parent is like a kind of social exile.

DL: Maybe that's why the Rabbis say these stonings will never occur: the parents won't want to publicize their child's rebelliousness and have them punished in this way, because ultimately, it could reflect poorly on them.

I think that is an interesting way of reading the verse, where the parents say to the court: "We've beaten him, and he won't listen to us."

When I read that text, I think, *Hmm . . . You've beaten him, and he continues to disobey. Did it ever occur to you that there might be some correlation there?* It's like that saying, "The beatings will continue until morale improves." Maybe if you had parented him differently, you would have seen different results.

AP: Of course, sometimes we all overcorrect as parents, and this is a reminder. So, let's end on the promise to never stone our children. How about that as a takeaway?

DL: I concur.

Ki Tetzei to Ki Tavo

Moses continues to explicate a wide range of divine laws governing interpersonal and religious conduct. These include the *mitzvah* to bury a person who has been executed by the courts (later understood as a general *mitzvah* to bury our dead); helping a donkey struggling under its load; sending away a mother bird before taking the eggs from the nest; building a parapet on a roof to prevent someone from accidentally falling off; and the *mitzvah* of *tzitzit*—fringes worn by boys and men daily as a reminder of God's commandments.

Laws of sexual morality are laid out, including a prohibition against prostitution, and what was a major innovation for the time: that a woman who was raped is blameless, and it is the man—the rapist—who must be prosecuted to the full extent of the law.

Other *mitzvot* include not returning a runaway slave to his master; not lending money with interest; allowing workers to eat occasionally from the crops they are harvesting; not withholding or delaying paying the wages of a worker; and the *mitzvah* to leave dropped stalks of wheat and forgotten sheaves of grain to the poor.

We are then told that a husband who wants to divorce his wife may not simply dismiss her but must first give her a *gett*, a formal writ of divorce. This extensive list of *mitzvot* ends with a prohibition against using false measures in business.

Moses then relays God's command to remember the evil that Amalek perpetrated on the Israelites, attacking them without provocation, shortly after leaving Egypt.

Ki Tavo

כִּי-תָבוֹא

AP: Ki Tavo is the parsha, and it means, "When you enter."

DL: Specifically, "When you enter into the Land."

AP: Here, Moses is preparing the people to go into the Promised Land. There's a lot of instruction and preparation.

DL: Yes, and at this point, Moses has only about a month left to live.

AP: The entire Jewish people are listening to Moses speak.

DL: Go ahead and read it for us.

AP: We're in Deuteronomy 26:1:

> When you enter into the land that the Lord, your God, is giving you as a heritage, and you possess it and settle in it, you shall take some of every first fruit of the soil which you harvest from the land that the Lord, your God, is giving you, put it in a basket and go to the place where the Lord, your God, will choose to establish His name.

Let's stop there for a moment, because while it's a very simple idea, it's also fascinating. Your *very first* thought when you get to this amazing land of milk and honey should be to give back. You have to think about who and what you *owe*.

DL: And you've put in all this work and effort, so it's very human to say, "I want to appreciate it. I want to take some of this for myself." But it's important to remember that God comes first, that's the way we express our gratitude. Everything we have is from God, therefore it's necessary to be thankful for the blessings that God has given us. And there is a declaration that tells the story of how we got here.

AP: I'll read that declaration from 26:5. It starts by describing Jacob and his journeys, and then continues. He went down to Egypt with meager numbers and sojourned there; but there he became a great and very populous nation.

DL: Then it continues in 26:8, "'The Egyptians dealt harshly with us and oppressed us; they imposed heavy labor upon us . . . God freed us from Egypt by a mighty hand, by an outstretched arm and awesome power, and by signs and portents.'"

AP: Isn't that a theme in our tradition—that you're constantly supposed to remember how you got here, how you suffered, and the miracle of your deliverance? You can't just revel and enjoy. In a way, you have to suffer it again; you have to experience your history and hardship again.

DL: I'm thinking about that line from *Crazy Ex-Girlfriend*—I don't know if you've seen the show—

AP: Wow, that's quite a detour!

DL: Yes, but the writer creates these great songs, and there's this one where they're doing the hora, and the lyric is, "Remember that we suffered."

AP: Every Passover is about remembering how we suffered; every seder!

DL: Right, but I don't think the seder is about connecting emotionally to suffering.

AP: Well, you're supposed to feel it again and experience it physically by taking the bitter herb into your body.

DL: I'm just not sure that's an important aspect of the seder.

AP: Really? It's not important that we are instructed to experience it "as if we came out of Egypt"?

DL: Yes, I certainly agree that it's important to remember *that* we suffered. What I question is the need to reconnect to the experience of suffering—to feel it in our bones. We are told to see ourselves as if we *came out* of Egypt. It's the coming out that's important. It's about re-experiencing redemption, not re-experiencing slavery.

AP: Once again, you're blowing up a central theme with which I was raised—that we are supposed to feel the discomfort so it connects us with the trials of our ancestors.

DL: That's a fair interpretation, but if we return to the declaration made when we bring the first fruits, I think we can agree that the focus is not on past suffering. It's more about acknowledging that, "You didn't get here all by yourself."

AP: And, "You didn't rescue yourself. You didn't take yourself out of Egypt."

DL: Correct. And it's not just about gratitude to God. It's a recounting of the national story. You're part of a people; your ancestors go way back. There is an arc to the history of this people that starts millennia ago and ends here—with you—in this moment.

AP: It strikes me that being required to bring first fruits means you have to wait for them—plant, tend, and harvest them. So every time you look at those fields, you have to pay attention—

DL: It's not just paying attention to the harvest. Every year you must "take the fruit to God."

AP: So gratitude becomes a discipline. The rigor of appreciation—we can't get lazy about it.

DL: And the idea that, "This isn't all mine" is reinforced by giving a portion to God before anything else.

AP: We've talked before about leaving the corners of our fields; you don't take it all. I want to move to a little bit later in the parsha, where Moses is giving instructions about what to do with certain stones, because it's connected to the "first fruits." I'm looking at Verse 27:2: "As soon as you have crossed the Jordan into the land that the Lord, your God, is giving you, you shall set up large stones. Coat them with plaster and inscribe upon them all the words of this Teaching."

There's this idea, again, that when you get to the Land you have to rewrite the Torah and create new tablets. The message seems to be: "The Torah is in your hands." You are going to physically engrave these stones with this law, and that exercise makes you revisit it, remember it, makes it indelible. It's something you can see every day. It's not just in your head—it's in your hands and always in your sight.

DL: I also hear you saying that it's almost a reenactment of Moses getting the tablets. But here, rather than God writing the tablets, the people are writing them, and there's something really stirring about that.

AP: That's the idea of authorship. It's not only ours to follow but ours to write.

DL: That's a really great way to look at it. The Rabbis add to that idea. They note that the last words of the verse are, "And thou shall write upon the stones all the words of the Law most distinctly." The Rabbis say that "most distinctly" means "in seventy languages." The Law—the Torah—was translated into *all* languages. That's a really strong statement because we all know that the act of translation is not a simple one-to-one matching of words; it's taking a set of associations from one culture and bringing them into another. Translation is interpretation, and in translating the Torah, you're taking these divine words and incorporating them into your reality and your life. You own them, which is what you were saying.

AP: If we bring it back to the "first fruits" of this parsha, here's how I'd connect them: Moses is telling his people, "These are your instructions when you get there. Yes, you must give a piece of your harvest to God; but the stones you're supposed to do right away. You're going to inscribe these stones *before* you bring in the first fruits." Again, the Torah comes first, but emboldening this population to do it themselves is a way to have them be Godlike and inscribe the law with their own hands.

DL: I really like that. God comes first when you enter the Land. The Torah is saying, "Take responsibility. Show gratitude." But showing gratitude doesn't mean submission or dependence. It's really, "Own the responsibility—follow the law—but also make it yours."

AP: And part of that responsibility is authorship.

DL: I'm thinking about the verse you cited that said the people were to coat the stones with plaster and then write the Torah on that plaster coating. Why not write it directly on the stones themselves? Maybe the impermanence meant they would constantly have to maintain it, rewrite it. If you want the Torah to be an active part of your lives, you must constantly be working on it—

AP: Inscribing it again and again.

DL: Translating it again and again, keeping it alive.

AP: There are all these built-in safeguards to make sure we don't get complacent. In the previous parsha, Shoftim, we discussed what a king needs to do.

DL: Exactly.

AP: Keep your Torah with you.

DL: Read it constantly.

AP: Copy it, etch it in stone, again and again.

DL: Right.

AP: We can put that on a T-shirt! "The Torah: Write it again." Hmm, actually, that's not very pithy. I don't think we'll sell too many T-shirts.

Ki Tavo to Nitzavim

The Israelites are told that when they enter the Land, they should perform a ritual involving the proclamation of blessings upon those who keep the Torah and curses upon those who violate its laws. Moses continues to lay out the terms of the rewards the Israelites will receive if they heed God's word and the punishments they will face if they fail to do so. The punishments describe illness, famine and hunger, war, exile, and enslavement—all in graphic detail—culminating in the return of the people to captivity in Egypt.

Moses then tells the people that they are all now standing together—men, women, and children, from the leaders of the tribes to the woodchoppers, and even those not physically present and those of future generations—to enter into God's covenant. They are again warned against idolatry and told that if they abandon God and the covenant, they will be exiled, after which, they will repent and return to God. In parallel, God will draw close to them, gather them from all the places that they have been scattered, and bring them back to the Land.

Moses ends this section by telling the people they have two paths before them: the path of life and doing good (loving God and observing the *mitzvot*) or the path of death and doing evil (abandoning God). Moses charges them to "choose life."

Nitzavim

נִצָּבִים

DL: Nitzavim means "standing." Here Moses is saying to all the children of Israel, "You're standing here together to enter into a covenant with God. You're about to go into the Land, and you must reaffirm your relationship with God."

AP: This is a pretty famous passage. I think it's been in some songs as well. This is Deuteronomy 30:11.

> Surely, this Instruction which I enjoin upon you is not too baffling for you, nor is it beyond reach. It is not in the heavens, that you should say, "Who among us can go up to the heavens and get it for us and impart it to us, that we may observe it?" Neither is it beyond the sea, that you should say, "Who among us can cross to the other side of the sea and get it for us and impart it to us, that we may observe it?" No, the thing is very close to you, in your mouth and in your heart, to observe it.

I just love that.

DL: Me too. It's has such great imagery: crossing the sea, going up to the heavens. You don't have to go look for it far away; it's right here.

AP: "*It* is not in the heavens, *it* is not beyond the sea, and *it* is in your heart." What do you think the "it" is, Dov?

DL: The Rabbis say this is about a life of learning Torah and connecting to Torah. We don't have to feel like it's in the heavens. Yes, God gave it to us from the heavens, but it's here, it's given to us, it's close to our hearts, accessible for us to learn anytime we want.

AP: These verses confirm that you don't need rabbis or prophets or intermediaries. This Torah is yours. Moses personalizes it and brings God's law down to earth. He also seems to be telling us, "Don't use as an excuse that you can't access Torah, because not only am I giving it to you, I am giving you permission to connect to this inheritance without me."

DL: In a way, this speaks to what we have been doing in our conversations these many weeks, in the sense that everybody should be learning Torah. Nobody should be saying, "I can't because I don't know Hebrew" or "I don't have enough background" or "My ideas are too heretical." The Torah is, and should be, accessible to everyone. That's very different from some other religions, which believe that only the priests should have access to the sacred texts, and that the general population cannot be trusted to study them directly or understand their true meaning. Here, the Torah is saying, "It was given to human beings; it's not still in the heavens. Everybody has the right and the obligation to engage with this book themselves."

AP: When it asks, "Who among us can go up to the heavens and get it for us," what does that mean? "Go get the law?"

DL: Yes. Another explanation is that you don't have to have a direct channel to God. The Rabbis take this one step further, saying that when it comes to adjudicating or interpreting the law, God doesn't have a vote. There's a famous story where the Rabbis are debating a point of law, and one Rabbi says, "If I'm right, let the walls of the study hall bend in," and the walls of the study hall bend in. Then he says, "If I'm right, let a tree be uprooted from its place," and a tree is uprooted." The other Rabbis say, "We're still voting against you." Then the Rabbi says, "Let a heavenly voice come out from the heavens and say that I am right," and a heavenly voice comes from the heavens and says, "He's right!" The other Rabbis say, "God, keep out of this! This isn't your business." And they quote this verse, "*lo ba-shamayim hee*"—"it's not in the heavens." In other words, "You've given us the Torah from the heavens, but it's no longer up there. It's down here now, and it's up to us to decide how to read it, interpret it, and apply it."

AP: That story is nice, but it takes the poetry away for me.

DL: What! It's a great story!

AP: Let's finish with the last line of that verse—30:14: "The thing is very close to you, in your mouth and in your heart." The phrase "in your mouth" is so strong: you can speak it without being taught it. You *know* it—it's in your DNA. It's like the idea that we all stood at Sinai, or that *midrash* that says we are all born knowing the entire Torah and then an angel touches the groove above the lip, and it all disappears so you have to relearn it. There is something empowering and intimate about this verse and this message: you have these Torah muscles from birth; you have this vocabulary from the start.

DL: I love that you mentioned the *midrash* about learning all the Torah in the womb and then forgetting it. If you were going to forget it, why did you learn it in the first place? One answer is because when you learn it afresh, you are rediscovering something that you always knew. It's finding something out about yourself, a feeling of coming home, that this is some truth you knew deep down but never articulated. There is a beautiful meaning in this verse that, not only do you have the skills, but deep in your heart you also have this knowledge, and you just need to rediscover it.

AP: I think we have to be honest about the barriers here, however. Many Jews don't feel that Torah is close to them. They *don't* feel as if it's in their mouths and in their hearts, and it's a hurdle to feel entitled to this story.

DL: It's true. There are so many translations, wonderful books, and countless ways to access it nowadays, but that doesn't mean people feel comfortable or that it is fully accessible to them. The Rabbis instituted a whole system of public education because they felt it was critical for everybody to have the skills, not just something for the priests to hold and protect from the people. But it's really a challenge for some. What would you advise in those cases, Abby?

AP: Just begin. That gets you over the hurdle. I remember feeling that it was too overwhelming even to start, that it was too late. But I've seen that when you begin to read and discuss the Torah, it gets closer. In a sense, it starts far away, and gets nearer the more you engage with it.

DL: That's beautiful, Abby. A great line to end on.

Nitzavim to Vayelech

Moses tells the people that he is now, on this very day, 120 years old, and that he will not be going with them into the Land. He calls Joshua to come before him, and in the presence of all those gathered, Moses charges Joshua with leading the people and bringing them, with God's help, into the Promised Land. Moses then writes down the Torah in a scroll, entrusts it to the *kohanim*, and charges them to perform the *mitzvah* of *hakhel*, a public ceremony once every seven years where the Torah is to be read to the entire people.

Vayelech

וַיֵּלֶךְ

AP: We're discussing Vayelech, which means, "And he went."

DL: Moses *went* to speak to the people before his death.

AP: Moses is finishing his long speech to the Israelites and preparing them for what they're about to do because he's going to be gone. It's poignant; he's departing—dying—these are his last days. Here we go. This is Deuteronomy 31:16. "And the Lord said to Moses: 'Behold, you are about to lie down with your fathers.'" Meaning, "You're about to die." God continues, "'Then this people will rise and whore after the foreign gods among them in the land that they are entering—'" God is saying they will worship false gods.

DL: Correct.

AP: "'And they will forsake Me and break My covenant that I have made with them.'" It's a prediction that the people will abandon God and monotheism.

DL: Yes.

AP: "'Then My anger will be kindled against them in that day, and I will forsake them and hide My face from them.'" That kind of feels a little tit-for-tat—a bit beneath God, in my opinion. "'And they will be devoured.'" That's quite a threat. The Torah goes on to say the people will believe these evils have befallen them because God abandoned them.

DL: Yet, all these punishments will happen because of idolatry. As modern people, we might ask if idolatry itself is deserving of all these punishments. I mean, let's say it's a moral society—would they deserve this just because they worshiped other gods?

AP: They're breaking the Second Commandment.

DL: Yes. There are a lot of commandments, but the focus on the sin of idolatry in the Torah underscores how central our relationship with

God is. We can never forget that we are living in the land that God has given us.

AP: Why does God believe people will lose their faith so easily? Where's the proof that we're so weak?

DL: Well, God does know the future.

AP: It seems like pretty bad parenting to say, "I'm sending you forth, you're growing up, but I completely doubt your ability to handle it and do the right thing." That can become a self-fulfilling prophecy.

DL: That's a really good point. God knows the future, fine, but what's the benefit of saying it and writing it in the Torah, undermining their sense of a positive future?

AP: Why is God so sure that we will lack fortitude and commitment? In a way, that says something about God: You're putting all the blame on us, but if we fail, aren't our flaws partly of Your own making? Why don't You author our qualities differently? Why build failure into our future?

DL: The Torah is telling us that failure will be met with exile, destruction, and punishment, and that's indeed what happened. The First Temple was destroyed, the Second Temple was destroyed, and from a theological perspective, those tragedies are always read as having been the result of our sins. So, God is saying, "When you stray, don't ask what you did to deserve this, because you've been forewarned."

AP: Moses picks up where God left off in Deuteronomy 31:27: "Well I know how defiant and stiff-necked you are: even now, while I am alive in your midst, you have been defiant toward the Lord; how much more, then, when I am dead!" He's basically telling the Israelites that he doesn't believe in them either.

Skipping ahead to 31:29:

> For I know that, when I am dead, you will act wickedly and turn away from the path that I have enjoined upon you, and that in time to come, misfortune will befall you for having done evil in the sight of the Lord, whom you have vexed by your deeds.

This is how Moses wants to go out? Chastising his people?

DL: Moses is saying, "I know from your character that you're going to falter." God is saying, "I know from the future that you're going to disappoint Me." Either way, as you rightly asked, how is this a helpful message? How is it at all useful to say, "I know you're going to take the wrong turn"? The Torah's answer is that then we will understand our suffering as a result—

AP: You mean we'll understand why we're being punished.

DL: Yes. Punished, exiled from the Land, the Land destroyed—this is because you disobeyed God and violated the covenant. And hopefully, that will spur us to repent and do better next time. But then the question becomes: is that victim-blaming? It was the Babylonians who destroyed us in 586 BCE. Aren't they to blame? Why are *we* to blame? What about all of our oppressors throughout hundreds of years of Jewish suffering—was that all punishment for our sins? While it might be helpful as a prompt for us to try to repent and do better, it can be very *un*helpful if it's blaming the victim.

AP: Let's turn to your idea that it's somehow constructive for someone to say, "I envision you failing here." Bringing it into the personal realm, have there been times when someone doubted you and said, "Dov, I don't think you can do this"?

DL: I'm sure that there have been. But I think those are usually very counterproductive messages. How about you?

AP: I've definitely had people doubt me, whether behind my back or to my face, and I hope that's emboldened me in some way, or, rather, "galvanized" me. That's a better word.

DL: I can see how someone doubting you can spur you to prove yourself.

AP: I'm talking about those times when you hear through the grapevine that someone said, "I don't really think this is her strength." If we were to psychologize the Torah, there might be some value in saying to the people, "You are going to screw this up."

DL: Yes, but I don't think it played out in practice.

AP: What didn't?

DL: They didn't repent. They didn't avert the exile. They sinned and they were exiled, as this parsha foretells.

AP: Did they abandon God?

DL: Yes. The First Temple period was rife with *constant* idolatry.

AP: It is very problematic—if we're going to cut to the quick—for God (or Moses) to say, "You are going to sin, and you are going to be punished" before either has happened. That's dispiriting. How does that guide or inspire people?

DL: Do you feel it would have been better as an "if" clause?

AP: Yes.

DL: So, "*If* you sin, you will be punished, and it will be because of your sins if that punishment comes to pass."

AP: This all reminds me of the *Kol Nidre* liturgy where we essentially say, "I'm going to atone for all these vows that I'm going to break." There's this assumption of falling short, and I don't really see the value in it, other than the idea I was trying—in my modern take—to imagine: that maybe there's something incentivizing when our failure is prematurely assumed.

DL: A deeply resonant message I've often heard about Yom Kippur is that the acknowledgment of human failure—that we're going to fall short—is a reason for God to have compassion on us and for us to be compassionate with ourselves and others. You spend the whole day of Yom Kippur repenting and asking for forgiveness, and you make all these commitments for the future, believe you are forgiven, and then the *very first sentence* in the evening prayer that we say after Yom Kippur is over is, "And God is compassionate and forgives sin." We are saying that we know we will slip up and sin again. And God knows this, too, that this is what it means to be human.

AP: It's reassuring to know that God still holds us at the end of the day. But it's pretty confusing to keep hearing the contradictory message that we humans, given the choice of sinning or not, will sin and let God down. And yet, God is the one who created us and controls us and our outcomes. So, when we are punished for our missteps, were we not wired to make them . . . by God?

DL: We are human, fallible, and we are going to make mistakes and get things wrong. That's why God is compassionate, forgives, and gives us Yom Kippur to atone for our sins. But we still have to try to do our best. We don't have license to do evil. If we willfully act immorally or violate God's commandments and don't try to rectify that, God will hold us responsible.

AP: It's about trying to do our best, not in a platitude-y, lip-service way, but *really* trying.

DL: I want to return to your main point about how it is predicted that we will sin and be punished. I know somebody who is so angry about these verses and verses like this, a very serious, learned, observant Jew—a bit of a maverick, admittedly—who blames all historical antisemitism on this construct. He says, "The Torah here is saying, 'We deserve to be punished; we deserve to suffer because we are sinful people,' and what else do you expect other than for people to have antisemitic attitudes?" I think that's quite extreme, and I don't endorse that, but it's a way of looking at how harsh these verses are and asking what function they're serving.

AP: Can you square that Yom Kippur message of, "You have some influence over your fate," with this parsha, where God is saying, "Your fate is already written for you"?

DL: No, I can't. That question gets to those deep theological questions of divine foreknowledge and free choice. "How can we have free choice when God knows things about the future?" This is God telling us, "Here's what I know about the future," and *teshuva*—repentance—is about the ability to change yourself and your trajectory . . . free choice.

AP: It's not just God saying, "I know the future." It's God saying, "I know you're ultimately bad instead of good."

DL: Well, Moses is the one saying that, but yes.

AP: Moses is saying we're stiff-necked. Does that mean that even if I'm that one person who says, "No, I promise I won't be stiff-necked," it doesn't matter.

DL: Yes. I wish I had a better answer for you. That's why we're having these conversations. But I do think it's important to balance this with what we read in last week's parsha. There it said, "You're going to sin, and God is going to exile you and drive you from the Land," but then it goes on, "You will return to the Lord, your God, and God will return to you, and God will ultimately bring you back to the Land." It's not the end of the story, what we have here. That is the important counterbalancing message—there will be a better day. But that brighter message doesn't occur in our parsha.

AP: It's a sorry statement on God's confidence in us, and I'm hoping for a little more faith in humanity, a more genuine chance to get it right.

DL: What if we look at it from a parenting perspective? A parent says to their child, "Look, I know you're going to mess up; we all mess up—you're a kid, you're a teenager, you're going to experiment, and you're going to make mistakes. There will be consequences as a result, but I'll always love you. I'll always be your father; I'll always be your mother—you'll come back to me, and you'll always be welcome here at home."

AP: That makes it a lot better. But it's not what's on the page.

DL: Well, we tried our best.

Vayeilech to Ha'azinu

Moses writes down the Torah—the collection of God's teachings—and tells the Levites to place it in the Ark of the Covenant. He then commands them to gather the elders of the nation before him so he can recite to them the Ha'azinu poem, which calls on heaven and earth to bear witness to the inevitability that the people will eventually grow complacent and forget God, worship idolatry, and be driven from the Land, but that ultimately God will redeem them.

Ha'azinu

הַאֲזִינוּ

AP: This is the penultimate parsha, Ha'azinu, which means, "listen" or "give ear"—correct?

DL: Correct! "Friends, Romans, countrymen, lend me your ears."

AP: This parsha is written as a kind of lyric. Tell us why it's unlike any other parsha, Dov.

DL: It's referred to as a *shira*, which is either a song or a poem. The words here are not common words; they're very poetic and sparse.

AP: We're going to read its beginning and stay with these very few verses. This is Deuteronomy 32:2, and Moses is speaking to the people: "May my discourse come down as the rain, My speech distill as the dew, like showers on young growth, like droplets on the grass."

It goes on to read, "For the name of the Lord I proclaim; Give glory to our God!" Then in 32:7, "Remember the days of old, consider the years of ages past; Ask your father, who will inform you, your elders, who will tell you."

Previously, in Deuteronomy 31:19 God had said of these verses, "Therefore, write down this poem, teach it to the people of Israel; put it in their mouths, in order that this poem may be My witness against the people of Israel."

It's kind of amazing.

DL: Beautiful imagery in the text and in the command in 31:19 to "write down this poem." "Put it in their mouths." The best book I ever read about how to read poetry was called *How Does a Poem Mean?* It says that a poem is not about the content but how it's said. There's something so affecting about the language and what it evokes; it resonates emotionally in a way that a simple narrative might not. The symbolism is striking: What does it mean to consider the Torah to be like rain? What are your thoughts?

AP: It's a perfect segue, since we are nearing the end of our journey together, to touch on what it means to reengage Torah, particularly with someone different from you (or me) in many ways. I hope, Dov, that we align very much on values, but we live our Jewish lives very differently—not just in terms of observance, but in terms of our communities, our orientations to ritual, tradition, prayer, and even discourse. The fact that we have not just chosen to, but forced ourselves to reckon with texts, whether they are resonant or alien, is exactly the gift of this ancient book. The Torah is like rain in the sense that it waters, quenches, nourishes. It brings very different Jews together and spurs us to ask us not just what our ancestors intended but what it means on the day we're reading it. Because if this book is not relevant today, I don't think you can argue that it should continue to be read.

DL: That is beautiful. Poetic, even.

AP: Let's not go overboard.

DL: Let me read a *midrash* that I found, where the Rabbis expound upon this metaphor of rain: "The verse says, 'Like rain on the grass.' What does rain do? It descends on the grass and causes it to grow. So are the words of Torah: they raise us up, and they cause us to grow." Then it continues, "What happens with rain showers? They come down on the grasses, and they make them healthy and beautiful. So too the words of Torah: they make us healthy and beautiful." The idea is that they cause us not only to grow but also give beauty to our lives.

AP: I'm allergic to the words "personal growth," probably because it feels overused and therefore unspecific and uninteresting, but putting my cynicism aside, would you candidly say this exercise of ours has caused you to grow in any way?

DL: Absolutely. I'm not the cynic you are. When I look at the opening word of this parsha, *ha'azinu*—"give ear"—it feels apropos to our study partnership. Because, as a rabbi—and this might come as a surprise—I tend to talk more than I listen. It's the opposite of *Hamilton*. What was the line?

AP: "Talk less. Smile more . . ."

DL: For me it needs to be, "Talk less, listen more!" I have a lot of prepackaged ideas about various Torah passages and verses, and sometimes I'm just downloading them to others. I remember when you and I were starting, I was sharing my ideas and not doing nearly enough listening. But in the process, I really learned how to listen better—you taught me that—and it has been a real growth experience for me. I have learned a tremendous amount from your insights and questions. So embracing that idea of "giving ear" is one of the key ways I have changed from this experience.

AP: Thank you for saying so. That idea of growth, much as I resist it, certainly applies to what I have learned from you and what this ongoing dialogue has given me. Part of it is, as you said, that we often sit in our certainty; we've made up our minds. Not only is Torah difficult because it's opaque on the page, but then when I peel it away and talk to you, our dialogues lead me not just to greater clarity, but greater connection. That is why the Five Books of Moses are magical. It's why it continues to give, give, and give again. What is that line in Talmud? "Turn it, turn it, for everything is in it." This exchange and friendship with you is a turning and turning of a text.

DL: I so agree with that. This parsha also made me think about the difference between rain and dew.

AP: You think about dew?

DL: I do.

AP: Ha! Okay. I'll let you expound on condensation.

DL: Seriously—rain is periodic, and when there is a lot of it, it has an immediate, powerful effect. Dew is constant; we can't survive without the dew. There's an aspect of each in our ongoing engagement with Torah. The low flame that is nurturing us is a constant part of our dialogue, and then there are these powerful moments.

AP: You switched metaphors abruptly there: from dew to fire.

DL: Touché. I was thinking back to some of those "Aha!" moments for me. I loved that discussion about whether we find God in the synagogue and when we talked about the importance of voluntary participation in building the Tabernacle. There was another discussion about *sotah*, when a woman is suspected of adultery: I was trying to contextualize the awful ritual, and you said, "You're turning yourself into a pretzel trying to hold on to the idea that the text is divine." And I said, "Well, I have to adhere to the belief that even this difficult text is holy, so can you see why I can't reject it?" I loved the honesty of that.

AP: I also remember our discussion about the stranger—the *ger*—and how I was shocked to learn that the stranger is never the non-Jew; it's the convert.

DL: In the Rabbinic mindset.

AP: Yes, but I still hold on to the idea that we should stretch ourselves beyond our Jewish family to "welcome" or even "love" the stranger who is truly from a different people.

DL: To do that is sacred work.

AP: Another reflection on our Torah dialogue was spurred by this week's parsha when it says in Deuteronomy 32:3, "In the name of the Lord I proclaim; give glory to our God!" I noticed in our conversations how often you brought us back to God and to the fact that this Torah exercise is anchored in faith. That's a very complicated issue for many Jews to articulate, let alone wrestle with. The practice of discussing God's Book means engaging and honoring the divine and being grateful in a way that has both challenged and deepened my Judaism.

DL: Thank you, I really identify with that. I would add one more reflection on the image of rain in this parsha: it falls from the heavens but comes to the ground. Another thing I've gained from you is that you often bring me back to earth. I sometimes went on and on about an abstract idea, and you would say, "Okay, but what does this have to do with your life or what's going on in the world?"

AP: I appreciated you letting me nudge you. Before we hit the last parsha of them all, let's end with the earth and the rain.

DL: Amen.

Ha'azinu to V'zot HaBracha

After proclaiming the Ha'azinu poem to the elders, Moses, along with Josuha, proceeds to read it to the entire people. Moses tells them that the Torah is "no empty thing for you, but it is your life" (Deut. 32:47). God then tells Moses to ascend Mount Nebo, from where he will see the Promised Land, never to enter it himself.

In a form that parallels Jacob's last words to his sons, Moses offers each tribe a final blessing as he is about to die. Contrary to the harsh rebukes that characterized his previous addresses, these blessings carry warm wishes for abundance, comfort, and protection, each one speaking to the tribe's unique character and social role. In his last few words, Moses extols his fellow Israelites as a happy, triumphant nation, cherished by God.

V'zot HaBracha

וְזֹאת הַבְּרָכָה

AP: We've made it to the end.

DL: Drumroll!

AP: It is powerful to come to the finish line—Moses's death—and the idea that this epic story does actually have an ending.

DL: But, in reality, we never end anything, because on the same Shabbat that we read this parsha, we make sure to also start at the beginning again. Learning, as you once said, is a lifelong endeavor. Let's get to it. The fifty-fourth and final parsha is V'zot HaBracha, which means, "This is the blessing," and it was Moses's final word to the people—for each tribe a different blessing.

AP: What's kind of amazing is that Moses is up on this mountain being shown the Promised Land he'll never see any other way.

DL: Right. After Moses concludes the blessing, God takes him up to the mountaintop.

AP: That's Mount Nebo. I would like to start, before we even get to the verse, with the memory of Martin Luther King Jr. and his last speech before being assassinated. I've heard it invoked so many times, though not so much connected to this particular parsha. But the text is obviously exactly what King was saying: "I've been to the mountaintop." Let me read the language of his speech; we all know these famous words:

> I don't know what will happen now. We've got some difficult days ahead. But it doesn't matter with me now. Because I've been to the mountaintop. And I don't mind. Like anybody, I would like to live a long life; longevity has its place. But I'm not concerned about that now. I just want to do God's will. And He's allowed me to go up

> to the mountain. And I've looked over, and I've seen the Promised Land. I may not get there with you, but I want you to know tonight that we, as a people, will get to the Promised Land.

DL: Wow.

AP: Incredible. That was April 3, 1968. He was killed the next day. I get choked up every time I read those words. And King is invoking this very moment in this parsha.

DL: Yes, absolutely. I'm awed by the almost prophetic nature of his speech. Moses knew he was going to die—God says, "I'm bringing you up to the mountaintop because you won't be going into the Land." You've talked before, Abby, about how heart-wrenching it is that Moses worked his whole life and sees the Land from this vantage point but is not allowed to go in. Martin Luther King Jr.'s take on it is, "I don't have to go in. It would be good for me, but I've brought you here, and the future is in front of you."

AP: What's also great about what you're saying is that Martin Luther King Jr. helped build that Promised Land, that better day—and Moses did too. It's not just, "We brought you to this moment." It's that, "We ensured that the world will be better for you than it was in the past." Their hands—Moses's and MLK Jr.'s—will always be felt.

DL: Absolutely, and the blessing Moses gives the people right before this moment presents a romantic view of the future. It's a nice counterbalance to all the curses and tragedy that we read in the previous parshas. Here, it's a vision—looking at the Land, its infinite possibilities, and all the blessings the people will have when they enter into it—that Moses was central in making happen.

AP: It's an important point because this is a kinder, gentler parsha. As the ending note, it seems kind of conscious on the part of the author—maybe God, or maybe human beings—to give us a dramatic finish, almost like a Hollywood ending. I'll read the language from Deuteronomy 34:10:

> Never again did there arise in Israel a prophet like Moses—whom the Lord singled out, face to face, for the various signs and portents that the Lord sent him to display in the land of Egypt, against

Pharaoh and all his courtiers and his whole country, and for all the great might and awesome power that Moses displayed before all Israel.

DL: What's your reaction to that famous line: "Never again did there arise in Israel a prophet like Moses"?

AP: It's a big statement. "No one else will ever be like him." No one will ever rise to Moses's strength, stature, or character.

DL: That's a constant theme in the Torah: Moses is singular. When Miriam and Aaron, Moses's sister and brother, complain about him and speak ill of him, God essentially says in Numbers 12:6–8, "All other prophets see me only in a distant vision; Moses speaks to me mouth to mouth." Moses's singularity is a pretty major theme, but here it's also being said about the future: there will not be another like him.

AP: It's interesting that someone so unique is also so flawed. He was really hesitant in the beginning. He didn't want to be a leader, and he didn't relish the job of taking his people out of bondage. Maybe I'm wrong to call it a flaw, but I guess I mean he's textured, ambivalent, human. He's not a polished, straight-out-of-central-casting kind of hero. He's a little awkward, self-doubting. He depends on his brother, Aaron, to speak for him. There are ways in which this paragon is not Superman.

DL: Yes! And the Torah does not say no *human being* ever arose as great as Moses; it says there was never a *prophet* as great as Moses. The one thing it says about his character was, "Moses himself was very humble, more so than any other human being on earth" (Num. 12:3). So, it singles out his humility, but it doesn't say he was a perfect human being. It says he was the greatest, unmatched prophet, and I think there's a beautiful message in that.

AP: "You're special *because* you're humble."

DL: I've been very influenced by Maimonides, who says Moses was chosen for his role because of his great intellect and because of how profoundly he was able to connect to God intellectually. But focusing on humility is saying that, key to his being a prophet was that his ego would not get in the way. Moses is the perfect vessel for communicating God's word because it's not about him; it's only about letting God speak through him. I like that.

AP: Go back to the words, "face-to-face" for a minute; how literally should we take that?

DL: This harkens back to the time at Mount Sinai when Moses said to God, "Let me see your face" (Ex. 33:18) and God answered, "Nobody will see me and live," and "You can see my back, but you won't see my face." What you're asking is about the anthropomorphism of that "face." Are we supposed to believe God has a face? I don't think any modern reader reads it that way. But it is an interesting point—

AP: It suggests intimacy.

DL: Exactly. Direct personal connection, not at a distance. It's about knowledge, not direct seeing. So even here, there remains some distance, some inability to *fully* know God.

I'd like to share a powerful Rabbinic teaching at the end of this parsha. It focuses on the final verses, which say,

> And there arose no prophet since in Israel like Moses, whom the Lord knew face to face. In all the signs and the wonders, which the Lord sent him to do in the land of Egypt to Pharaoh . . . which Moses did in front of the eyes of all of Israel.

So again, there's this sense of Moses as a vessel. God is doing these miracles for Israel through Moses. And then Rashi—

AP: The medieval commentator.

DL: Yes, the eleventh-century French commentator, who is seen as the standard commentator for the Torah. Rashi quotes the very last words of the last verse of the entire Torah, which are: "Which Moses did in front of the eyes of all Israel." And Rashi says, "What did Moses do in front of the eyes of the children of Israel? He broke the tablets. And when he did so, God said to him, 'Well done that you have broken them!'" I love that. The very last comment Rashi makes on the last line of the Torah is not that Moses is just this vessel for God, doing God's miracles. It's that Moses's greatness is the initiative he took to break God's tablets when the Israelites sinned and God's subsequent affirmation of that impulse. Rashi is making a point about the need for human agency—the active role we play in bringing God's Torah into the world.

AP: It also underscores that precious things sometimes need to be broken to prove their value. I want to finish by saying that the title of this parsha is apt—V'zot HaBracha translates to: "And this is the blessing." Because it has been a blessing to study Torah and discuss it with you, Dov.

DL: Thank you, Abby. I really couldn't have said it better.

ACKNOWLEDGMENTS

First and foremost, thanks to our publisher and editor, Fredric Price, who believed in this book from the start, made all the right demands of us to make it better, clearer, and tighter, and who walks the walk when it comes to truly caring about the Jewish story and making sure it not only expands but endures.

Thanks to Aaron Wildavsky, who wrote the first draft of all connecting narratives between parshas. His wise curation of key plot points—and his keen eye for what we'd left out—are deeply appreciated.

Mayim Bialik's Foreword captures the essence of her scholarship, humor, and heart. Thank you, Mayim, and to all those who gave us such generous endorsements.

Thanks to Ethan Klaris for doing the initial transcription with such thoroughness and curiosity, and to DJ Schuette, who completed the final edit with invaluable input.

We applaud Christine Van Bree for her beautiful cover design incorporating the painting we love—*On the Way to Sinai* by Yoram Raanan.

Huge gratitude to *Tablet Magazine*'s top editors Alana Newhouse and Wayne Hoffman for saying yes when we told them we wanted to talk about Torah in a regular podcast series and for matching us with wonderful producers Josh Kross, Shira Telushkin, and Jacob Siegel.

We will never forget those who enjoyed the podcast and pushed us to collect our conversations into one readable volume. Your encouragement was its own manna.

Most precious of all are our families. So, to Devorah, Kasriel, Netanel, Dave, Ben, and Molly, thank you. We'd be lost—and much more stressed—without your patience, insights, and love.

ABOUT THE AUTHORS

ABIGAIL POGREBIN is the author of *My Jewish Year: 18 Holidays, One Wondering Jew*—a finalist for a 2017 National Jewish Book Award—and *Stars of David: Prominent Jews Talk About Being Jewish*. She's written for the *Atlantic*, *New York* magazine, the *Forward*, and *Tablet*, and moderates conversations for the Streicker Center and the Jewish Broadcasting Service.

RABBI DOV LINZER is the president and Rosh HaYeshiva (Rabbinic Head) of Yeshivat Chovevei Torah, an Orthodox rabbinical school and Torah center, which promotes a more open and inclusive Orthodoxy. He has written for the *Forward*, *Tablet*, and the *New York Times*, and has hosted highly popular Torah podcasts.

Photo Credit: Michael Nagle